I0819721

Art History after Modernism

Art History after Modernism

HANS BELTING

Translated by Caroline Saltzwedel and Mitch Cohen
with additional translation by Kenneth Northcott

THE UNIVERSITY OF CHICAGO PRESS/CHICAGO & LONDON

HANS BELTING is professor of art history and media theory at the State College of Design in Karlsruhe, Germany. He has written numerous books, including *The End of the History of Art?*, *Likeness and Presence: A History of the Image before the Era of Art*, and *The Invisible Masterpiece*, published by the University of Chicago Press.

Originally published as *Das Ende der Kunstgeschichte. Eine Revision nach zehn Jahren* © C. H. Beck'sche Verlagsbuchhandlung (Oscar Beck), Munich 1995.

An earlier draft of chapter 20 appeared as "Marco Polo und die anderen Kulturen" in *Neue Bildende Kunst* 4–5 (Sept. 1995).

The University of Chicago Press, Chicago 60637
The University of Chicago Press, Ltd., London
© 2003 by The University of Chicago
All rights reserved. Published 2003
Printed in the United States of America

12 11 10 09 08 07 06 05 04 03   1 2 3 4 5

ISBN: 0-226-04184-0 (cloth)
ISBN: 0-226-04185-9 (paper)

Library of Congress Cataloging-in-Publication Data

Belting, Hans.
[Ende der Kunstgeschichte? English]
Art history after modernism / Hans Belting ; translated by Caroline Saltzwedel and Mitch Cohen with additional translation by Kenneth Northcott.
p. cm.
Rev. ed. of: The end of the history of art? 1987.
Includes bibliographical references and index.
ISBN: 0-226-04184-0 (alk. paper) —
ISBN: 0-226-04185-9 (pbk. : alk. paper)
1. Art—Historiography. 2. Art criticism—Historiography. 3. Art, Modern—20th century. I. Belting, Hans End of the history of art? II. Title.
N380 .B4413 2003
709'.04'5—dc21

2001006547

♾ The paper used in this publication meets the minimum requirements of the American National Standard for Information Sciences—Permanence of Paper for Printed Library Materials, ANSI Z39.48-1992.

Contents

Preface to the English Edition

"Art History after Modernism" is the new title of an essay originally called "The End of the History of Art?" The title change alludes to the changing significance of art, which has repercussions on the discourse of art history whether or not art historians accept the connection between the two. Modern art, which has had a longer history in Europe than anywhere else, has always been more than an artistic practice; it is also a model that allowed art history to establish an orderly, linear progression. "Art history after modernism" means not only that art looks different today; it also means our discourse on art has taken a different direction, if it is safe to say that it has taken a clear direction at all. We have since discovered that modern art was rooted in a much longer artistic tradition, which the advent of modernism negated. Willingly or not, we are also confronted with the dissolution of the universal significance of Western art and its historiography. We have recently begun to admit the changes that affect even the canon of art history, which now reappears as a local Western concern, despite its universal pretensions. This does not mean that the traditional discussion of art history is on the verge of collapse, but it invites us to reopen that discussion to communicate with others from non-Western traditions.

The essay does not conceal its highly personal view, one that does not wish to dispense with method or a generally accessible discourse, but one that eschews the claim that it speaks with the voice of history or from a position beyond history. The American reader is invited to test his or her tolerance of a decidedly European way of describing the contemporary scene. The aim of this book is not to offer a definitive truth but to present the author's view as one based on personal history and professional experience. I feel no need to apologize for this; on the contrary, I am convinced that this is necessary to avoid an intransigent dogmatism that claims to possess an overview of our world. Only by learning to listen to one another and to accept that the other's experience is as legitimate as our own will we be ready to accept the future.

I wrote this book more than nine years ago, which is a long time when dealing with a contemporary topic. Moreover, I wrote it in German; a translation will inevitably alter some of the original nuances. An English-language edition was paradoxically necessitated by the views I expressed in an earlier U.S. publication, *The End of the History of Art?* (1987), which no longer represents my thinking about the topic today and which I did not want to see in a new edition. I have dispensed with the section on Vasari, which did not need restatement, and have added some new text that did not even appear in the latest German edition, whose title translates as *The End of the History of Art: A Revision after Ten Years* (1995). All views on the contemporary art scene are open-ended; we cannot capture its meaning once and for all. Some experts on modern art take a stand against anything that no longer conforms to their own artistic experience, thus raising the question whether they are still truly engaged with art itself or whether they are merely defending themselves against the flux of events.

This does not mean that no firm view can be taken, nor does it imply a surrender to a cinematic course of events to be blindly followed. But it does mean that we are in control not of these events but only of our own particular viewpoint. We may be attracted to a school of thought that is briefly fashionable in academic circles. But we have adopted, if only unconsciously, a given tradition of thinking: in my case, a tradition rooted in long experience of art history that both shapes and limits my perception of the contemporary scene, a scene that in turn reacts to this tradition. Dissent and sometimes a secret rivalry are growing between established art criticism and its living artistic counterpart. But there is also a growing dichotomy within art criticism itself, which seems to be rejecting the intellectual symbiosis that developed between the United States and Europe in the postwar decades. This dichotomy, which has recently become my experience as well, caused me to hesitate a moment before venturing upon the present publication. No one wants to appear obscure or, worse, uninformed, although information is itself a matter of selection and local preference. My confidence in an ongoing dialogue within the West has encouraged me to take the risk of agreeing to publish the present volume despite my doubts. I was once trained to believe in this sort of close dialogue; so I was eager to know whether such a belief is still justified.

The first part of this volume has no equivalent in the original book. It begins with a balance sheet defining the difference I see between our current situation and what we call modernism. At the same time, I feel better prepared now to formulate the thesis of the end of art history than I was twenty years ago. Moreover, I can now refer to the discussion that has since arisen on the theme of my original book (for instance, in the writing of Arthur C. Danto). The art discussion has since become the playground of both art critics and artists, making it clear that the traditional narrative of art history was pursuing a different purpose. Style and history were in fact issues of early twentieth-century art, which the discipline unconsciously or intentionally keeps alive. The periodization suggested by the phrase "the late cult of modernism" moves outside art-historical or art-chronological periodization and reflects my view that our perception of art and the path of art history are colored by our own cultural experiences.

At the center of part 1 is a triad of larger themes that did not actually originate in the history of art but that have, nevertheless, changed and will continue to shape the development of the discipline. Only by writing this text did I grasp their inner connections. I began chronologically with the idea of Western art following the Second World War, when the United States led the way in cultural as well as in other matters. Today, however, after its own East-West dichotomy was suspended for so long in a "Western partnership," Europe has suddenly become self-absorbed again in its preoccupation with the reality of Eastern Europe. So far, art history still remains silent on this matter. Furthermore, world art is on the rise, a chimera of global culture that challenges our well-trained Western definitions of art. Finally, minorities are also claiming their own place in a canon of art history from which they feel excluded or in which they were never considered.

The last three chapters of part 1 tackle three other themes whose current significance is generally known. First, the categories of "high" and "low," long central to our understanding of art, have lost their firm boundaries. Second, with its working structures and temporality, media art, whether installation or video, has raised completely new questions that cannot be treated with traditional historical methods. Third, as institutions, the museums of contemporary art are increasingly being transformed in a way that no longer permits them to be used as the usual explication of art history.

Part 2 developed out of the original book. It begins with reflections on how contemporary artists present the history of art, then traces the art historical discourse back to its origins. After Hegel, art history detached itself from these origins, much to its detriment, thus immediately calling its critics into account. Even the coexistence of art history and the avant-garde, which always resulted in antagonism, allows us in retrospect to take a position toward the discipline in the present context. My inspection of the rules of this academic game is not intended as a formal exercise but as an opportunity to understand the historical reasons for certain notions and theorems that we must not confuse with articles of faith.

The reality of the work of art, which occupies the central position of part 2, resists concerns with the end of art history, since the work of art stimulates a discourse of its own. But in contemporary art, the concept of the "work" has itself come under dispute. My review of media history therefore examines anew the problems emerging in the present art scene. The concluding chapters form a new body of thought by engaging modernism and today's posthistory in dialogue, thus comprehending the peculiarities of each as seen from the art historian's vantage point. The artists' posthistory, I suggest, developed before that of the historians. I then discuss a film by Peter Greenaway, who, to my surprise, treated the same themes of frame and image that I had already used to describe the relationship between art history and art. It is strange that a text begun in 1983 discusses a film, shot in 1991, that unexpectedly reflects some of my earlier ideas. Chapter 20 is entirely new and thus demonstrates the flux of time in the book's argument.

PART I

Modernism in the Mirror of Contemporary Culture

1 Epilogues for Art or for Art History?

Those commenting on art or art history today see each theory they might seek to promote already devalued by any number of other theories. One can no longer take a position that has not already been advanced in another form. It is best to insist on the standpoint one has decided upon and to accept that others will find it mistaken or, if they agree, probably have misunderstood it. This is a time of monologue, not of dialogue. Naturally, common themes still exist, but those who share them, may understand them in very different ways. One of these common themes is the epilogue. Epilogues have been fashionable for so long that one would dearly like to write an epilogue on the age of the epilogue. It is not important whether these epilogues refer to the end of history, of modernism, or of painting. The important thing is the continued need for epilogues that characterizes an age. Where nothing new is discovered and the old is no longer the familiar, then epilogue is what suggests itself.

But today the epilogue is also a mask quick to express reservations about one's own opinions in order to avoid overstraining the readers' or listeners' tolerance. Whether referring to "art" or "culture," "history" or "utopia," each concept is put in quotation marks to permit its continued use while demonstrating the requisite degree of skepticism. One also expects another, different understanding, but not consensus. Each concept is tagged with a visiting card that introduces its user and serves to confine the general concept to an individual sense. Anyone speaking about culture is soon informed that such a thing no longer *really* exists except on a market of the media. Concepts and theories have met the same fate that art met long ago: the only way they find legitimacy is by simultaneously calling themselves into question. Of course, many earn their living by contributing to the changes in the debate that keep it alive. But today, theory, whatever it acquits itself of, is geared toward epilogue in all its themes and speech rules, just as at the outset of modernism it had the aspect of prologue, being militantly future-addicted and intolerant of the present. In the past, the enemy was the very notion of history that we fear to lose today, since what we now treat as history is the same modernism that they once hoped to bring into being.

An epilogue to a former paradigm measures the present against models it can no longer satisfy. In our case, this model is the culture of modernism, with which we identify ourselves just as emphatically as our forebears once identified themselves with religion and the nation. This collective identity is not linked with a part of the world but with a nostelpy for battles and utopias in which all eyes focused on an ideal future. The loss of such a perspective does not, however, mean the end of modernism but rather the impossibility of ending it, since we possess no alternative to it. This is the reason why I sympathize with the term "surmodernité" or hypermodernity as it was coined by the French anthropologist Marc Augé to define our present time.

Modernity has taken a thousand shapes, and we argue about whether it lives on in them or whether it has already been abandoned. History, too, long since and for good reason declared dead, refuses to lie down and ubiquitously continues to make heard its unsolicited voice. Finally, the classical arts, which we have so often ceremoniously and finally left behind us, continue to exist as if against all expectations and derive new power and freedom from precisely this fact. Yet this does not mean that we still live with the old challenges and opportunities that once obsessed "classic" modernism. Every glance at *this* modernism can only be retrospective, as it emphasizes our different situation and the new cultural experience clearer than ever. This is why the argument as to whether the present still retains the old profile of so-called modernism has long been superfluous. We are in the process of expanding the concept of modernism, just as we have always expanded the concept of art whenever we wished to continue using it.

The new media arts, to give one example, react to a media world that, as is well known, did not even exist in classic modernism. The media are inherently global and thus suspend all regional and individual cultural experience. They reach and adapt themselves to everyone, which is why their chief purpose became the consumption of information and entertainment at a high level of technology and a low level of ideas. The commonplace concept of art can no longer cope with this. Everyone knows that art with an implied capital A has meanwhile fragmented into a spectrum of resistant phenomena that are accepted as art long before we are able to define them. The very loss of a binding definition of art prevents us from holding a well-founded position on media art. The question is not whether the media arts are capable of being art but whether artists are willing to create art with the new technologies.

Art is still bound to an artist who uses it for his or her personal expression, and to a viewer under this spell. That makes it the secret opponent of technology, whose raison d'être is functionality and whose information is geared not toward a spectator but toward a user. This is why technology has always been indifferent to every personal worldview as it had always been mirrored in art. Put in extreme terms, technology does not interpret the given world but invents a technological world in which all physical and spatial reality is suspended. It thus dramatizes the crisis of individualism that has emerged in modernism and since the exhaustion of bourgeois culture. Philosophers have already declared the human in a text as superfluous or outmoded, and the new artistic currents are being acclaimed as "posthuman," a slogan containing the most terrible and (one hopes) the most erroneous epilogue in our time.

At the same time, a gradual countermovement is forming in the sense that it is precisely media, whose audiences continue a belief in new technology, that trigger a call to return to personal and physical reality. The body is the theme of philosophical conferences and also emerges as the target of new installations, such as those by Gary Hill (see p. 94). Film directors like Peter Greenaway forsake the world of the surrogate as it emerged on celluloid and in video photography and organize exhibitions that physically involve the viewers. The good old stage play, of all things, which once claimed appearances as its own prerogative, has now become a refuge for lost reality, for it is far more real than any analogical or digital medium can ever be.

But the problem of how to make use of new technology and how to gear it to a new aesthetic has accompanied the discussion of modernism from the beginning. The debate has always suffered from the fact that the innovators were in open conflict with tradition, while the others always defended every inch of it. In the process, each side invoked the famous logic of history in their attempt to win the argument, and the analyses assumed the character of epilogues; but there were two intentions involved: break with or defense of the old. Incidentally, this has been the case for as long as bourgeois culture has existed: it had to be sufficient unto itself and yet continued to worship models from history that it could no longer live up to.

Modernism thrived on the contradiction between these two models, the one turned toward the future and the other toward tradition, and thus found a necessary resistance against its own utopias. The practice of culture, as soon as it became politicized, inflicted such deep wounds in the twentieth century that, in retrospect, its victories appear just as doubtful as its defeats appear justified. Today, modernism itself has become tradition, which is why its guardians are so ready to conjure it up again in an epilogue, while its opponents, true to the proven pattern, are all the quicker to announce the end of a modernism they never cared for.

Whether we were talking about the "loss of aura" that Walter Benjamin saw as a historic opportunity for a new art or of the "loss of the center" lamented by Hans Sedlmayr in a modernism gone off the rails, the epilogue was always handy. The same is true of the deconstruction of the concept of the "work," which was augured from such phenomena as Fluxus or concept art. The individual work that—as a museum picture—represented a norm in the public's appreciation of art appeared to have been replaced by a fleeting artistic spectacle in which there were now only spectators and bystanders. In media art, video tapes only are visible as long as they have been played, or installations before they are dismantled. The permanence once inherent in the presence of art is thus replaced by rapid impressions that fit the fleeting nature of modern perception. For some decades, the pressure on art to innovate has been increasing as the possibilities for innovation in the fine arts have dwindled. The pace of new artistic invention is accelerating, but the weight of these innovations has diminished in the same measure as has their ability to shape a new style. Several styles have long been allowed to exist side by side, and artistic production no longer carries the banner of progress that has been replaced by the frivolous or lethargic "remake." The institutional culture of modernism that adopted progress as a program of identity has become an exercise of memory.

Looking back over classic modernism in light of present practice, we notice a range of fundamental changes that elude all simple comparisons, as the following topics make clear. From today's distance, modernism's erstwhile universal claim proves to be a view that was never ready for globalization. Modernism's erstwhile goal of "freedom from taboos" lost its value when art lost its ability to provoke. Belief in the ideal of a technological world of art as a living environment for humankind was supplanted by the fear of the loss of nature. The challenge to bourgeois culture presented by an antibourgeois avant-garde, invented by modernism, collapsed because the demise of the bourgeoisie also meant the loss of the avant-garde's enemy. This debate on the image of an elite culture loses its meaning on the level of a mass culture in which everyone can make his or her own choice. Finally, history—the locus of identity or of contradiction—lost its authority to the same extent that it became omnipresent and malleable. This also means that art history can no longer be the guiding image of our historical culture—which brings us to our theme.

2 The Meaning of Art History in Today's Culture

When I published the first draft of the present book in 1983 under the German title *Das Ende der Kunstgeschichte?* (The End of Art History?), I appeared to be contributing to the production of epilogues, but I did not intend to write an obituary for art or for art history. Instead, I asked myself whether art and the narration of art to which we had grown accustomed were still compatible. The opportunity to publish a new book on the same topic is also a chance to review and update the argument; this is possible only in the individual steps I undertake in the following chapters. But I must again insist on the initial argument that the rhetorical figure of speech dealing with the end of art history does not mean that art or art history is over but that, both in art and in the discourse of art history, we can foresee on the horizon the end of a tradition whose familiar shape had become, in the era of modernism, canonical.

I spoke of the farewell to the guiding model of an art history with an internal logic, which was favored in describing shifts of style from one period to another. The more art history as a coherent discourse disintegrated, the more it was absorbed into the whole cultural and social environment of which it was a part. The debate about method lost its edge, and historians replaced the one, mandatory art history with several or even many art histories that exist side by side, much as do today's artistic styles. Artists, for their part, took leave of a linear conception of history that had forced them to carry art into the future while waging war against its old form. They freed themselves from both a model and an incompatible history, and they abandoned such old genres and media whose rules constantly demanded progress to keep the game going. No longer did artists continually reinvent art, for it had been institutionally and commercially established—incidentally, with the admission that it was and remained a fiction, thus denying art's relevance to real life. Art critics ceased writing art history in the old sense, and artists stopped paying their debt to this kind of art history. Thus, the old play is interrupted if we haven't already been to a new play for some time, while we continue to consult the old textbooks, therefore failing to understand what happens. Talk of an end should not be confused with a longing for an end of art itself, which, like a picture in its frame, found a fitting framework in art history. The ideal art history was a narrative of the meaning and course of historical art. If today the image bursts out of its old frame, then we have reached the end of an old and most successful academic game. It was the frame that turned all it contained into a picture. It was art history that gathered the art of previous centuries into the picture, where we learned to see it. Only the frame provided inner cohesion to the image. Everything within it was, as art, privileged over everything outside, just as in a museum, which collects and displays only art that has already gone down in art history. The age of art history as an academic discipline coincides with the age of the museum.

The age of art history? Once again, we must define concepts. The idea of a general history of art was not established until the nineteenth century, while the material it gradually accumulated came from all previous centuries and millennia. Let us put it another way. Art had long been produced without any idea that it was fulfilling the course of art history. The comparison with the museum suggests itself again. Museums, too, filled up with artistic works that were created long before such institutions existed and without reference to them (fig. 1). But later, artists lived with museums and conscious of the idea of art history or else in opposition to it. We can distinguish the age of art history from all other ages that still lacked a framework for viewing art. My argument addresses this framework. It seems that taking art out of this frame has led to a new and uncertain art discourse that transfers itself onto art itself. Accordingly, artists have for some time abandoned what they call the "rigid frame" of artistic genres, which they find restrictive. They believe the public is also forced into a "rigid stare" at such a frame, even if, as at the movies, the frame contains a great deal of movement. Every genre proved to be a frame defining what was to become art. But the meaning of the frame, which keeps the viewer at a passive distance, also applies to the general situation in which culture manifests itself. It appears that the prevalent concept of culture was restricted to that of a historical culture that might, in retrospect, just as easily be resisted as revered. The struggle over "art and life" is, therefore, telling, suggesting as it does that art was only found outside life's reach: in the museum, in the concert hall, in books. The expert's gaze at a framed picture was a metaphor for the cultivated person's attitude to culture as an ideal. He or she always remained the audience, while artists and philosophers "made" culture.

Today, in contrast, people no longer appropriate culture for themselves but like a collective spectacle. There may be several reasons for this, for example, that we are not as much producing culture but repro-

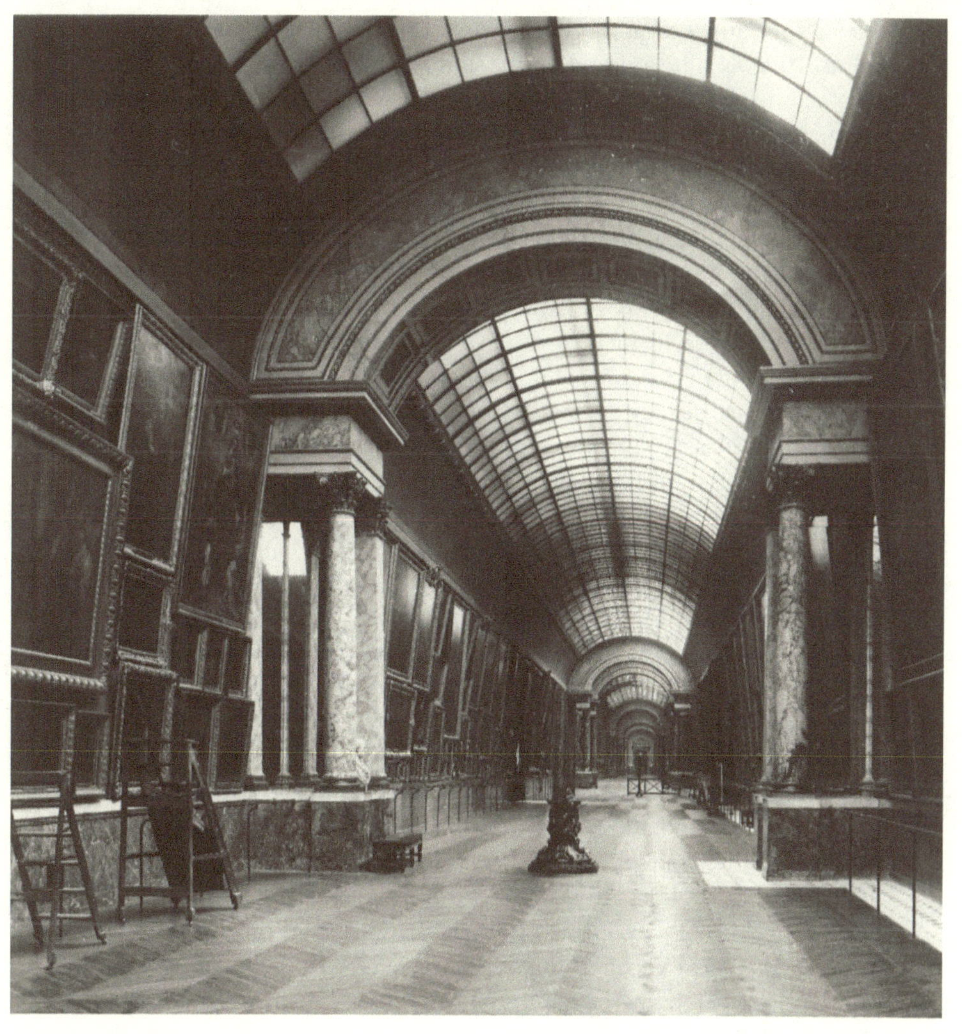

1. The Grande Galerie in the Musée du Louvre, Paris. Nineteenth-century photograph.

ducing the culture of other times. And therefore the desire is growing for culture that is entertaining rather than instructing and that offers a spectacle in which we take part. Artists react to this desire for entertainment and are performing art history as "remake" with a mixture of nostalgia and freedom that rejects the historical authority of art. Rather than continuing to represent culture and history, art engages in either rituals of remembrance or (depending on the given audience) resistance.

New exhibition types confirm the observation that the relationship between culture and art is shifting, providing another argument for the "end of art's true history" (see figs. 26, 27 below). Until now, it was taken for granted that art exhibitions were about art and served the experience of art history, in the sense of autonomous art; now more and more exhibitions are staging culture or history as art's messages for a viewer of a museum rather than for the reader of a book. The reason for organizing such exhibitions has less to do with art itself than with culture, whose visible performance requires art to be convincing. For the Biennial in 1995, Jean Clair's concept was not a retrospective of modern art but, under the title *Identity and the Other*, a synopsis of ideas about mankind and human nature in which art was to mirror the dramatic changes in the concept of the body and especially of the "self."

Since art has always been a privileged category of culture, it enjoyed full autonomy on its own terrain, where it felt free not only from social constraints but also from other cultural tasks. It was a culture's pride to tolerate free art and allow it to run its own course. Encroachments came from outside whenever art was forced into an ideological or political mold. But today, claims to get hold of art are increasing and are not primarily ideological or political. Rather, the culture is mustering its last reserves to achieve recognition; it rises or falls with the business of self-promotion, whereby art is requested to act as a convincing mirror.

Such general observations leave aside the question of who participates in and who profits from art history. Artists, art historians, and art critics do not share the same image of art history, in which, nevertheless, the are all involved. The alliance between artists and critics, both of whom had a share in the production of art history, was long put to an uncertain test. Artists were responsible for the future; art historians, for the past. History, which would bring out who was right (in art), was the concern of critics and historians, although this ceased to be true when marketing strategies of galleries began to dictate what would make subsequent art history. For a long time, the battle between art historians and artists was fought at the doors of the museum, which one group strove to defend from the other. This, too, changed after each side wanted to have the last word in the museum and to turn a temple into a stock exchange of art. Now, museums and art fairs can hardly be distinguished from each other: works seen at art fairs have already found their way into museums elsewhere.

Artists, who for so long resisted the authority of art history, now became its beneficiaries. The less they were able to speak with their work alone, the more they invoked a history that gave their art meaning. They themselves continued the path of history when they continued to produce art, and they followed history when borrowing from history their models. Sometimes a work is better explained by the time it recalls than by the time to which it belongs. Artists today use the history of art (against "low art" and popular taste) for cultural recollection of what the meaning of art has been. Art has long since ceased to be an elitist affair: it now is requested to represent cultural identity where the institutions fail to do so. Experts are no longer required to judge but only carry out the expected ritual. Where art no longer creates conflict but guarantees a conflict-free zone within society, experts cease to offer orientation. Where there is no expert, there is also no lay public.

These observations remain valid despite the unprecedented boom that both the art scene and the academic discipline of art history are enjoying. We have reached the climax of a development marked by a explosion in the number of artists and galleries. In New York, whole areas of the city are refurbished when the artists and galleries move in. The success of art (which, provided it is modern and preferably contemporary, is also collected by banks and hung in public offices) is not affected by complaints of art's blurred profile. Pandora's box gives each his own, so that the investment advisor replaces the art expert in social prestige. The success of art depends on who collects it, not on who makes it.

This boom is matched by the boom in art history. In Germany, for instance, the huge crowds of art history students are significant for the book market. *The Dictionary of Art* published by Macmillan, with 533,000 entries on world art in thirty-four volumes, is a sign of the worldwide development of interest in this field. The posters announce this event with the astonishing news that "6,700 scholars have joined together to change the world of art history" (fig. 2). The team of editors consists of just twelve well-known scholars, one of whom has already died; yet the number of art historians in business today must outrival the 6,700 listed here, since no one I know has worked on this project. The world of art history has grown very large, so large that it now communicates through dictionaries: and this produces a situation in which the

6,700 scholars
have joined together to change the world of art history.

2. Press notice for *The Dictionary of Art*, 1994.

former meaning and the cultural norm of a single, definitive art history fade away.

Art theory finds itself in a similar situation. In the realm of the humanities, art theory has split up among so many different disciplines and professional groups that it says more about the discipline in which it is practiced than about the art to which it refers. This has also been true of the philosophy of art ever since philosophical aesthetics fell into the hands of specialists who write philosophy's own history but have no new models to offer. The few models to arise in the last century—I mention here only Jean-Paul Sartre, Martin Heidegger, and Theodor W. Adorno—emerged within the framework of a personal philosophy. They were as incapable of founding a dominant theory of art as art was to attain inner unity. Artists' theories have seized the space previously occupied by art theory. Where there is no general theory of art, artists assume the right to express their own personal theory in their work.

A collection of essays edited by Dieter Henrich and Wolfgang Iser in 1982 concluded that there is no longer any integrative art theory. In its place are many limited-liability theories following each another, each dissolving art's aesthetic unity and chopping it up into "aspects." Discussing the functions of art is preferred to discussing art itself, and aesthetic experience itself is no longer self-explanatory (Iser). Many concepts we read harmonize surprisingly well with "contemporary art forms" that suspend "historical systems of symbols" and link them back to individual functions in "the social process" (Henrich). If a work of art oscillates between the mere *idea* of art and a mere *object,* then what it loses is the old claim for autonomy. If a work transforms itself into theory or, conversely, if it denies any aesthetic profile that art theory would distinguish from the everyday world, then classical art theory rapidly loses its ground.

The problem, if it is still one, arises only where the philosophy of art asserts a monopoly, which in modernism is as impossible to sustain as the idea of a linear and homogenous art history. Why should there be many art currents if they all fit into a single theory? Theories, works of art, and art movements all vie with each other on the same level; even discourses adopt a playful, polemical, and artistic form, something previously known only in creative practice. A new anthology of more than eleven hundred pages presenting twentieth-century *Art in Theory* in a solely *chrono*logical succession is, in its colorful variety, like art history itself, and is fittingly subtitled "An Anthology of Changing Ideas."

In 1984, at the same time as my previous essay appeared, Arthur C. Danto published his views about the end of art history, which coincide with a statement on art theory. In a revised version of 1989 that appeared in the periodical *Grand Street,* he maintains that, now after art had started to pose the philosophical question about the essence of art, it "was doing philosophy" in the medium of art and was therefore leaving its old territory behind. In his earlier publication, *The Transfiguration of the Common Place,* Danto had already insisted on the fact that art, no longer phenomenologically distinguishable from everyday objects, yielded to become a philosophical act. In a Hegelian phrase he added that "[a]rt has come to its end by becoming something else, namely philosophy." From now on, we read, artists no longer are required to define art for themselves, and thus also are freed from their previous history, in which they had to do what philosophy now could do for them.

I have exaggerated his point in order to reveal a philosopher's dream within it. But the question Danto posed has been intrinsic to art history for a long time, perhaps as long as anyone has reflected on art. The question has long raised the suspicion that the notion of art could be a fiction. This view of a phantom was only overcome where "the arts," as a plurality of artistic genres with a writable history, took its place. That is why Danto is right in saying that an end to art, in the sense of a particular "narrative of the history of art," can be conceived of only within the framework of an internal history, outside of which no predictions can be made and, therefore, can be no talk of an end.

We can now discern what is stirring people's minds when art loses the internal mirror of all the particular genres in which it has been created for so long. This is where progress, the life force of the individual arts, ceases to keep the old sense. Progress is exchanged for the concept of the "remake": let's repeat what has been done before. Any new manifestation is no better, but also no worse—and yet it comes as a reflection on previous art where the latter could not (yet) reflect on itself. The genres always provided a solid framework, which now begins to dissolve. Art history was a framework of a different kind, designed to put art's course in perspective. That is why the end of art history is also the end of a story: either because the story is changing or because there is, in the received sense, nothing more to tell.

Such media as we know today (film, video, etc.) approach the same problem whenever they are summoned to perform the drama of art and are equally liable to lose their proven profile. In an interview Peter

Greenaway gave in 1994, he justifies himself for questioning movie production while gradually preferring to put on exhibitions. It is the situation of cinema, whose fixed frame already held the viewer's gaze as much as in painting, that he wishes to "abandon." That is why Greenaway tends to rework some films for the stage, although he considers the stage, too, as restricting the audience's aesthetic experience. "All rules and structures are simply constructs" from which it is difficult to free oneself. Greenaway, art historian and artist in one, kept returning to the old masters in his study of lighting and composition and thus ceased to pay customs to the guardians of modernism. He sees technology as a means of expression and therefore as a constant, and not just a modern, precondition for art. On the one hand, Greenaway admits in his interview, he would like to release a baroque *Gesamtkunstwerk* in which the audience experiences the natural world as if in a film; on the other hand, he has recently made a black-and-white film whose "theme is that history does not exist, but is construed by historians."

In making such statements, Greenaway casts himself as a protagonist in a culture of posthistory in which the end of art history as a narrow framework is unavoidable. Art scholarship is unable to treat this theme with the same freedom, because to do so would risk its own legitimization. It prefers to engage in the allegory of its own tradition or in the archaeology of its accumulated knowledge, as found, for instance, in Donald Preziosi's book *Rethinking Art History*. The book sees itself as "a series of connected prolegomena for a history that will have to be written if we want to know where it is going," in other words, a clarification of the real story of art history as produced by the specialized literature. A chapter on Paleolithic "art," which, as we know, never drew the discipline's attention, arrives at the paradoxical conclusion that because art as we know it did not exist in the distant prehistoric past, it is also questionable today whether we have a proper understanding of art. In the final chapter, the author punningly leaves it to the reader to decide whether to read the title as referring to the "end" or the "ends" (i.e., purposes) of art history. The text concludes with a description of the Acropolis as if seen through the "frame" formed by the Propylaea, much as art history can be understood only in the light of its own narrative. The frame is the continually recurring notion in today's discussions whereas we had previously failed to notice it. In our case, Preziosi's discovery that all art history was a theory of history is the discovery of the frame.

The end of art history is practiced today in a multitude of books that never even mention this end. Our own culture is no longer the stern judge before whom we have to justify our scholarship, but rather, a beautiful stranger we encounter on the path to seduction. In other words, there are many ways to get lost in the labyrinth of historical culture once Ariadne's thread has been broken. In doing so, we now use our ancestors' original motifs to interrogate the exercise of art history. In a book published in 1994 on Winckelmann and the origins of art history, Alex Potts poses an unsettling question about the fascination for naked marble figures, or to quote the title, the question of *Flesh and the Ideal.* The question is answered with a homoerotic close-up photograph of a detail of the statue of Antinous, the once famous lover of Emperor Hadrian, in the Vatican Belvedere. But our historical distance from the homosexual writer Winckelmann and his archaeology is subtly substantiated by Walter Pater, who published a Winckelmann essay in England in 1867 in order to express his "theory concerning perverse sexual self-experience in cultural education and criticism"—admiring for his own part, as Pater puts it, the "sexless beauty of the Greek statues." Potts continues: "It would be somewhat anachronistic to envisage Pater as exploring what we would call a gay identity; we are with him, nevertheless, on the boundaries of a new modern consciousness of sexuality as playing an essential role in definitions of the self."

3 Art Criticism versus Art History

In Western culture, the problem of the literature of art was long apparent in the way it approached modernism. The study of the old masters focused on methods that were of little use in capturing the contradictory profile of modern art, encompassing all the crises and schisms of the modern world. Not that there were not plenty of attempts to do so; but their authors forced the image of modern art into the mold of art history, whereby art lost all resemblance to itself in the process. Despite all doubts, the needs of art history and its well-established paradigms effortlessly won the day. When we speak of the "history of the history of modern art," we have come to accept written history, not lived history, as the frame of reference.

I previously understood the problem as residing in the inadequate methods of the discipline; today, accumulated experience with a number of methods has caused me to change my view. There is no "right method" available for an academic discipline concerned with the "wild" freedom of recent art. The critics either want to serve a work by willingly providing the expected commentary or, conversely, to dominate it by imposing their own view. A critic is not expected to usurp for him- or herself the artist's freedom nor to allow his own commentary to rival art. That is something better left to poets, who, as we know, anyway were the first interpreters of art. Good old ekphrasis, which even in classical times was used to describe a work of art by the poet's own word-picture, has always remained in fashion. Admittedly, its protagonists in this area today are writers and philosophers rather than specialists in historical art. And artists have finally grown eloquent themselves and happily provide interviewers with the explanations they desire. Others have discovered art as the last domain in society that still offers them the freedom to develop grand visions and unleash speech. Art sometimes seems to be a preserve of the past; and the literature of art, an old ritual that we so love to relive.

The problem of method addresses the relationship between the commentary of art and the work of art. Art commentary has repeatedly sought to suspend its difference from the work and substitute itself for the work, in other words, to establish a mimetic relationship to the work of art—commentary as art. This temptation grew in the same measure that works lost their formal autonomy and became incommunicable except through commentary, which competed with art itself. Art *criticism* took on the tasks of art *theory* ever since philosophers and men of letters began writing manifestos for a group of artists: Filippo Marinetti for the futurists, André Breton in his role as spokesman and taskmaster of the surrealists, to name only the first in a long line. The continually burgeoning production of new theories reduced each individual theory to a slogan around which a group of artists gathered in a joint effort, and each slogan forced each work to represent their collective credo. Thus the work was in principle bound to a theory that subsequent critics would be expected to respect. Art essentially appeared to be shrinking into individual free zones whose bounds were marked by theories. Art historians played only a small part in this game. In the end, their methods served more their own specialized needs than to describe what happened in contemporary art.

The relationship between commentary and work shifted with the growing claims of theory-bound art criticism, as soon as artists versed in theory joined the debate. The texts artists had for a long time written gained a new quality with Marcel Duchamp, who mirrored his works in texts that soon became impossible to distinguish from his visual creations and thus caused more confusion than the works themselves. For example, he wrote the first texts of what later served as commentary to *The Large Glass* before this central work even existed (fig. 3). Joseph Kosuth declared that Duchamp had given art back its true identity when he posed "the question of its function" and discovered that "art is [nothing else than] the definition of art."

In my book on the "invisible masterpiece," I recently tried to reveal the commentary in Duchamp's work and the work in his commentary without distinguishing what Duchamp himself had not separated. *The Large Glass* preempted all other commentaries on his work as commentary on the artist's commentary, which was already part of the fabric of his work. André Breton, without having seen the work himself, used this opportunity more productively than anyone else. Duchamp effectively ran through all the possible variations of art commentary by publishing his work himself and by continuing to reinterpret it for decades, thus determining and wrapping in mystery the course of its reception. In this way, the place of *The Large Glass* cannot be distinguished from its place in (or its gradual withdrawal from) the history of reception. Work and text became tautological in this process. Traditional art scholarship can derive little use from such a situation, since it must restrict itself to reporting on the genesis (and completion) of the work, that is, to describing events that in this case seem merely secondary.

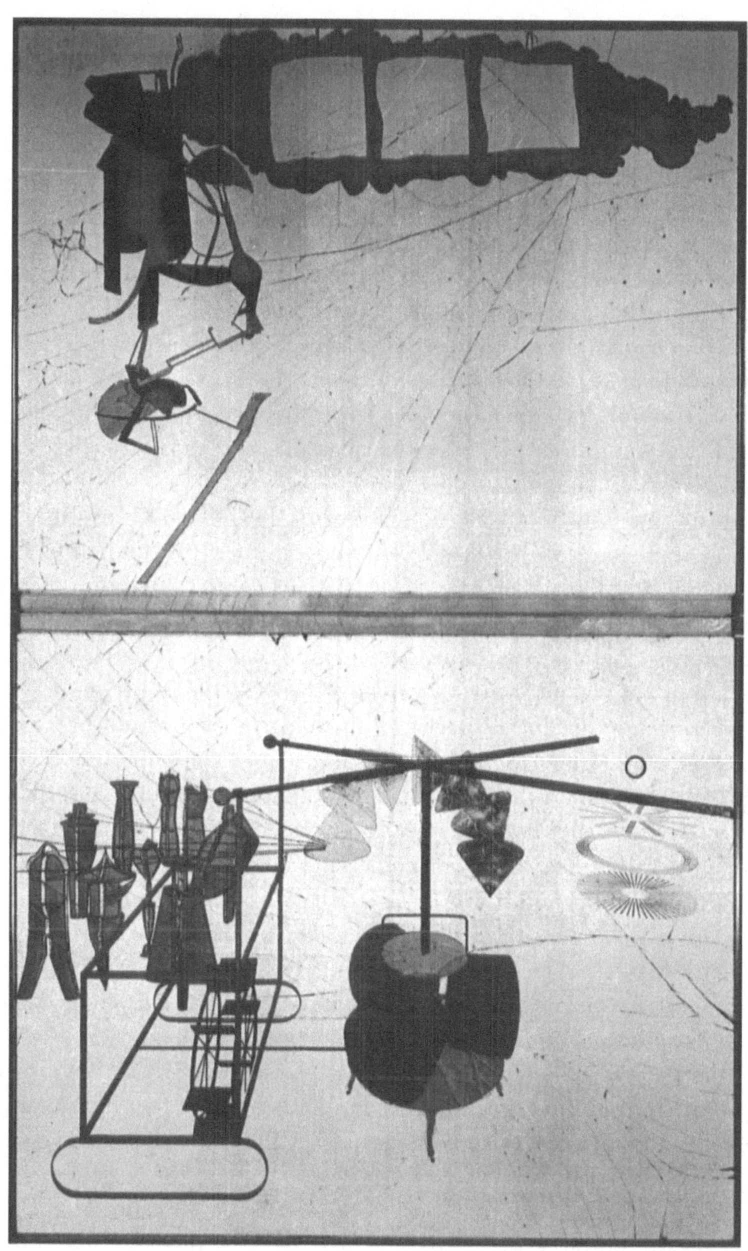

3. Marcel Duchamp, *La mariée mise à nu par ses célibataires, même* (The Large Glass), 1915–1923. Philadelphia Museum of Art, Philadelphia. © 2002 Artists Rights Society (ARS), New York/ADAGP, Paris/Succession Marcel Duchamp.

The question of the role of commentary shifted again when conceptual artists arrived on the scene and accused traditional art of being "formalistic." The respective artists were determined to address the concept of art as such, which also meant that they gave their own "propositions" priority over the usual works. As Joseph Kosuth stressed in *Art after Philosophy* (1969), such artists no longer wanted to create works but only to pose questions. Making art, as they understood it, meant casting doubt on art itself and producing commentaries on art. The high point of this new campaign was reached when, in 1969, the periodical *Art and Language* discussed the question whether the keynote article belonged "to the category of the work of art," if the concepts of art were simply expanded and the text exhibited in a gallery. The *Art and Language* people played with the assumption that concept art had rendered traditional art theory superfluous.

In a famous 1965 installation *One and Three Chairs,* Kosuth exhibited a single chair in three different versions (fig. 4): the real chair, a photograph of the same chair, and the chair as explained in a dictionary—that is, the chair as principle. The juxtaposition of picture and description is tricky, since it aims at placing image and text on the same level, thus wiping out the traditional distinctions: the picture here is also reduced to mere definition. Seen as a whole, the commentary triumphs over the work, which it causes to disappear. All the same, the text exhibited on the wall usurps the position of a picture. Kosuth's installation proposed a thesis that could have been voiced at any time, even a century earlier. But the proposition could not have been exhibited as *art* until the mid-1960s, and it was so associated with the Kosuth installation that any similar exhibition today would refer back to it. Seen in this light, art history suddenly appears strangely insubstantial and arbitrary. Thus, perhaps entirely in the spirit of the artist, I feel tempted to reproduce Kosuth's installation, not in an "original photograph" as it would appear when exhibited today or as it first appeared in 1965, but after an illustration from Robert Atkins's art guide, where the chair no longer appears as a trinity but as something quite different: a slogan in modern art history, concept art.

A few years later, the art critic Germano Celant introduced his book *Art Povera* with a two-page statement that turns this idea on its head and, instead of reducing a work of art to a text as Kosuth does, transforms the text into a work of art (fig. 5). Where once a group of artists agreed on a manifesto, now it is the art critic who introduces the respective movement in art with his own theses. The book in which Celant

CONCEPTUAL ART

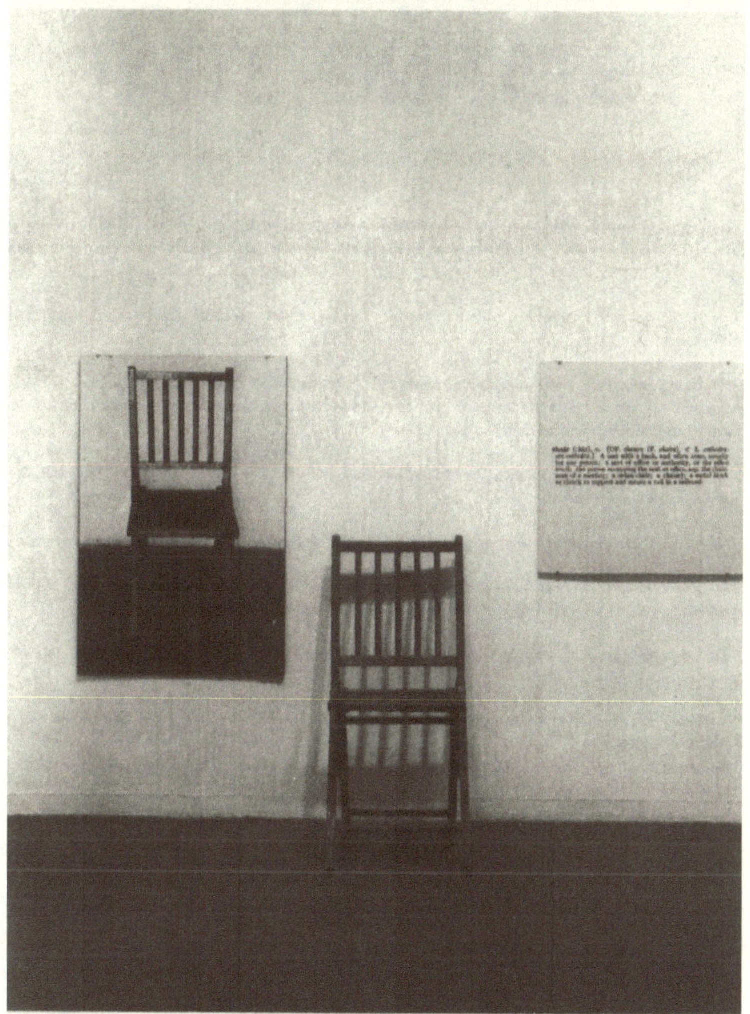

JOSEPH KOSUTH (b. 1945).
One and Three Chairs, 1965. Photograph of chair, wooden folding chair, and photographic enlargement of dictionary definition of chair, photo panel: 36 x 24 1/8 in.; chair: 32 3/8 x 14 7/8 x 20 7/8 in.; text panel: 24 1/8 x 24 1/2 in. Collection, The Museum of Modern Art, New York; Larry Aldrich Foundation Fund.

4. Joseph Kosuth, *One and Three Chairs*, 1965. From Robert Atkins, *Art Speak: A Guide to Contemporary Ideas, Movements and Buzzwords* (New York, 1990), 64. © 2002 Joseph Kosuth / Artists Rights Society (ARS), New York.

STATING THAT

This book does not aim at being an objective and general analysis of the phenomenon of art or life, but is rather an attempt to flank (both life and art) as accomplices of the changes and attitudes in the development of their daily becoming.

The book does not attempt to be objective since the awareness of objectivity is false consciousness.

The book, made up of photographs and written documents, bases its critical and editorial assumptions on the knowledge that criticism and iconographic documents give limited vision and partial perception of artistic work.

The book, when it reproduces the documentation of artistic work, refutes the linguistic mediation of photography.

The book, even though it wants to avoid the logic of consumption, is a consumer's item.

The book inevitably transforms the work of the artist into consumer goods and cultural goods, a means of satisfying the cultural frustrations of the reader.

The book proposes a way for the public to take part in artistic events, but does not impose it upon them.

The book narrows and deforms, given its literary and visual oneness, the work of the artist.

The book is a precarious and contingent document and lives hazardously in an uncertain artistic-social situation.

5. From Germano Celant, ed., *Art Povera: Conceptual, Actual or Impossible Art?* exhibition catalog (London, 1969), 5.

selected his artists "does not attempt to be objective since the consciousness of objectivity is false consciousness." Readers may ask themselves what they are entitled to expect from such a book. In the very next sentence, Celant questions the role of "criticism" as a mirror of artistic production and accordingly "refuses" to comment on the photographs as reproductions of works in his text. The book, he says, is meant for cultural consumption but cannot replace a visit to an exhibition: indeed, the very book as medium is as different from the artist's work as possible. These are of course truisms, but they are so affectedly and provocatively delivered that this commentary on art stages itself as an art product in its own right. The typography alone, and even more so the diction, reveals the text's claim that it is itself art.

It is only logical, then, that Celant's rival Achille Bonito Oliva should construe his own texts as literature fulfilling literary demands rather than informing about the art world. His smile adorns the cover of his book *The Dream of Art,* painted by one of "his" artists, who is included as accomplice in the portrait (fig. 6). If the boundaries between art criticism and art are thus blurred, this is merely an echo of the transformation of art into art commentary, as discussed above. The painting by John Baldessari (which I describe in detail below; see p. 173), brings this situation to a head: the painting is no longer anything more than the medium of art commentary in art form. Here the commentary consists of a short epigram: "Everything is purged from this painting but art; no ideas have entered this work."

I personally prefer such playful commentaries to the mountain of dull verbiage on art that expects the reader to mistake it for information. But the issue here is not to judge the value of art commentaries but to identify them as a critical genre for the discipline of art history. As a genre, art history is itself a form of commentary—historical commentary—which is why it is put in question when its very subject is a commentary, unless it turns into a history of ideas. Here a general remark is in place. Commentaries on contemporary artistic events are different in intention than historical texts that remember old events. The former aim at a meaning in the present; the latter, at a historical one and thus usually insist on the fact that everything happened just as they have it, and that what they thus authentically narrate is history.

It is amusing to see the same individuals who had written the commentaries now writing—after a decent interval—"history," either by revising the commentaries of years ago or, more simply, using their own memories as the proof of art history. "I remember that it was thus and not otherwise." Fact, information, and interpretation coalesce, and the

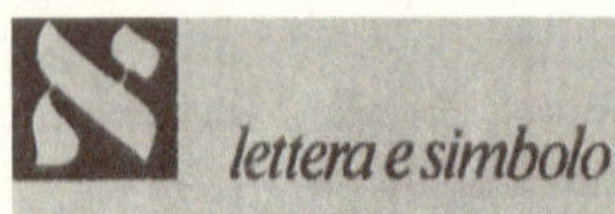

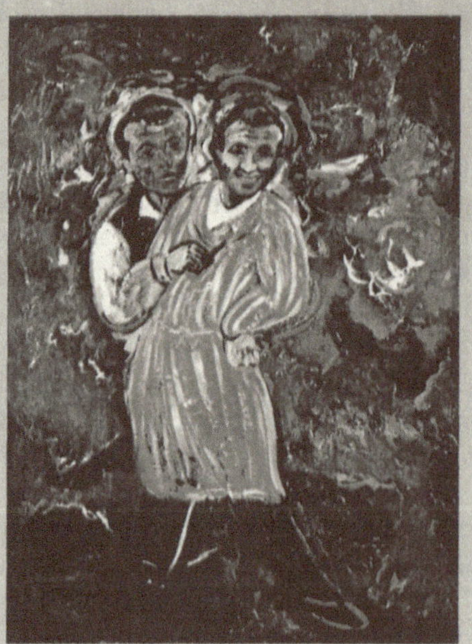

6. Sandro Chia, portrait of Achille Bonito Oliva. Cover illustration of Achille Bonito Oliva, *Il sogno dell'arte* (Milan, 1981).

authors use their own source material, just as the artists do. We begin to sympathize with this practice when still other authors, who cannot be a source, cease to find pleasure in the historical report, indeed in information *tout court,* and invent their own theories in order to have a personal entrance into the crowded market of art literature. In every theory there is a measure of aggression or surrender—if we leave aside its place in the writer's academic career. If we were honest, we would much rather know how things really were and understand what Western culture had been rather than listen with hesitation to the confusing concert of theories that, in the end, characterize only their authors.

4 The Unwelcome Heritage of Modernism: Style and History

Our understanding of modernism and our uncertainty whether we still live in it also applies to the argument of written art history, which, as an object of scholarship, is itself a product of modernism. Art history began with a concept of *history* and extended it to the concept of *style.* While the concept of history was a legacy of the nineteenth century, that of style materialized in the early twentieth century. Style was that quality of art for which a logical evolution was to be traced. In a book published in 1893, *Stilfragen* (Questions of Style), Alois Riegl laid the foundations for an art scholarship dedicated to pure form, and the book concentrates on nothing but ornament; the author did not involve any questions of meaning. The "will to art," as he summarized the dynamics of the art process, was in the end a declaration of style. Heinrich Wölfflin's famous book *Kunstgeschichtliche Grundbegriffe* (Fundamental Concepts of Art History), published in 1915, carries the telling subtitle *Das Problem der Stilentwicklung in der neueren Kunst* (The Problem of the Development of Style in Newer Art).

In Wölfflin's view, however, "newer art" referred to Renaissance and baroque art, which he viewed as representing the very essence of art itself. This reveals a conflict in early art scholarship that has had far-reaching consequences. Although this scholarship began in the modern age, its focus lay in the art of the old masters, whence it derived its categories for dealing with art per se. On closer look, however, analogies emerge between the views of artists and art scholars; the artists judged their own work with similar concerns for pure form that their contemporaries, the art historians, applied to the study of old masters. Key terms such as "impressionism" or "optical subjectivism," used in written art history to describe even the art of late classical antiquity, are symptoms enough of this. But the contradiction remains that modern art scholarship focuses its energies on the art of the old masters.

That is the reason a figure like Max Raphael (1899–1952) never had a chance to make a career in the discipline. His first work, *Von Monet zu Picasso* (From Monet to Picasso; 1913), was rejected as a doctoral thesis by Heinrich Wölfflin. Its subject was too modern, and its argument seemed not focused enough on the history of style; rather, the theoretical section attempted a "Versuch einer Grundlegung des Schöpferischen" (An Essay on Creativity). Nonetheless, it appeared as a book, went into a third edition as early as 1919, and was widely read outside the discipline. In the 1920s, when Raphael was involved in adult education in Berlin, he became acquainted with the socialist movement and studied Marxism, although he remained faithful to the notion of creative autonomy. After he went into exile in 1933, he could no longer publish his writings on art theory. In New York—where he was equally unsuccessful—he expanded his oeuvre with a study of Picasso's *Guernica.* Not until 1968, sixteen years after his death, did an English translation appear, titled *The Demands of Art.* The German original was finally published in 1984, almost half a century after it should have had its effect, under a title that by then seemed outdated and all too didactic: *Wie will ein Kunstwerk gesehen sein?* (How Does a Work of Art Want to Be Seen?). Of course, this tragic biography is a special case, but in fact Raphael faced a problem in his own discipline, in which modernism, as a theme, was still far off in the future.

Only a few outsiders, above all, writers, made modern art their theme. But they shared the basic conviction in art history that art's "internal history" had always been the history of style. Julius Meier-Graefe, as I have shown elsewhere, or Werner Weisbach charted the history of contemporary art as if it proceeded by plan and using an argument that could not have been simpler. The art of the old masters, they claimed, was primarily "style," and as such followed a course of "history" that continued in modernism. If art was reduced to style, that is, to an item of evolution, then not even the loss of figuration seemed to be a break with the past, since abstract art emerged as an ultimate triumph of form. Here, style no longer even needs to be abstracted from content, since it has become content in its own right. The historians of modern art, whatever their intellectual sympathies, had one and the same objective: to maintain the integrity of a single art history, regardless of differences between old and new. At the same time, they thus pursued the aim of allaying their readers' fear of contact with contemporary art, which they celebrated as an embodiment of the "law of history," on the path of progress.

The early project of art history and the enterprise of modernism are connected in a willful and almost paradoxical way. In the conceptual pair, history and style, we can see the true physiognomy of modernism, which today stands accused of having a one-sided picture of history and a tyrannical will to style, a charge that is beyond dispute. The great political movements designed the future, just as the arts did, by their own different means. Both movements were inspired by utopian ideals they hoped to realize in the future. Social and aesthetic intentions were closely linked. Both movements felt the need for liberation from the historicism of the nineteenth century, where their roots lay, and proclaimed the advent of a "new history" or a "new art."

The result is what we call modernism today. Just like "true" style in art, the imperative logic of history was more than a mere concept. It was based on models that society could identify with or assail. This explains the iconoclastic debate in twentieth-century art as a political issue. The hope placed on a new art that would initiate a new way of life frightened its opponents and discouraged its followers whenever the promised utopias failed in art. It was soon architecture and design that, as symbols of a new society, were to change the environment in which, it was hoped, people would also change.

These well-known facts and theories seem less harmless if, instead of explaining the early history of modernism in art, they reveal what lurks beneath the surface of beautiful ideals. At that time, style and history rapidly took not just a polemical but even a militant tone, which is all too readily excused when viewed in innocent retrospect. Today, we see the results of artistic modernism, but we prefer to forget the very ideas that brought them about, or else we regret to be excluded from the euphoria of these times. I therefore, in a short digression, will add a few colors to the picture of pure art and true style.

The contemporary critics understood the period before the outbreak of the First World War either as a time of new beginnings or of doom. But for all concerned, it was a time of suffering, which the revolutionaries saw as the catalyst of great changes. In this spirit, the Italian futurists, visiting the artistic capital Paris in 1912, had a group photograph taken of themselves, as if to intensify the impact of their movement and present a living manifesto (fig. 7). The central figure, towering over the others and with a self-esteem to match, is Marinetti, the man of letters and writer of their texts who enlisted his fellow artists in a common program. Futurist paintings and sculptures may still look modern—in fact, more modern than anything today's art has to offer—but these gentlemen themselves do not. They were still young then, but their very clothing reveals how old modernism has meanwhile become. They look as if they are in costume, wearing the clothes of the bourgeois society against which they have declared war. But this intention does not make the era any less remote from us.

I do not need to outline here the idea of futurism, which fills the first chapter in the history of modernism. A few key words will suffice to recall the slogans that marshal the concept of "history" against hated "tra-

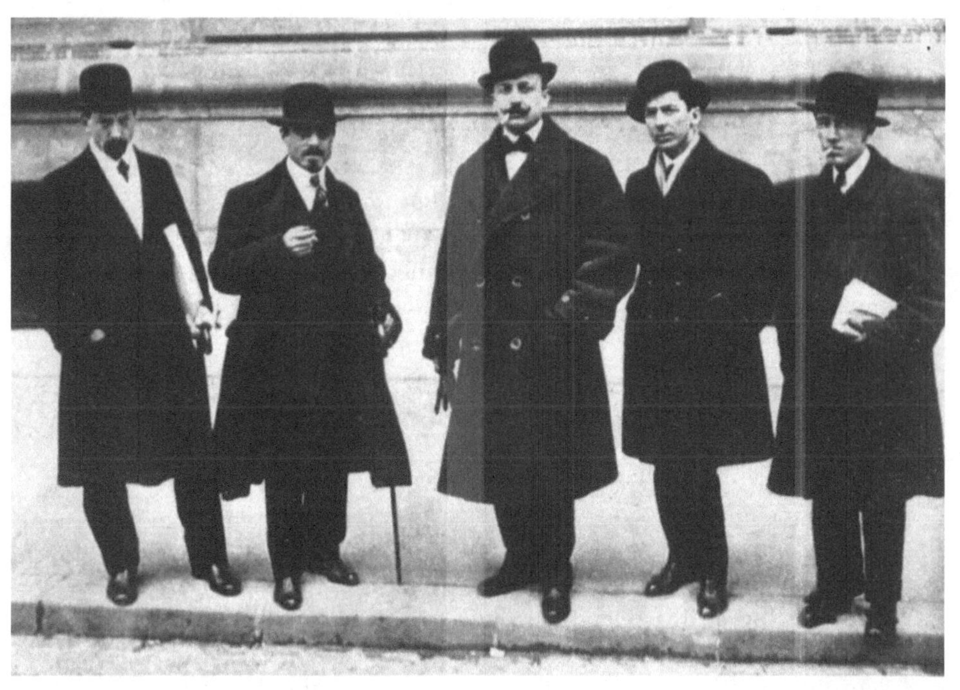

7. The futurists in Paris, 1912. From left: Luigi Rossolo, Carlo Carrà, Filippo Tommaso Marinetti, Umberto Boccioni, and Gino Severini.

dition" and that declare "technology" to be the successor of humanistic "culture" and the new "style," produced by the people for the people, to be the true replacement of the author and "individual" of the bourgeois age. Even the coming war was greeted joyfully as a force that would turn society upside down all the more swiftly. The *Mona Lisa,* which had recently been stolen from the Louvre (what an omen!), represented the epitome of an immobile culture that artists were keen to eliminate—although they tied themselves up in contradictions by producing paintings and sculptures that, on the other hand, disclaim their remoteness from time and movement.

A year later, Julius Meier-Graefe, who had always been a stalwart advocate of modernism, wrote two texts against the state of culture and art, which he published under the title *Wohin treiben wir?* (Where Are We Headed?; fig. 8). To anyone who believes in prophets, they are a disappointment, since seen from our perspective, modernism began at the time he was writing, whereas the author believed he was witnessing the demise of his own modern age. In this essay Meier-Graefe, who was then still working on his celebrated *Entwicklungsgeschichte der modernen Kunst* (The Development of Modern Art), had lost touch with his times and thus was in error. Nonetheless, when criticizing his own time he tells us things that are no longer obvious to us and thus elucidates a stage in the debate that deserves to be reconstructed when we speak of modernism.

What alarms him is the break with tradition, since this signifies to his mind a decline of the ideal of the creative individual, which he deeply respected, having grown up in bourgeois society. At a remove of twenty years, he recalls his first visits to Paris with unreserved nostalgia: "At that time Manet had been dead for years, Cézanne had vanished, Degas had become an embittered anchorite. Of the younger artists, van Gogh had recently died and Gauguin had gone native. What, however, was to be seen were their works. It was like a whole panorama, palpable. Every day a new work was revealed, every week, another series." Contemporary art and the cubists, whom Meier-Graefe only reluctantly accepted, could scarcely assert themselves in the face of such reminiscences. He was instead inclined to ask whether the new movement was leading to the death of culture, as had once happened in the Late Classical age "when the ancient world was overthrown by the barbarians and a completely new intellectual world replaced the old world formed by the gods."

To readers who now raise their eyebrows and think they have caught me in the act of professing my view, I say: patience, the colors in

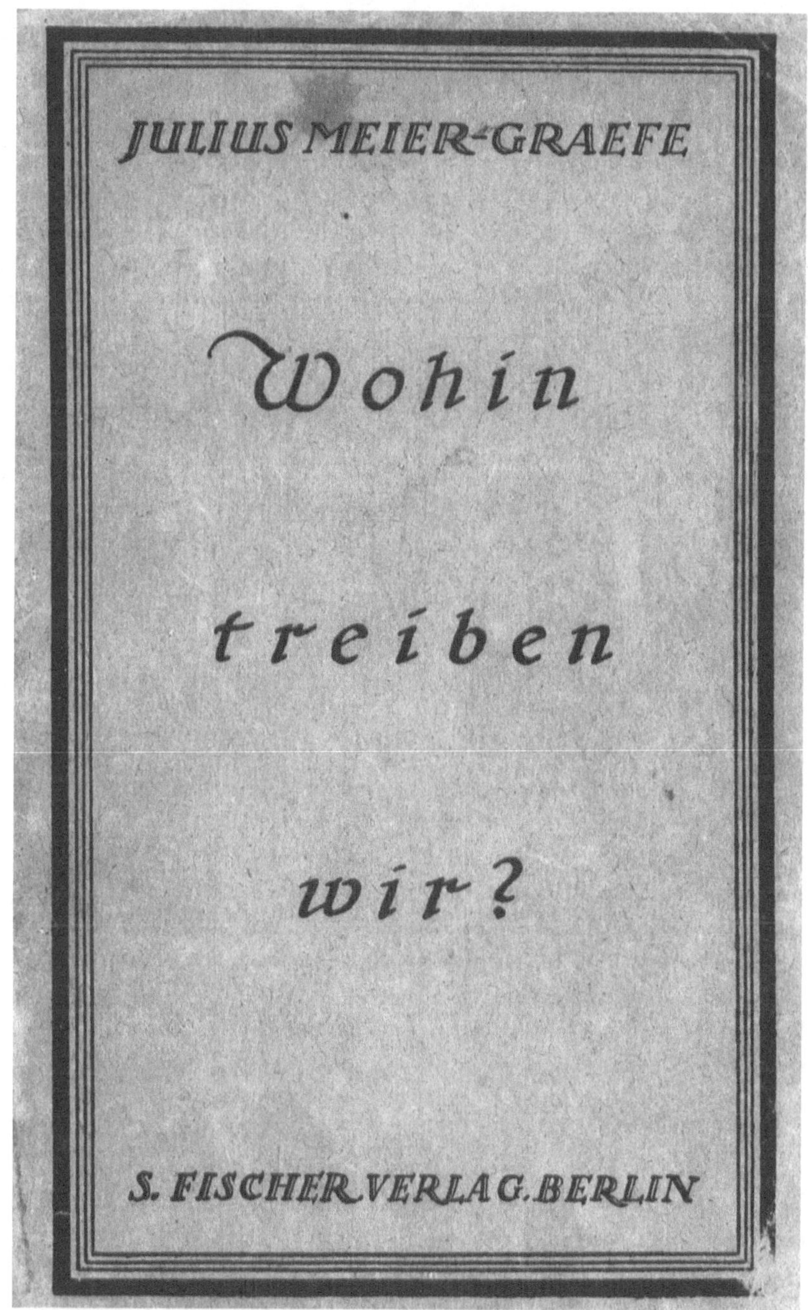

8. Cover, Julius Meier-Graefe, *Where Are We Heading?* (in German; Berlin, 1913).

my sketch are not yet complete. Meier-Graefe laments his age with comments such as "images have become slogans," "concepts are so hollow and constructed that they appear to be mere theatrical props," "Finding no style in the old masters, we have become stylists," and by ignoring all of Paul Cézanne's other ideas, he brutally reduces him to "the logic of his color system." When Meier-Graefe speaks of "barren concepts" and of seeing only "surface artists," "flat people," at work, this cheap criticism reflects an experience we no longer know today: the experience of the many riches that were washed out of art—and how much narrower art appeared when it strove for complete purity!

Equally disquieting was the attempt, in the new age, to denounce "personality" and "humanity," which formerly had been considered the highest ideals. These qualities embraced the notion of tragic genius, which was at the time loudly denounced as obsolete. Thomas Mann wrote its elegy in 1912 when he visited the Lido in Venice and published the short novel *Death in Venice*, whose hero, the composer Gustav Aschenbach, resembles Gustav Mahler, whose "princely dying in Paris and Vienna" could be followed daily in the newspapers. Thomas Mann recalled this in his essay "On Myself," written in American exile in 1940. There he adds that this melancholic and ironic portrait of the decadent artist was appropriate to that turning point in history where the "whole individualistic problem of a bourgeois age about to culminate in catastrophe" exhausted itself.

The First World War put an end to the debate over the views about which side would win. The dadaists, meanwhile, were in a better position to satirize traditional artistic concepts, but they put even more effort into exorcizing any expressions and ideas related back to the bourgeois individual. In 1921, Raoul Hausmann constructed his *Mechanical Head*, which he subtitled "The Spirit of Our Age" (fig. 9). "The spirit of Everyman in all his limitations," he commented later, was only "sensitive to what has been glued to his skull from the outside by chance." For Hausmann, dadaism meant "to see things as they are" and thus to accept that "people have no character; their faces are images made by the hairdresser." This was antithesis and mockery in the same breath, and colleagues with spiritual or abstract leanings instead worshipped the coming of pure "style."

A Dutch movement gave itself the name De Stijl and, in 1918, published a *First Manifesto* of its ideals, which they took back in the *Third Manifesto* to some extent. The "predominance of the individual" had to be abolished, even "destroyed," before the "universal" would triumph.

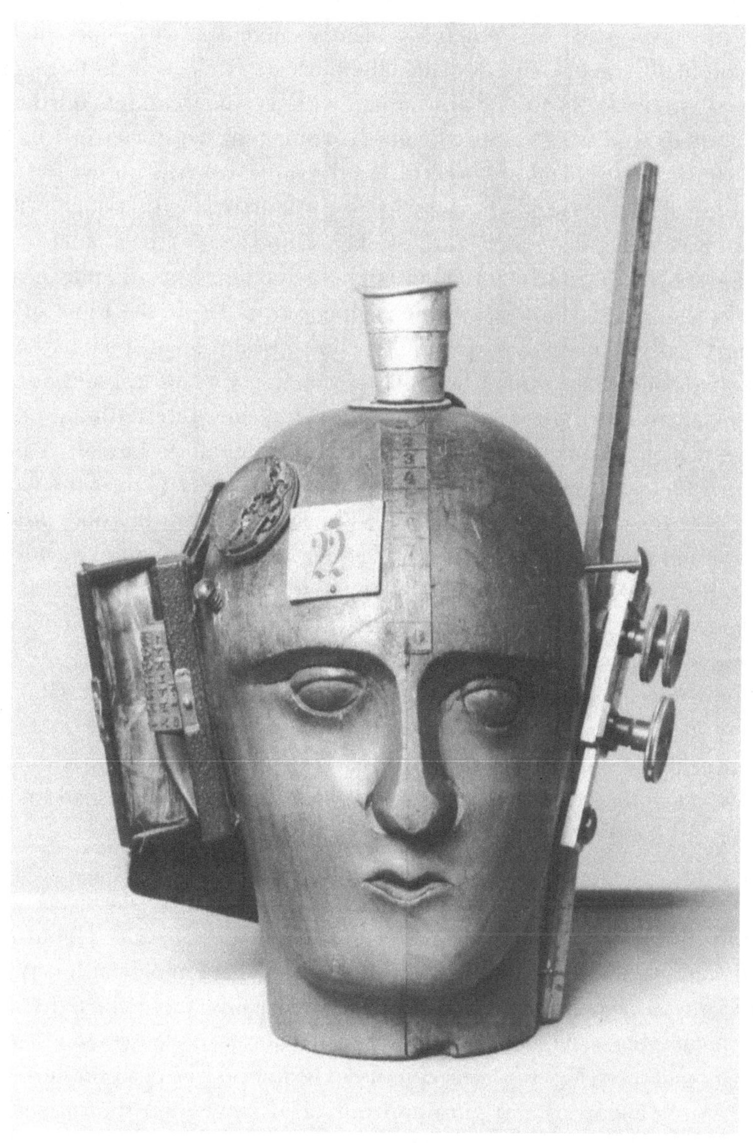

9. Raoul Hausmann, *Mechanical Head: The Spirit of Our Age*, 1921. Musée d'art moderne, Paris. © 2002 Artists Rights Society (ARS), New York / ADAGP, Paris.

But the "universal" was much less clearly defined: it was a formula for a general abstract clarity in which all objects, as well as all feelings, dissolved into pure "forms." "Tradition," with its wealth and its burden of heredity as well as its surfeit of competing ideas and historicisms, was to fall victim to this ideal of poverty; and the same was true for every "natural form" that "stands in the way of pure artistic expression." "History" was to begin anew, regardless of cost, and lead to the victory of the universal "style" in which the human being no longer would play a role.

In the *Third Manifesto,* which appeared in 1921, the topic of the "spirit" only comes as a surprise if one links the notion of spirit to the individual. But we encounter here another meaning of spirit, not the spirit of socialism nor that of capitalism, but rather an "International of the spirit which is spiritual." A new spiritual religion, as has often been longed for, was to proclaim the dominion of the "spirit" over the world and over the individual. Theosophical ideas long latent not only among individual members of De Stijl loomed behind the horizon of a cool rationalism that was to enable art to shape a new society. Utopia also has a dark side, as Beat Wyss has documented from within its hidden depths: the myth of beginning was the enemy of tradition. Mysticism and technology entered then into a strange alliance. Kazimir Malevich, who left a late suprematist manifesto in Berlin behind, became a mystic and militant critic of culture when he wrote, "The art of figuration is doubly dead, since on the one hand it depicts a culture in decay, and on the other, it kills reality in its attempt to represent it."

Written art history, too, at about the same time sacrificed biography and anecdote to "stylistic laws" and changes of style. The historical sources about art collected in the course of the nineteenth century suddenly appeared redundant after art history now was to be read from the forms themselves. Artists and their lives were no longer the principal themes. "Style," too, was conceived of in opposition to the individual, symbolizing instead pure and universal perception that appeared unconnected to particular cultural traditions. The analogies between art and art history speak for themselves. Curiously, even this notion of style offered identity, much as modernism itself did, once it was sparking the first great controversies: controversies in which two ideologies, "new art" and "new society," vied for the upper hand.

As long as art was the subject of open debate, that debate reflected expectations that always exceeded the purview of art. The Soviet Russians rejected any art that did not reflect the new society as they understood it. The constructivists appeared to be following only the goals of pure art, not those of the Party. The Nazis, on the other hand, were appalled when they saw art reflecting the ugly face of the modern world: the realists and the expressionists revolted against the aestheticization of politics and life with which the fascist state celebrated itself. The ruling Party, in both cases, demanded the ideal, even for the prize of kitsch. If the age was "sick," at least art was to appear healthy. The talk of the "artistic ideal" actually meant the ideal of the Party's own philosophy, just as conversely (and with equal militancy) artistic circles would speak of the "new society" as an environment in which to assert the "new art."

This debate was soon extended from art to written art history, which under public pressure obeyed the task of justifying the desired art. Art and art history were thus rapidly bound up in the course of modernism in diverse and confusing ways, even if art only seemed to follow its own laws and art history seemed to present nothing but the unsullied scholarship of its discipline. The high point of the debate was reached when the Third Reich issued its veto on modern art, just as the Soviet Union had done earlier, and when that veto was also applied to written art history, in which hated modernism was no longer permitted to be discussed.

The artists' slogans and the discourses of the art historians were surprisingly connected. "Abstraction," which removed itself from all nonartistic reality, and formal analysis, which neglected content, corresponded to each other and this also applies to "concrete art," in which mattered nothing but form and color, while everyday topics and themes became irrelevant. But pure art, like pure style, was quickly abandoned in favor of analysis and realism. The realists turned a critical eye on their own society to portray the "naked truth," while the art historians turned to social history even when studying the old masters. The surrealists sought, on the other hand, the unconscious in order to portray an "inner reality." Soon afterward, iconologists were examining the symbols of mankind, but instead of studying the unconscious, they concentrated on the realm of cultural knowledge, and instead of looking at the irrational images of individual dreams, they remained attentive only to the rational elements in tradition.

Written art history, then, did not arise in the rarefied atmosphere of pure scholarship and was not, as one might wish to believe, entirely dedicated to the inner needs of its own special field, but engaged in the debate of its time, even if indirectly or contradictorily. In early modernism, its thoughts were always concentrated on the abstract image of an art history that followed its own laws; and in this it corresponded to the artists' self-reflection, since all their activity was to culminate in an objective and universal art of the future. Art historians and artists were similarly committed to a collective ideal of modernism. Only those who agree on this sympathize with the argument I discuss in this book, the argument about the history of the history of art and the latter's present tasks.

5 The Late Cult of Modernism: Documenta and Western Art

Two events, however, separate early modernism from the present, and they permanently affected both the fate of art and the image of written art history. I speak of events, since they were not part of any artistic evolution but came from the outside world and dispensed with the pleasant ideas of continuity. The cultural policies of National Socialism represented the first event, and the new cultural hegemony of the United States in or over Europe was the second event to be discussed in any retrospective on twentieth-century art. These events, which radically changed all subsequent art and significantly shifted the conception of art history in the light of recent modern art, can be explained easily enough, but certainly not in terms of the so-called laws of art history. The debate that raged about "degenerate art" was only the high point of an already long-simmering controversy on modern art (fig. 10). What was new was the state veto that affected both art and art criticism. Modern art, in Germany the victim of politics, became the hero of international culture. Art criticism, which was silenced first in Germany and then in wartime France, became in exile the voice of this new international culture. After the war, a new criticism initiated a program of "restitution" for "lost modernism," casting a rosy glow over "classic modern art" and giving it a flawless profile. Modern art occupied a sacred space in which only veneration was possible and where critical analysis was out of place.

It is usually overlooked that the first Documenta exhibition in Kassel in 1955 did not exhibit contemporary production as it does today but was conceived as a retrospective of modern art as it had survived the period of persecution and destruction and that was now celebrated as a new classicism. It was precisely in Germany, where museums' collections had been plundered, that an attempt was made to recover the presence of prewar modernism, which Werner Haftmann, who organized the Documenta exhibition with Arnold Bode, had described in the first edition of his *Malerei im 20. Jahrhundert* (Twentieth-Century Painting). Naturally, this exhibition also overcame the national barriers that had been impermeable before the war, and European art emerged as the victor over nationalistic madness. For this reason, the Americans at first remained in the background, although from 1948 on an increasing number of

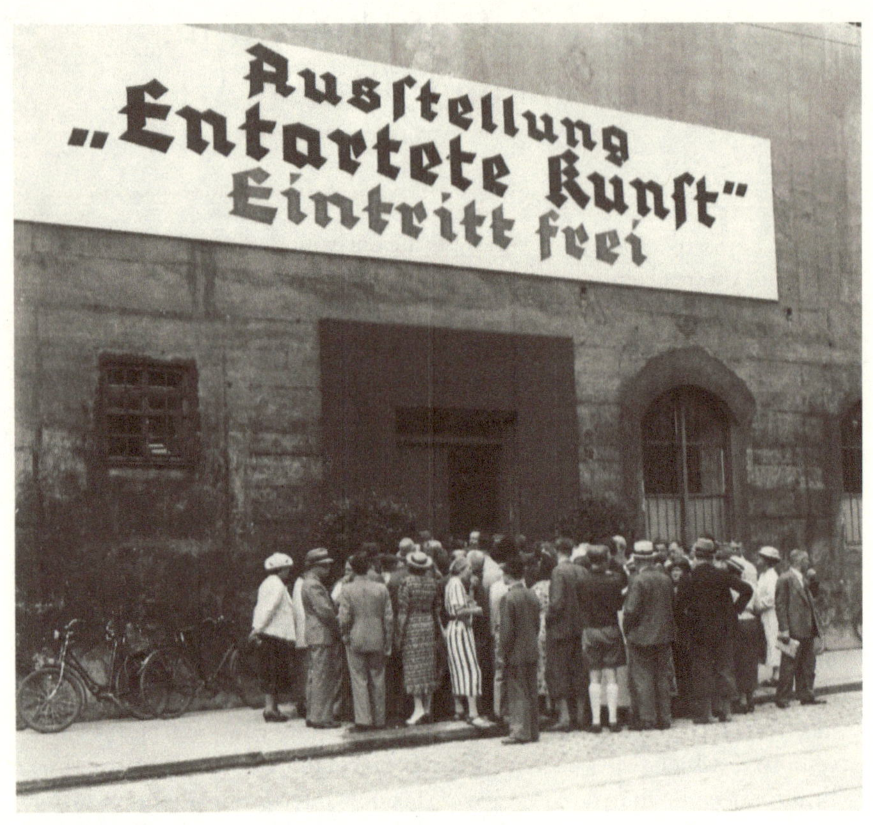

10. Visitors at the entrance to the exhibition *Degenerate Art*, shown at no. 4, Gallery Street, Munich, 1937.

exhibitions of American abstract art, for instance, in Baden-Baden, already had presented the new world power's ideal of freedom.

Whoever studies the photographic records of the exhibition rooms that housed the first Documenta exhibit is both struck and bewildered by its templelike aura (fig. 11). The very museum building, damaged by the war, conveyed the idea of new life springing out of the ruins. As they made their way up the central staircase, visitors were welcomed by Wilhelm Lehmbruck's *Large Kneeling Woman*, as if she, along with all the other masterpieces on exhibition, had returned from exile. Modern art, which had so often led the charge against the established culture, seemed in retrospect to be the true culture that had been repressed in the now-ended period of barbarism and that finally enjoyed its deserved rehabilitation. This cult of modernism was a mirror image of the censure it had formerly suffered. The new idealism is only too comprehensible if it is measured by the desire to purge guilt and bad memories. But it also went its own way in that it supplanted the history that had actually happened with its purified image in terms of longed-for and recollected history.

The critics, however, still faced doubts and prejudices as they tried to reveal the image of pure innocence in the works of classical modernism. They still remembered the old accusations that this was not art but degenerate art, in other words, art reflecting deracination, sickness, and incompetence—at any rate, an inability in terms of an ideal of humanity. To produce such an ideal by force, the Third Reich had enthroned pure kitsch. Now came the opportunity to dispel the old reproach and to rehabilitate the hidden human and artistic ideals immanent in early European modernism. To do so, it was necessary to retrospectively identify art's safe and unequivocal ideals—although many should have known better. "Safe" meant that art had not known any element of doubt, and "unequivocal," that it had materialized in the classic art genres. For this reason, technical media (photography) and dada, with their social satire, remained largely in the background, while painting and sculpture were to represent a humanism that appeared undamaged by any kind of collective slogan or any declared belief in the machine.

For obvious reasons, humanism had become the central theme of postwar Europe. The barbarism of the war and of racism, with its traumatizing effects, had created the urgent need to profess once more the lost humanistic ideals "after Auschwitz." The Darmstadt Talks of 1951 provided the opportunity for philosophical consensus yet ended in

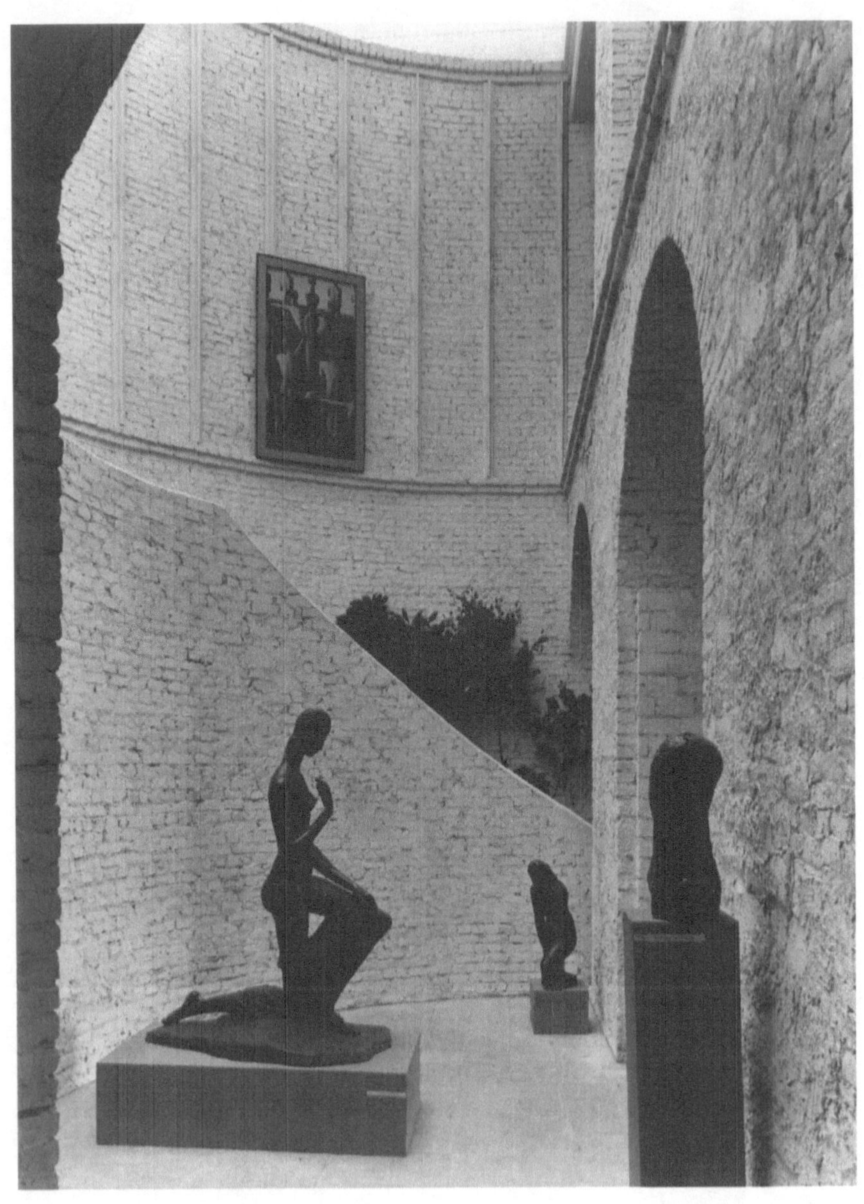

11. View of the staircase in the Museum Fridericianum during the first Documenta exhibition, Kassel, 1955.

controversy, after enemies of modernism such as Hans Sedlmayr, who had just been appointed to the chair of art history in Munich, chose precisely modern art as the target of the "loss of center," which they understood to mean the loss of a humanism in art. This argument sounded strangely similar to the previous Nazi ideology, even if now representing a Christian standpoint. Long before, an international critic, as it is summarized by Ortega y Gasset's slogan of "dehumanization," had accused art with charges that could just as easily be leveled at the whole of intellectual development.

Werner Haftmann therefore declared in his speech opening the Documenta that the old "view of the world" no longer sufficed to represent the essence of humanity. In presenting modern art as both cerebral and meditative, he made an appeal for the acceptance of so-called abstraction and of its anthropological truth. Art had become the great exemplifier of a new "sphere of experience" in which we encounter our own nature. "The modern image is a total adventure in the totally unknown." *The Unknown in Art* was also the title of the book that Willi Baumeister finished in 1946 and that invokes art as an unknown and indescribable mystery. The whole debate reflected a conscious, if unspoken, nostalgic view. "The modern image" was no doubt modern in the sense of the name of an epoch, but not modern in the sense of still being contemporary.

While the agenda of the first Documenta launched the program *This Is History*, a year later, the Whitechapel Gallery in London staged the first exhibition of English pop art under the militant title *This Is Tomorrow*. Here the mass media, which had been so carefully expunged from the "icon of modernism" in Kassel, were now for the first time introduced into High Art, in response to the call for the arts to open themselves up to "popular culture" (see fig. 24 below). But from the Documenta perspective, mass culture was the very opposite of culture: it was a counter-culture, although not in the sense that Jean Dubuffet meant in the lecture he gave in Chicago in 1951 when he spoke of "anticultural positions." In England, Richard Hamilton called for a break with purely formal aesthetics; and Lawrence Alloway, the spokesman of the "Independent Group," demanded more orientation toward the democratic mass media. Dubuffet's model was rather that of "primitive cultures," which he sought to give new life in his "art brut," and he declared: "Our culture is a garment that no longer fits. It is like a dead language and has become estranged from real life like a mandarin culture." This was spoken in the true spirit of modernism, the target of his attack was now the culture of established modern art.

Many could easily tell from the first Documenta that the artistic canon it promoted would not go without contradiction. A modernism that had already become historical was being declared a timeless ideal that the "modernists" might identify with, but in the process they became the keepers of a new tradition. Above all, this raised the pressing question of what was now to follow if modernism had already fulfilled its role in history. The only thing to do if one wanted to hold onto the official ideal of modernism, which appeared to have established itself worldwide in abstract art, was to invoke the idea of continuity. Yet the subsequent Documenta exhibitions progressively altered this image and were the occasion for continual revisions, finally resulting in a deep sense of uncertainty that cried out for a new synthesis. It is no mere coincidence that this synthesis was organized twenty-five years later in Germany.

The 1981 exhibition in Cologne, *Westkunst* (West Art), was designed by Laszlo Glozer and Kasper König to show "contemporary art since 1939," which meant that it took up the story where the historical reach of the first Documenta had in principle left off. The claim of "fresh" modernism that it could never be historicized was transferred from prewar to postwar art, which was received into the canon as a second wave of modernism. This claim, however, was self-contradictory, since "contemporary art" was only followed to 1972, and the true contemporaries were represented only in a rival exhibition, *Heute-Kunst* (Today Art). Nevertheless, there was a distinct program invoking a universal modernism that was controversial even then.

The formation of a canon was complicated by circumstances that had not existed at the emergence of modernism, namely, that it had not been preceded by any temporal break or conflict, factors that would favor critical distance and facilitate public admiration. Its authors assembled key works and exhibitions over the course of several decades in a great effort to communicate the idea of art history running its regular course in a manner that would be clear to all. They exhibited not only individual works that had made history: whole exhibitions that had since entered history were reconstructed. Richard Hamilton and Joseph Beuys undertook to reconstruct several of their own earlier exhibitions. History and exhibition in (and of) history thus became one and the same project, borne by a contradictory though understandable purpose: on the one hand, to raise this second modernism to its place in history, and, on the other hand, to celebrate it as a living presence.

Seen in this light, the 1981 project appears profoundly similar to that of the first Documenta, since the purpose of that exhibition had also been to establish a canon. The 1955 exhibition had also canonized its views on art history in order to shape public opinion. *Westkunst* was synonymous with a second modernism following on from the modernism of the first Documenta like the second chapter in a great epic. But this analogy was simply another case of wishful thinking—like that in the first modernism—and all it actually did was to put the retrospective in the light it needed. What had been subsumed under this new heading in fact had been much more heterogeneous and contradictory than it seemed now, and the choice of respective works was premature, making *Westkunst* a less successful exhibition than the earlier Documenta, even though the earlier success was due to the mood of the times.

The title *Westkunst,* left unexplained in the catalog, is as significant as the exhibition's reference back to the year 1939. In 1981, "Western art" did not yet imply contrast with "Eastern art" (i.e., from Eastern Europe, as everyone today would understand it), since Eastern Europe was not yet of general interest. The term was to be understood more in the sense used by Americans. Moreover, 1939, the year to which the exhibition referred back, was the year of the great wave of emigration that brought so many European artists to the United States. It was the same time that young American artists were beginning to assert their own profile in what Barnett Newman has called "new painting." The concept of *Westkunst* thus integrates European modernism with American art, giving a name to that historical symbiosis which progressively determined postwar events.

In the period immediately after the war, the fate of modern art briefly appeared uncertain, at least in Germany, where the tradition had been interrupted for more than a decade. The followers and the opponents of this interrupted modernism engaged in a discussion about basic principles and traditional values; its outcome could not be foretold. The reinstallation of Bauhaus architecture and abstract painting, reimported from the United States, initially appeared to come down to an attempt to restore modernism, which points out the contradiction intrinsic to this process. Since then, the fear of the loss of modernism, as the latter was more episodic than we believe, has resurfaced several times. This fear has also molded the course of the postmodernism debate, particularly in Europe, where the loss of modernism has been equated with the loss of cultural identity.

6 Western Art: The Intervention of the United States in Postwar Modernism

Shortly after 1945, the second wave of abstraction was led by American artists who, until then, had not figured much in the art annals of modernism. They felt freer in their attitude toward art history than the Europeans, but now they decided to enter this very history. Some of the art movements emerging in the New World had been a generation behind or took a different course than corresponding movements in Europe. A good example is primitivism, which came to prominence in the United States only around 1940 and was markedly different from the primitivism that had held artists spellbound in Paris around 1910. Since the 1930s, Adolph Gottlieb, who was to become one of the foremost representatives of abstract expressionism, had been collecting African art, and in 1989 his collection was exhibited together with his own paintings in the Brooklyn Museum in a show entitled *Image and Reflection* (fig.12). The exhibition of the African "models" was reconstructed according to an old photograph of the artist. But the "primitives" chosen for American art were now sought on the same continent.

The invocation of "Indian art" or even pre-Columbian art, which was exhibited in 1944 by none other than Barnett Newman, contradicted the European traditions the New World artists sought to break free of. *The Ideographic Picture,* as propagated in a group exhibition of 1947, was the successor to a "native art" that in olden times appeared to possess access to the true myths of life. In 1948, Newman therefore chose the epithet of "sublime" when he wrote about the "failure of European art" in its two leading movements, geometric abstraction and surrealism. Here he called for "the liberation from the burden of European culture" yet refused to join the ranks of "the professional Americanists," as he contemptuously called the patriotic movements of the 1930s.

It was no longer enough to offer a safe haven for an international culture dominated by emigrants from the Old World. American artists now wanted to lead the international of art. The American Foundation of Modern Painters and Sculptors, founded in 1940, therefore, condemned "all forms of artistic nationalism" and urged the nation "to finally accept cultural values within a truly global framework." Art critics like Clement Greenberg supported a campaign in which American artists

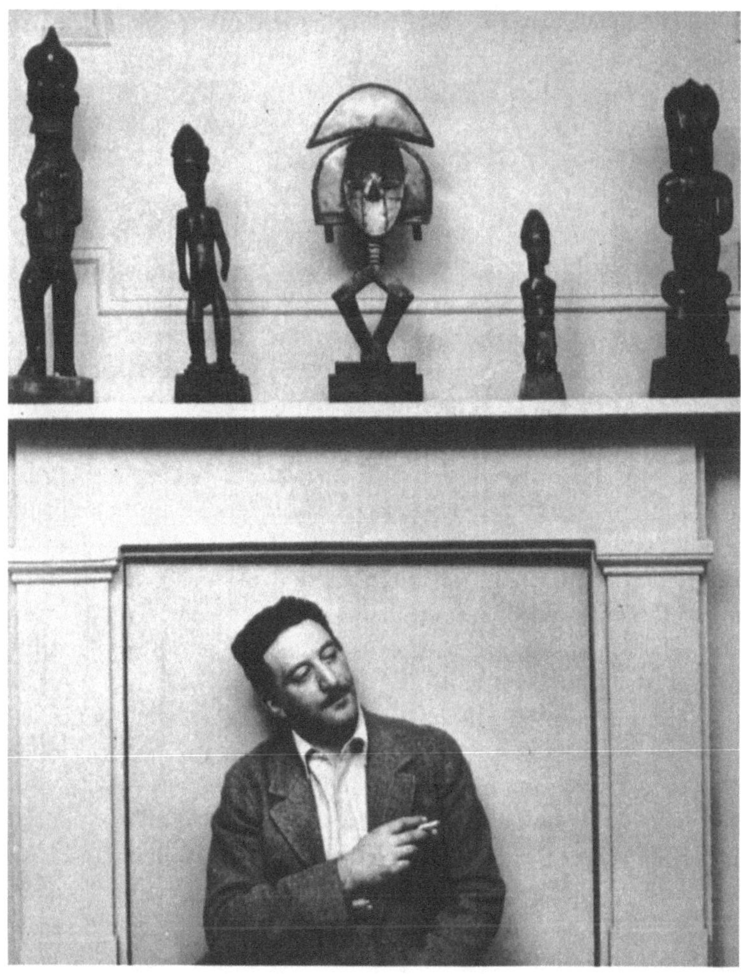

12. Adolph Gottlieb with his collection, 1942. From the leaflet accompanying the exhibition *Image and Reflection* (New York, 1989). Photo by Aaron Siskind. Courtesy Robert Mann Gallery. Copyright Aaron Siskind Foundation.

were invited to assert their own significance and to provide the necessary arguments. Some of the traumatic obstacles that were to be overcome are described in the biography of Jackson Pollock by Steven Naifeh and Gregory White Smith. In their view Pollock was destined or felt it was his destiny to become the "American Picasso."

The term "second modernism," though frequently used in another sense (I only mention Heinrich Klotz, who identifies thus a late modernism after it has been transformed by multimedia culture), may conveniently describe the postwar era in which modernism began anew, this time not in Europe, but in the United States. At that time, there was a widespread movement in the United States to establish a truly American modernism, a movement that at first kept its distance from the European scene, where the first act of modernism had been performed under dramatic conditions. This distance still is to be felt in an installation by George Segal, who, in 1967, staged the body of Sidney Janis holding an original Mondrian painting that the collector had bought from the artist in 1933 (fig. 13). The work went beyond the portrait of an art collector and introduced a historical distinction between European and American modernism by embracing not only two genres but two different conceptions of art. A new American realism had replaced European geometric abstraction, which—as a sort of historical icon—had become a quotation in the installation.

The artistic events at the end of the war, retold countless times, have long become part of the myth of modern art and remind Americans of the heroic moment of their cultural debut, which came disturbingly close to America's political and economic ascent to world power—disturbingly, because one would rather like to give different reasons for cultural success than economic and political success. American modernism, at least in a few centers in the United States, manifested a culture on an international scale in which Europe soon became restricted to a second voice and reacted more than it acted. Only now did the two hemispheres take a simultaneous course, and it soon appeared that only one culture would remain, tied as it was to the market they shared.

Despite this, the dialogue between the Old World and the New continued to determine artistic events for some time. In Europe, the avant-garde seemed to be freeing itself with increasing success from the burden of the history of art, and yet—or perhaps precisely for this reason—to be liberating art itself. A new "zero hour" for art came in 1960,

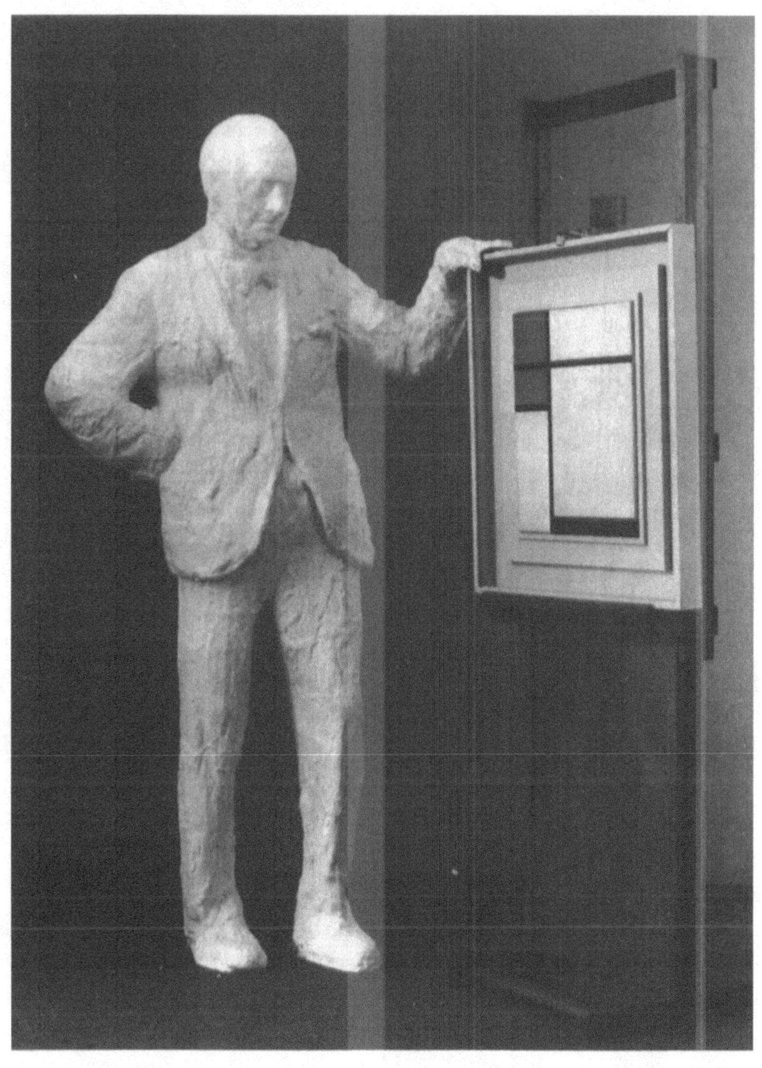

13. George Segal, *Portrait of Sidney Janis with a Mondrian*, 1967. Museum of Modern Art, New York. Collection of Sidney and Harriet Janis. © The George and Helen Segal Foundation / Licensed by VAGA, New York, NY.

when the German Zero Group seemed to be introducing an art beyond abstraction, an "absolute art" in which idea and work would merge. These were confident times when people boasted of having freed themselves from figuration and when Yves Klein entertained hopes that the history of art had reached the climax where all historical change would finally collapse. But this utopia proved to be yet another fiction.

In 1960 and 1961, the well-known art critic Pierre Restany made a last desperate attempt to draw the line between the art of the Old World and the New. The "new realists" in France, whose voice he was, were soon embroiled in a hopeless competition with the Pop artists of New York, who, in turn, were for awhile (despite their protests) defined as neodadaists. Both seemed to take as their ideal the ready-made, which was no longer understood as the "acme of refusal" to make art, but as a new means of expression in which "reality overtook fiction." In a joint exhibition of French and American artists in 1961, Restany used every available means to create a distinction between his compatriots and the "romantic" Americans with their "modern object-fetishism."

A year later the case ended in favor of American pop art, when the same Sidney Janis, whom we have met in Segal's installation, opened his gallery to both groups in an exhibition he gave the European title of *The New Realists.* The catalog promoted a new "international art" that was to be a kind of "urban folklore" springing from the very same mass culture that Restany so profoundly despised. The triumph of the "popular image" began with the touring exhibitions of 1963 and 1964, in which only the terminology remained briefly European. Pop art, initially misunderstood in Europe as a criticism of consumerism, actually tore down precisely that barrier between culture and the commonplace that the art historian Meyer Schapiro, in his panegyric of abstract art, had believed insuperable. The Europeans' "total art" turned into its opposite as soon as the mass media reentered American art. Never again was it possible to divide events between what had been two cultures (and may become two cultures again in the future).

Twenty years later, in 1981, a first revolt against U.S. predominance emerged in the exhibition *A New Spirit of Painting* at the Royal Academy in London, an exhibition shown in Berlin the following year under the name *Zeitgeist.* It boldly proclaimed the return of painting and the Central European expressionist tradition. The Americans remained in the minority here, and American art critics were accused of having towed an orthodox line for too long. "They declared everything made by New York artists to be the only art of universal significance, against which everything else should be considered provincial." Yet the Documenta and the Venice Biennial continued to present the unified culture of the Western hemisphere. Exhibitions like the 1988 *Binationale*, which showed German art in the United States and American art in Germany, repeatedly made the uncomfortable attempt to define each culture in contrast to the other, though the art of the two cultures was often indistinguishable; each time, the loudly announced "marriage" of the two unequal partners rendered such attempts futile. As early as 1986, in *Artscribe International*, Donald Kuspit referred to the "myth of internationalism."

While this alleged unity of Western culture was emerging, for the first time there was no dominant artistic current, as had hitherto characterized each generation. Perhaps the Euro-American synopsis was simply unable to cope with such a guiding model. Art took positions mutually exclusive and that also could no longer be subsumed within a common framework. As the pace of artistic invention accelerated, written art history became rather chaotic. It was forced into continuous response, just as art itself was continually changing direction. Paradoxically, the established pattern of a historical narrative was still accepted, although the rhythm of change became ever shorter, and each current set the tone for at most two years. It followed from this that art criticism increasingly lost track of what was happening in art, if one can still speak in terms of distinguishable events. Whatever entered the scene since 1960 never had a chance to exhaust its intention—often it did not even develop—with the short validity the market would grant it before the gallerists would announce the next trend. The critics often cannot keep pace with the pulse of the art market, and many simply capitulate and take the market for the movements, assuming the function of market analysts.

Today, one may ask whether the two hemispheres still form the unity we call the "West" in terms of art and culture. The conflict around the photographic work of Robert Mapplethorpe, which culminated around 1990 in the campaign of Senator Jesse Helms, stirred up old puritan fears and the resistance to any public support of art not in conformity with American ideals and morals. I am here referring to Robert Hughes, who in his controversial book *The Culture of Complaint* identifies modernist culture as a foreign or marginal element in U.S. society especially in view of the uncompromising internationalism so characteristic of modernist art. Hughes describes modernism as a "brilliant adaption" in American culture where it gave birth to the "idea of a therapeutic avant-garde" propagating aestheticism in its purest manifestation, as the agency both of a new culture and new morals. It is for these reasons, he continues, that it was such a short distance to the "political correctness" that emerged in the art scene as soon as the attraction of aestheticism faded away. When this happened, artists hurried to "address issues" such as racism and sexism, thereby adding self-censorship to the previous practice of public censorship.

Due to its Puritan traditions and to the advanced state of its multicultural society, such phenomena emerged in the U.S. earlier than elsewhere. A society in discord and yet striving for self-confidence and the American way of life will not want to quarrel about art's pictorial concepts so much as about contents and issues, if we exclude the advanced gallery scene. Wherever art has ceased to generate conflicts on its own terms, it will easily tend to represent such controversies as exist in its own society and thus attract public discussion. This temptation is all the more obvious as art is one of the few areas left in present-day society where opinions not only are free but are allowed free expression. Art still enjoys its institutional protection and therefore profits from its privileges in a way that so often has been the subject of court proceedings. Yet in the guise of "political correctness," art misuses this freedom while only allowing one position, its own, and excluding any other in the name of a "silent majority." In this case, the mechanisms are particularly effective in that they link the issues of public ideals with those of high culture (art).

Such issues may seem alien to the notion of art history, which is my subject. But I would insist on the importance for my subject whenever artists, instead of referring back to a history of the arts with its implied concepts of culture, establish a sort of horizontal relationship with the society of their time, thus shifting the balance between history, as the artist's heritage, and society, as the artist's mirror and mission. What artists are doing and how they are thinking is not so different from what art historians as their contemporaries are writing, even when they do not explicitly refer to each other. North American culture, as it has been described from a German point of view by Gert Raeithel, is based on a different system of values whose effects are already revealed in the academic scene. The domestic battles in U.S. scholarship make it difficult, and sometimes impossible, for European visitors who have not learned the latest passwords current in the respective discussions. Art history has often been described as a European import when it was taught by émigrés in American universities. "New art history" therefore appeared as an attempt to liberate the academic discipline from this burden and to americanize the topics and methods. Today, art history, seen in a global framework, seems to have become an American property whose products, like books and periodicals, are distributed on a global scale due to the power of institutions and the advantage of language. Thus, the situation has been reversed in relation to European traditions. American scholarship enjoys worldwide predominance in art writing and, therefore, must ask itself which concepts of art history it makes use of, given its new responsibility, in the future.

The unity of Western culture, which for so long seemed undisputed, now reveals subtle cracks. Nonetheless, the cultural or academic elites in both hemispheres insist on their consensus in an air either of ostentation or fear. But the impression of total unity will not stand up to scrutiny. The two hemispheres are turning away from one another more than we are ready to admit. It is with equal reason that we may doubt whether Western art can still be narrated in the same terms. Although artistic exchange continues on an unprecedented scale, the artists involved entertain very different views of what they are doing, how they see history, as a meaning of their work, and how they interpret each other. We may even speculate that the old narrative of a unified art history was bound to collapse as soon as the "symbiosis" within Western culture after the Second World War was achieved. Its interaction for a while favored the idea of a common art and a common place in art's history, but this wishful thinking more and more proved to be a necessary fiction that best survived on the art market.

The protagonists in the two hemispheres to remain within the art scene once were Andy Warhol and Joseph Beuys, whose contrast revealed a deeper conflict. Many still remember the two artists' appearance, each embodying his own myth of modern art, in 1980 in a gallery in Munich, where Warhol was exhibiting his Beuys portraits (fig. 14). This was only a few years after Beuys had captivated the American art scene by using almost atavistic incantatory rituals (the "coyote episode") and had been hailed in the Guggenheim Museum as a European prophet of art. Warhol, the virtuoso oracle of American society, at first was rebuffed by Beuys's cult of nature. It may be that each was acting out the role of a protagonist who would speak for his own culture. It may also be that they stylized their art for or against the mass media in an opposite sense. Nevertheless, they offered the spectacle, not of a merely personal encounter, but of one between two hemispheres that, with its illusions, were as much connected as they remained separate.

It may be remembered that nobody expected a portrait of Warhol from Beuys. Everyone knew then, as we know now, that Beuys did not do portraits. Everyone who visited the exhibition could again convince themselves that, to put it paradoxically, when Warhol depicted someone

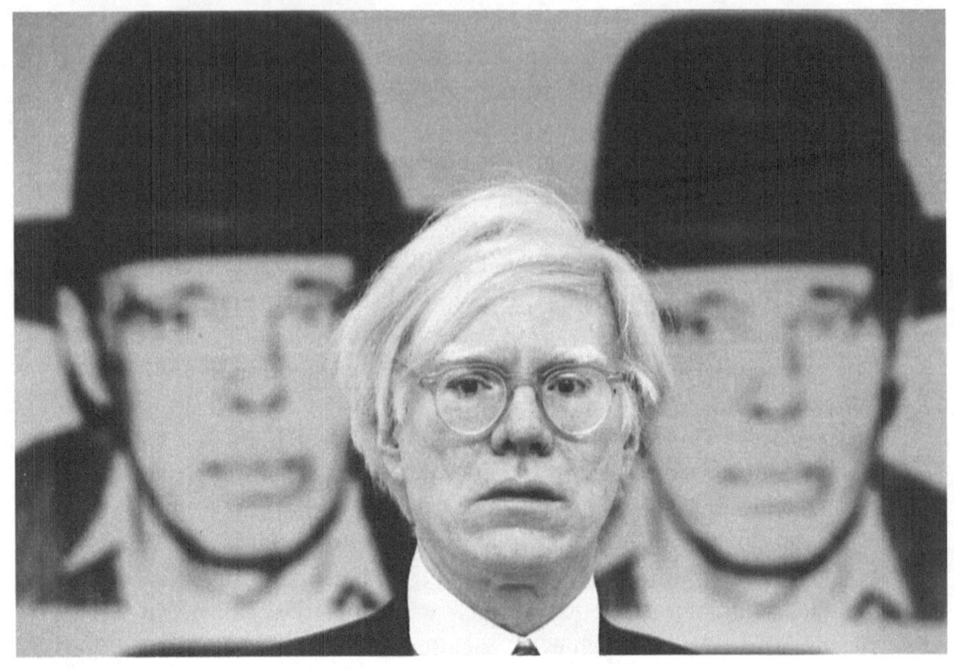

14. Andy Warhol in front of his double portrait of Joseph Beuys in the Schellmann-Klüser Gallery, Munich, 1980. Photo by Isolde Ohlbaum.

he was not making a portrait either. The mere fact that he had placed many heads of Beuys next to one another, works containing one Beuys head or several, was proof of this. They were, as always with Warhol, clichés conveyed by the public media that reduced not so much the person as the "image" to a visual slogan. It was precisely here that Warhol represented American commonplaces that, whether one likes them or not, he aestheticized rather than criticized—in other words, transferred them to an art form that was completely incomprehensible for European critics in 1960, when he first became known.

One may argue on and on over "Western art," but perhaps one should not spend too much time on this issue, since the aims of art meanwhile have turned in other directions. If art today refers at all to history, it is less and less to the so-called history of art and increasingly to the history of a particular group or of a belief seeking a mirror in art. There is no better proof that old art history was always a locus of a cultural identity and therefore able to survive only for as long as the tradition remained alive in the minds of the majority. When art appeals to social or political convictions borrowed from individual groups, it is a successful ploy to reestablish itself as the medium of identity. When it speaks in its own name, this happens only in the context of its debate with the pictorial mass media. But that is another theme.

7 Europe: East and West at the Watershed of Art History

The unity of Western Art, which has become uncertain, gained its common profile from the contrast to that of East European art. One culture lived at the cost of and perhaps with the collusion of the other. With the collapse of this safe borderline, it is difficult for the two cultures to keep their former self-reference. Each lived from a tradition that was defined against that of the other. This is why the open frontiers that resulted from the collapse of the Soviet empire gave rise to such hysterical reactions in the West, when it became clear that matters of identity had to be defined in substance rather than by demarcation. The Western art markets' irresistible pull on the East, however, seemed to confirm the Western self-assessment that the only art worthy of the name came from the West.

For the greater part of the twentieth century, East and West had no shared art history. The interrupted success of modernism in countries like Russia, whose avant-garde once had also stirred up the West, gave rise to the erroneous idea that modernism had taken place only in the West, as if it had not repeatedly been suppressed in Eastern Europe (and as if its development had not greatly differed from one Eastern European country to another). In this part of the world, modernism soon had become an unofficial culture and, as an underground movement, was therefore denied public access. The loss of modernism was traumatic for countries for which it had served as the door to European culture (and art history), since their native art, if it was thought at all worth discussing, had long been considered merely a product of Western colonialism. We usually ignore the degree to which we have imposed a Western view on the East by recognizing only Western traditions and by writing art history such as to exclude Eastern Europe.

West Germans had their own problems with looking eastward, since their view was already obstructed by the existence of the "German Democratic Republic" (GDR) next door. The culture of the GDR was by no means typical of Eastern Europe, even if, perforce, it declared itself faithful to the collective identity of the Eastern Bloc: cultural reality was something different from the official way of self-representation. For a time, it appeared as if East and West Germany no longer were rooted in a common history, and the cold war made them compete over the true German heritage. The two German states staged their opposition like a German drama complete with adversaries, heroes, and victims, whereas all other roles readily labeled traitors. Each side granted the other its part of the world, and this agreement left no room for further discussion.

I do not, however, consider the double history of German art—as I have discussed it in the book *The Germans and Their Art*—only a topic of the East-West conflicts as they existed for so long. It only provided an opportunity to discuss such conflicts in a German context, while, however, nobody seems prepared to engage in this, in spite of the importance of this topic for the process of reunification. In a catalog for the exhibition *Resistance* held in 1993 in the Haus der Kunst in Munich, I therefore made the (of course utopian) suggestion that art from the two Germanys be exhibited in juxtaposition, to promote a critical position and to overcome the suppression of the topic. The history of GDR art is as impossible to wish away as to simply incorporate into that of Western art. It is obvious why this topic meets with resistance from both sides, since the two narratives cannot be integrated into each other. Even the West German side would have to admit its adherence to a political system where it was taken hostage in the name of freedom.

Since the frontiers fell, we are realizing how little we know about the history of so-called Eastern Bloc art. Not until 1988, in Cologne and Aachen, did it become a subject of public concern; there, a heated debate ensued over Peter Ludwig's collecting practice: he had broken taboos by including Eastern bloc art. Russian artists like Ilya Kabokov and Russian writers like Boris Groys live in the West, where they opened a debate that had before practically lived from internal Western topics. Yet the Hungarians who emigrated to the West in 1956 and the Czechs who left their homeland in 1968 have long become champions of Western culture, which they propagate with a conviction far exceeding Western expectations.

The complexity of the task to reopen the debate about European art in an enlarged framework is illustrated by the case of the Hungarians, who with some justification insist that they belong to a culture that is Western European, because Latin and Roman Catholic, and from which they were cut off in 1948. Only now can they work through the continuities and breaks in their own modern art, which fell victim to official amnesia. Their brilliant avant-garde, which had come to prominence in the revolution years 1918–19, only entered modern art history when their leading representatives emigrated to the West; the others are only now being discovered. After 1945, the "postponed revolution" in Hungarian culture was taken up again, and the so-called European School was founded, a collective movement of avant-garde artists that was once more suppressed by Stalinist cultural doctrine in 1948.

The de-Stalinization policy introduced after the Twentieth Party Congress of the Soviet Union changed this monolithic culture within eight years, but at the same time it triggered the Hungarian Uprising of the same year, 1956, which the Soviets brutally suppressed. It was not until the late 1960s that an alternative art scene began to gain influence—the sort of influence, paradoxically, that state-supported art in the GDR had long wielded. Ever since the forgotten native representatives of an unofficial modernism began coming to light, they were enthusiastically celebrated in exhibitions like the 1991 show organized by the Museum Ludwig in Budapest. Only today, the discussion of Stalinist culture has become possible, and we are learning to understand that Stalinism, whatever its Hungarian part, was regarded as a foreign import. On the other hand, the discussion of international modernism in Hungary still divides the participants who either wish to rehabilitate the Hungarian contribution to modern art or fear a fresh defeat of the national culture in this mirror. Stalinism, it must not be forgotten, was an international culture, whose end released long pent-up nationalist feelings.

Western culture, which claims for itself the idea of freedom and the presence on the market, now emerges as the universal heir of history, simply swallowing up the Eastern culture that was so much compromised. But can or should Western art simply be exported into the East, the same way Western currency was exported for the purpose of buying up the land and the people east of the border? Even before the frontier was opened, dissident artists from the Soviet Union had spectacularly extended the Western art market. The open frontiers produced a strong pull by which the artists from the East gained power on the market but lost their former clientele.

The attraction of Western culture in the East, where for a long time it was inaccessible, proves irresistible, as long as people are not enough acquainted with it to realize how poorly it fulfills their overblown expectations. Whatever can it be expected to offer, when it already offers almost everything? The media, at any rate, are mesmerizing people in Russia with advertisements for commodities that cannot yet be bought there. True to the practice of advertising, they promise more than they can keep. Art, in a similar way, cannot keep its promises as there is as yet no market for it. In the process, we see that Eastern art has always lived off the Western market where artists from the East also find a niche, if they are prepared to work for it and, for example, to exhibit their works in New York's Greene Street. Culture and the market are indistinguishable here, since both are omnivorous and utterly undiscriminating.

But the issue is not exhausted with this kind of discourse. Rather, it challenges us to engage in an unprecedented comparison of the two cultures, in which we can (or must) get to know our own culture better. As Ilya Kabokov frequently said, Russian artists encounter a different public in the West, one that scrutinizes art with a professional eye and that forces the artists to develop new strategies if they wish to succeed. In Russia, they produced an "informal but unalienated" art that "was not separate from life." Now, even in the East, art has to be "professional" in that it is "paid for, exhibited and institutionalized."

For this Russian artist, art was formerly "a necessity of life, not a professional activity." Today these two roles have reversed and art loses its "place in life" to the same degree that experts bestow autonomy upon it. But this means the artists lose their Eastern European lay public, which had always sensed in art the adventure of freedom, and gain a Western public that collects art and visits galleries. Perhaps they are a kind of art public, which their Western colleagues often seem to have forgotten. Nonetheless, many feel well received in the Western "paradise," whose blessings they so longed for while languishing in the "Soviet hell." Yet the Western paradise that has become their new home makes some of them feel in exile.

The Russian "dadaists," Vitaly Komar and Alex Melamid, the Eastern counterparts of the Western twins Gilbert and George, have been conducting a subversive yet playful strategy ever since they emigrated in 1977 and, after a year in Israel, settled in New York. In the early 1980s, they had already surprised with pseudo-Mannerist paintings that portray a phantom unity of East-West art artistic unity in an unexpectedly joking manner. Then they exhibited pictures that, on the basis of a statistical survey, combine all the clichés of the average American citizen. The choice of motifs and colors represents the taste of eighty per cent of all Americans. Such subversive strategies in art live from an interaction of East and West, which has become a new phenomenon in the art scene.

Compared with the West, art in Eastern Europe in retrospect mostly appears retarded in the general development and at another stage of development which means that it was performing a different social role, two conditions that result from its historical lack of contact with Western modernism. Where it did not join the permanent crisis of modernism, art remained in a state of innocence, as it were, especially since it could easily justify itself by its resistance to official state art. It was not disputed that there was art. Whether in terms of the "right" and the "wrong" kind of art, official and subversive, there was still conviction in the power or art, something that had vanished long before in the West. Progressive art, which once was cut off from any public impact, in the meanwhile has become as official as state art once was, but it turns into art for the market, and its mechanisms will represent an extension of the Western art market until a comparable market will develop in Russia.

However, Western culture cannot simply expand in such new spaces without confronting questions it cannot currently answer. Western identity that gradually took shape in the constant dispute over modernism will not remain the same once Western culture has lost its image of the "enemy." Above all, it has no right to feel chosen by the logic of history for representing a unified culture of East and West. The disparities between East and West cannot be eliminated without giving rise to new differences and boundaries, which will alter the West, too. The hour of truth is imminent.

But Western plans for facing the new situation are often astonishingly simple. In Dresden, for instance, Frank Stella was at one time commissioned to build an art gallery to represent "international art of this century" and signal "the beginning of a new era." In that museum, art was to be chosen from private collections and sponsored by Western patrons. Against the baroque architecture of Dresden, the neobaroque of the museum's architecture, whose pavilions and garden would have given the whole ensemble a festive air, was to establish links with local tradition, much as the museum collection was to offer links with the concept of international Western art, whose long absence it was to make good.

In contrast to such rushed actions designed to nullify an undesirable history (of art), all attempts to introduce the art of the former GDR into the discussion at all meet with resistance fed by the fear that this could lead to the GDR's being retroactively recognized. This resistance reveals the refusal to reexamine the completed canon of West German art as a part of Western culture. One would rather escape straight into the general issue of East European art, where no German feelings were involved. Thus, we gain insight into what the much-invoked "House of Europe" means, where the Germans are not in the foreground. But this does not mean that the participants would liberate themselves from patterns of thought to which they had been accustomed for long. A large-scale exhibition in the Bonn Kunsthalle in 1994, titled *Europa-Europa,*” presented the astonished visitor with the flawless image of an Eastern European avant-garde which met Western tastes, while the bulk of art production in this area was missing, since it would have spoiled the desired image. Instead, the gallery accepted into this group portrait all the avant-garde artists from the Eastern bloc who had spent most of their lives in the West and had long been part of Western art history. The argument that, after all, Eastern Europe belongs to Europe as a whole, was understandable only from the standpoint of the Polish curator. Here, of course, Eastern Europe is measured against its Western profile, to make it accessible to a Western public.

But in a few cases, museums offer a place for critical reflection, when raising questions about the encounter between the victorious culture of the West and the defeated culture of the East. In 1991, Wim Beeren invited thirteen artists from East and West—that is, from within the extended boundaries of the old Europe—to take over one room each in the Stedelijk Museum in Amsterdam and stage it with a personal view of his or her own journey between the two cultures. *Wanderlieder* (Songs of Travel) was the exhibition's title, but the only artists who traveled were the Rumanian, the Pole, and the Czech painter, while the Western participants, without any recognizable doubts about their previous roles, exhibited with complete self-confidence. They produced installations that could be easily dismantled afterwards, while the Eastern European artists painted murals on the walls temporarily put at their disposal, an act betraying their inexperience with the Western art market. The Romanian Jon Grigorescu, who covered a whole wall with one painting (fig. 15), avoided all forms of narrative innocence by joining splinters of personal memories with clichés from Christian iconography and symbols from Rumanian history in a strangely hesitant, broken monologue in which only his style of figuration appeared unfamiliar to Western eyes. There was little opportunity for comparison, since these productions allowed none, at least none that would have struck a chord with Western art connoisseurs. The latter, to protect their own superiority, would retreat into a smile in order to keep their own standards and expertise.

East and West is a European theme that appears to be replacing the former theme of *western art* and that, on the other hand, differs from the theme of world art. Present-day Europe has lost sight of its former history; its Western half was long ago seduced by the immaculate ideal

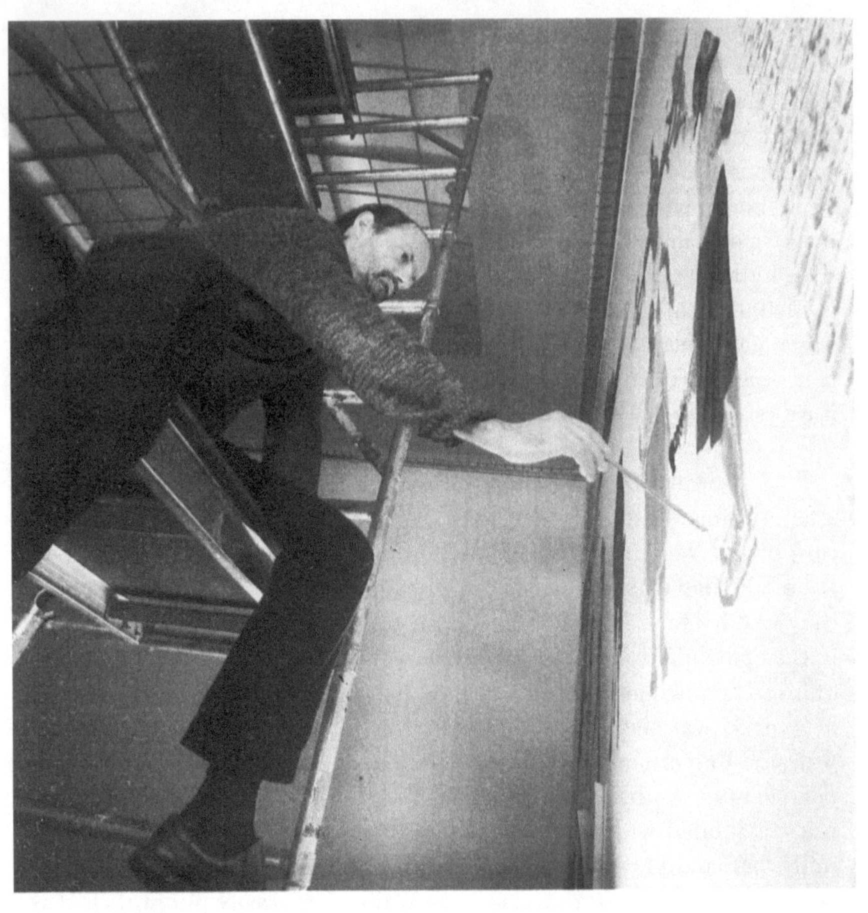

15. Jon Grigorescu painting his mural for the exhibition *Songs of Travel* in the Stedelijk Museum, Amsterdam, 1991. Photo from *Vrij Nederland* (1991): 5. Photo by Quentin Bertoux.

Occident in which Eastern Europe no longer had figured. To compensate for this lacuna, the catalog *Songs of Travel* has a text by Heiner Müller that reproduces a then-recent interview that had questioned "The State of the Nation," as the titles says. In this interview, the author posed the question whether, "historically speaking, this one Europe existed at all." Müller refers to the film director Krystof Zanussi, who, like many before him, used to refer to "two Europes": the one shaped by Byzantium, the other by Rome. Müller adds, "This is vital to any reflection about Europe, and many misunderstandings between East and West result from insufficient knowledge of this historical fact." The question of what will become of Europe is not yet settled, but it is already clear that Europe, in its near extension, can no longer evade the topic of East and West— which in our case would necessarily be an art history written from two points of view or, so to speak, with "two voices" hopefully in harmony. The political and economic project of extending "United Europe" to new member states also leads to the project of rewriting European history and art history, as an emblem of identity, whereas any other, pseudonational concept would only support the danger of a new kind of colonization on its own territories. Europe was rightly proud of its national identities as they were mirrored in English or French art, etc. But at the beginning of the new century, the task is to find a European profile that, in the case of art history, means the coexistence of very different and sometimes contradictory narratives.

8 Global Art and Minorities: A New Geography of Art History

The figure of the frame, which can be used to describe art history as a locus of identity, can also help us to understand the problems that play a role in today's so-called global art. Art history as a discourse originally was invented for a particular culture, in other words, for a culture with a common history. By contrast, minorities that have surfaced in a given society feel that they need not be represented in such a frame, as they do not share the other's view on history. So now "political correctness," the battle cry of minorities and those who identify with perceived minorities, plays an increasing role in many countries. The connection between culture and history, like the conception of art history as an emblem of one's own culture, becomes obvious as soon as we focus on consensus and dissent. There was a time when dissent was the trademark of avant-garde artists who attacked culture as the trademark of the educated bourgeoisie. The creed of modernism was formed in such attacks. Today, dissent is rather to be found among art's audience, who demand that artists represent the claims of minorities and that the historians rewrite history to suit. The more individual groups in a given society no longer recognize the cultural heritage as their own, the less they are willing to accept its official image.

What we refer to as the history of art has long been a narrative about European art, in which, despite all claims of national identity, European hegemony was undisputed. But this pleasant image now provokes contradiction from all those who no longer find themselves represented by it. The protest arose first from the United States, which now dominates the art scene. It has been a long time since the Museum of Modern Art divided its exhibition rooms equally between European art before 1945 and postwar American art. It is even longer since Alfred H. Barr Jr. wrote in the 1930s his legendary exhibition catalogs, in which diagrams represented the history of modern art from 1890 to 1935 in a didactic and almost missionary way (fig. 16). European art there still monopolized this history and was presented chronologically according to a structure normally used to describe genealogies and scientific evolution.

These days, not only is American art before 1945 being rewritten: minority art and especially women's art have come very much to the fore as a new issue. The "neglected" part of history gave reason for the

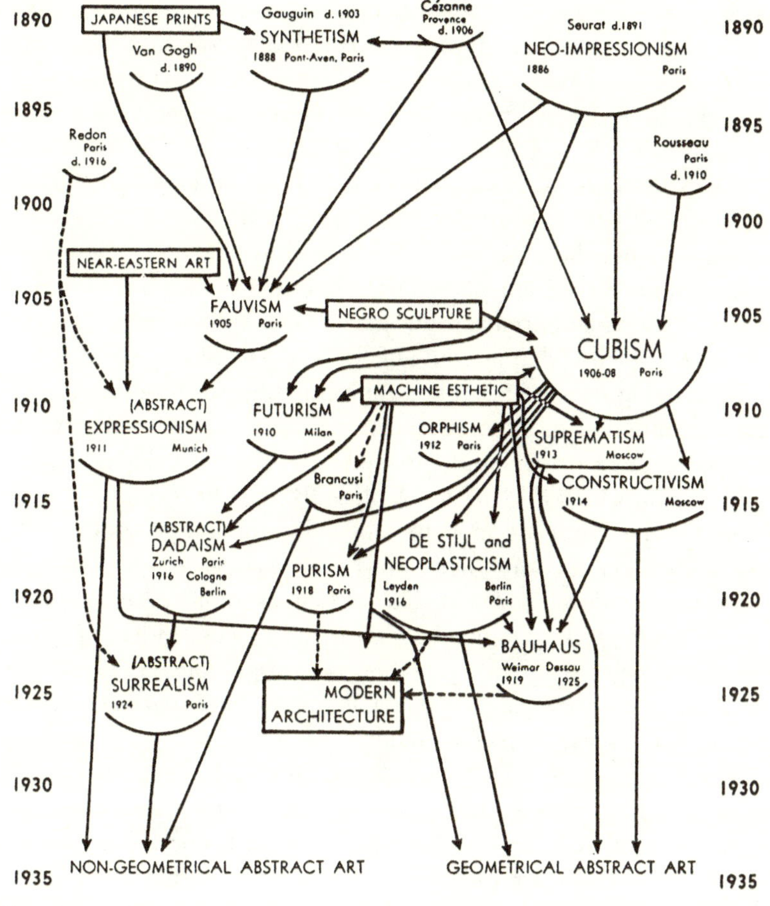

16. Diagram showing the development of European modernism. From Alfred H. Barr, Jr., *Cubism and Abstract Art in the Museum of Modern Art*, exhibition catalog (New York, 1936), i.

suspicion that official historiography had simply been "invented"; the demand arose for the latter's "revision." In Europe, where a multicultural society is not yet fully developed, it is as yet feminism that claims attention for women's part in the narrative of art history, in order to retrieve a forgotten identity and to finally give women's art the appropriate weight. In the United States, regional interests are requesting a revision of art history: the American West or Northwest are themes of regional exhibitions, and local artists share the invention of regional traditions. Usually, the dispute over the "true" history of art rages on in such exhibitions where visitors are expected to "discover" things that they cannot find in written history. Exhibitions of this kind are either organized by individual groups or meant for such groups.

Even so-called global art, in which every part of the world is to be represented, has meanwhile staked claims that, justified as they may be, will contribute to a disintegration of art history in the familiar way. A world culture, as represented, for instance, by UNESCO, demands a unifying frame in which also art has a place. But art history as it was developed for the European model is not a neutral and general tale that could easily be applied to other cultures that lack such a narrative. On the contrary: it developed within a particular tradition of thought in which it met the task to remember culture as a locus of identity. Intrinsic to this was the historical cycle that, in Europe, ranged from the ancient world to modernity and that formed the cultural space in which art continually fell back on its own models. Seen in this light, Europe was the place where a historical cycle of a special kind has occurred that, in turn, shaped those referent narratives by which history is narrated. This does not mean that I cherish a Hegelian view of history, as it excluded the rest of the world from history in the "proper"—that is, in Hegel's own—sense. I only insist that art history, as a given discourse, needs structural changes when extended to other cultures and cannot simply be exported such as it is to other parts of the world.

Boris Groys, in his discourse of a "cultural archive," which he distinguishes from the "profane sphere," claims that innovations originate outside or against this archive, yet gain significance only when they become part of this archive and thus provide the "cultural memory" that society guarantees. Cultural criticism, he maintains, comes from the groups that have failed to find "cultural representation in the established archives." The image of art history to which I refer is precisely this "cultural archive," in which the events that have taken place in art, arranged according to their importance, form elements of that very construct we used to call *the* history of art.

But the framework within which culture becomes a meaningful memory is not as firm and immutable as this schema suggests. The archive cannot absorb everything without fundamental change to its own content and significance. The more and the faster it incorporates what is new, the less it can guarantee the hierarchy it represented. Protection against the new only meant that the archive was admitting the new only after it had become compatible with the existing hierarchy in the archive. The mechanism of constant extension does not by itself guarantee the continuity of cultural memory. Likewise, expanding the archive in the direction of other cultures cannot fail to change the former. We are already witnessing similar developments in the political world: the old states are dissolving into ethnic cultures with which individual groups or regions wish to identify.

Here we are broaching questions that belong in a wider context. In a planetary civilization, the Western project of the technological modernization of the world has become a threat to cultural diversity. It all too easily creates the misunderstanding that Western modernism also contains all the blessings of a global culture, just as missionaries in earlier centuries sought to spread Christianity all over the earth. "Only the West elaborates the rhetoric of universalism," which recognizes "no difference between near and far" because it is "unconditional and abstract," writes Hans Magnus Enzensberger in an essay on universal human rights, "Aussichten auf den Bürgerkrieg" (Prospects of Civil War). From a Western viewpoint, every historical conflict amounted to a "crisis in the ongoing process of assimilation. Global modernization is seen as an inexorable, linear process." We may add that so-called world art offers a folkloristic compensation, which is not expected to seriously compete with the Western model and which presents "third world" culture only under the conditions of an exotic "reserve."

For this reason, Constantin von Barloewen pointed to the mistake that living in the project of a global modernization respects nations but not cultures. This mistake is aggravated by the fact that modernization is always seen as synonymous with the import of Western media, which not only inform about the Western world but produce the mirage of proximity to and of the accessibility of the West, including its culture. Basically, this is a new colonialism which, in terms of the art scene, only allows the choice to "take it or leave it," while "ethnic allowances," once they maintain certain limits, are tolerated as a welcome alibi.

The global triumph of mass media transforms every cultural event into a media event, as if it had occurred in the media or had been created for the media. Individual cultures deliver the occasions for a memory globally available as soon as it is stored in the digital archives of a computer's memory and distributed by the mass media. Global culture celebrates its own omnipotence because it replaces personal memory with an omnipresent technical memory. Global culture is thus actually a phantom of the media, which promise the same share of culture to everyone, regardless of origin and social status. Similarly, world art, being free from language barriers, is hailed as the symbol of a new world unity, though it only delivers ingredients of a new media culture that is, again, controlled by the West. The concept of world art would need to be grounded in a history of world art that does not and cannot exist as a common model of memory. The so-called Imaginary Museum that André Malraux propagated after 1945 when accumulating world art—in texts and photographs on the printed pages of a book—was a European idea with a European meaning.

Literary and academic culture, in which the narratives of art history have always had their place, are now being replaced by media culture, which has very different criteria. In its own way, world tourism facilitated the error that the traveler understands whatever he can visit. The presence of the world as it is represented via its presence in the mass media creates the error that world art is available as well. World art has been physically collected in the West for a long time and thus seemed to have become the possession of Western culture—while the native cultures seemed to lack any appropriate discourse. Outside the Western world, interest in one's own culture has a different purpose, as natives have the impression that they were robbed by Western civilization, when they involuntarily handed over their own artistic heritage.

Global art, which belongs to everyone and to no one, does not create identities of the kind that arises within a culture with common traditions but still suffers from confusion with exotic or primitive art. The so-called primitives had been in demand in early modernism when people were tired of their own cultures and when their own art history seemed exhausted. But even this escape from art history inevitably became an event in the same art history. Primitivism is an inseparable component of Western art history, as the great exhibition organized by William Rubin in the Museum of Modern Art in New York in 1984 underlined in a secretly tendentious way. But what is true of primitivism was by no means true of the "primitives" themselves, whom we expected to find outside the boundaries of any art history. They offered the welcome counterimage of our own culture, to use the title of Karla Bilang's book *Bild und Gegenbild* (Image and Counter-Image), whose subtitle speaks of "Das Ursprüngliche in der Kunst des 20. Jahrhunderts" (The Quest for Origins in Twentieth-Century Art).

The ethnographic clichés long blocked our view, as Clifford Geertz repeatedly stated also for anthropological studies. The counterimage we expected lived from the doctrine that tribal cultures, to take just one example, had never made the experience of history. The kind of history we found there was so unlike our own concept of history that it was mistaken for a mythic form of life in which time had stood still. It is, however, evident that history does not live solely from the patterns of a linear history or from the dynamics of change that steer the course of technological modernization; it also is manifest in the use of social models and cultural traditions. So it was the lack of chronology (one of the most striking characteristics of the "primitive" idols) that discredited any attempt to write "primitive" art. But since archaeological research has begun, even the "dark continent" has asserted its own right to an *Art History in Africa*, as the Belgian anthropologist Jan Vansina chose for the title of his 1984 book. Once this progress will be recognized by Western humanities departments, we will be well on our way to an art history with a different meaning and a different practice.

In global art, of course, we deal not only with "primitive" cultures but also with early "high cultures" in which art history, if it has any tradition at all, does not have the same tradition as we would accept. The example of China reveals the otherness of a non-European tradition of art history. And finally, long before any of the known historical cultures, including our own, there existed the prehistoric culture of the *Frühzeit des Menschen* (early mankind), to quote the title of a book by Denis Vialou. For obvious reasons, the latter culture resisted any attempt (including Theodor W. Adorno's *Aesthetic Theory*) to integrate it within a history of art. The question of art and the aesthetic phenomenon implicit in today's term was always out of place there. Our art discourse was not invented for and did not apply to any prehistoric material. So-called art history is thus a discourse with a limited use and for a limited idea of art.

There is the question whether tribal culture—yes, I dare to say it—has *no art,* even while its images display the highest artistic skill. They served other purposes like religion or social ritual, which may be more significant than creating art as we understand it. This topic became an embarrassing one for any attempt to exhibit world art and to avoid the art topic at such occasions. Thus, the major exhibition staged in 1989 in

Paris revealed Jean-Hubert Martin's desperate effort to reopen the contemporaneous phenomenon of world art. The title *Magiciens de la terre* avoided the word art, whose idea nevertheless was the ultimate reason for exhibiting these "magicians of the earth" in an art museum where artists and artisans shared the contemporaneity of their visitors. It is not my intention to discredit this early attempt to deal with the new coexistence of Western and non-Western artists who do not share a common concept of art. Rather, such attempts reveal the conflicts that emerge on either side of the barrier enclosing the territories held by traditional art history and the latter's way of thinking.

The critics have then asked the uncomfortable question as to what the work of the minimalist Richard Long, titled *Mud Circle*, had in common with a ritualistic item of the Yuendumu, a group of Australian aborigines, which was its neighbor in the exhibition (fig. 17). The pair of exhibits offered formal analogies, which readily lend themselves to the contemplation of pure abstraction. But in the end, Richard Long could not be dismissed from his place in Western art history any more than the aborigines could be incorporated within it. This contradiction was, however, further obscured by the practice of labeling every exhibit with the artist's name and with a date of the work, as if these data—as normal and necessary as they are in the Western art scene—were even remotely relevant to many of the products of non-Western world art. In the case of the aborigines, not only the alleged analogy but also the open contrast lured the visitors into a trap, because the aborigines meanwhile produce for the Western art market, which places a high value on "indigenous art," so easily distinguished from its own products.

World art increasingly engages in the transcultural argument when non-Western artists express themselves in Western media and technologies in which they continue their native traditions, while at the same time carrying on a critical dialogue with Western culture. This may result in unusual works and conceptions, but Western culture cannot claim credit for them, nor will they play a role within it until Western art is capable of a creative response. For the time being, the cliché of "otherness" is more a hindrance to perceiving the other. Eleonor Heartney, commenting on the Paris exhibition in the July 1989 issue of *Art in America*, notes that, thanks to its present trendiness, the theme of the "other," as it was solemnly presented in this context, is in the process of being received "into the pantheon of the ruling myths of twentieth-century art."

A special case in today's world art is the alliance of non-Western art with Western media culture. This has created a meeting place for

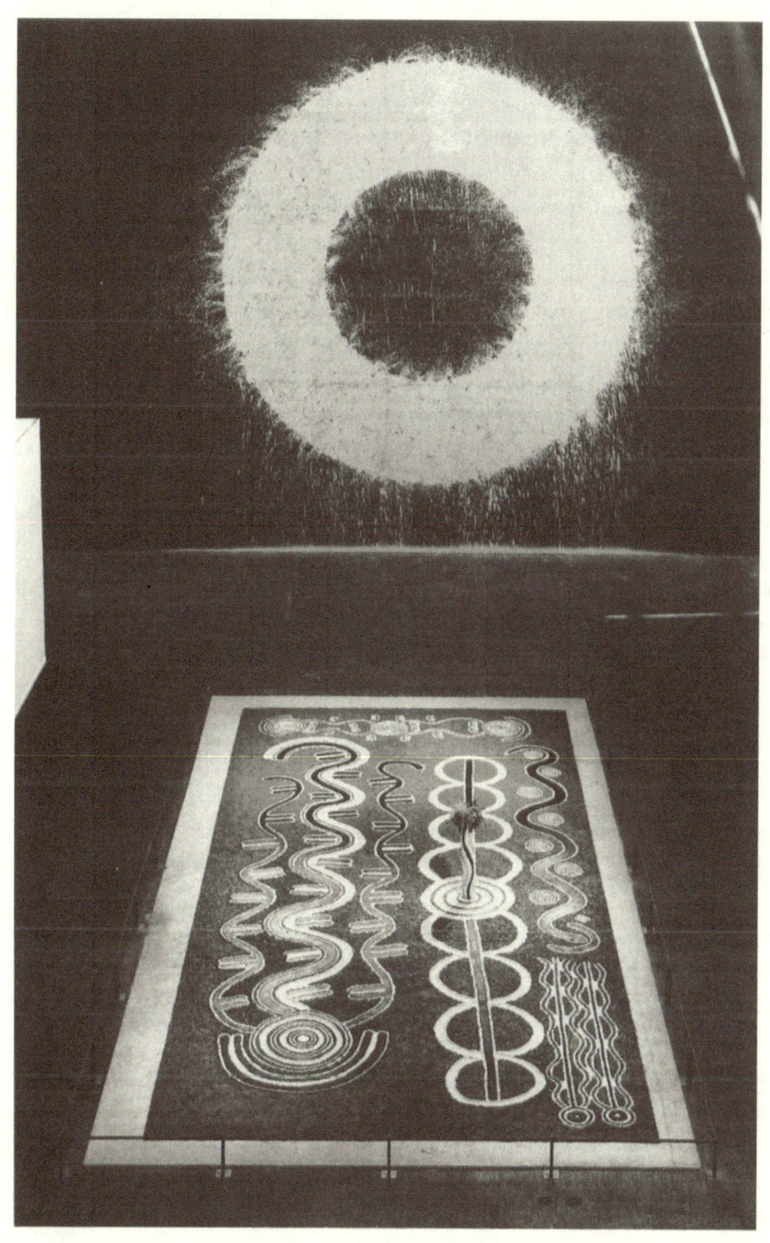

17. Exhibition *Magiciens de la terre*, Paris 1989, showing *Mud Circle* by Richard Long alongside a composition by a member of the Yuendumu tribe, Australia.

artists from different cultures, who use the ubiquitous technology of networking to produce works without reference to place or time and to participate in joint artistic events everywhere and at any time. Their protagonist is the Korean-born Nam June Paik, who long ago has entered Western art history as the "father of video art," where he is being remembered jointly with John Cage and Joseph Beuys. In a very personal way, Paik has introduced his own culture into the Western art scene, whose concept of an artist he adopted in paradoxical ways. Thus he does not qualify for any evidence of global art but has become a famous outsider of Western art, within which he was more celebrated than understood. The former key figure in the Fluxus scene, who likes to hide his own silence in a noisy Western potpourri of images, has repeatedly played with ideas of non-Western origin that seem familiar because of their Western manner of expression. Paik has been subtly addressing the theme of his own cultural migration, for example, in the summer of 1993, at the Venice Biennial, where he staged the voyage of Marco Polo in the garden of the German Pavilion (fig. 18), or in the fall of the same year, when he launched the companion exhibition entitled *Eurasian Way* (fig. 19) in the Watari-Um Gallery in Tokyo almost like a reversal of the Venice show, at least in the direction of East-West.

The revisions in conceiving culture, now on the agenda in many societies, are more contradictory than it appears at first glance. Western culture, which once felt up to the task of representing all ethnic cultures via exploration and exploitation as collection, is now proclaiming the future of a world culture in which it again claims the leading position. Non-Western cultures, on the other hand, are retreating in a kind of countermovement into their own histories in order to rescue a part of their identity. To Western eyes, such moves make them look nationalistic—a telling misconception. But while Western culture fosters its global ideas, its own cultural unity is disintegrating: that very unity that was supported by the educated class of bourgeois culture has long ceased to survive as a common ideal or canon.

Art history for a long time offered a favorite image of Western culture and its past victories. The objections to this image, which, as we have seen, began with the feminists, were raised much earlier by the artists themselves, as will be seen below. Minorities are now filling the void left by the "canon" with the "invention" of their own brand of art history, in which artists can meet an audience whose sympathies match their own. Where no minority can articulate itself, topical issues produce consensus and justify the production of art, whose topics are more important than its artistic creeds.

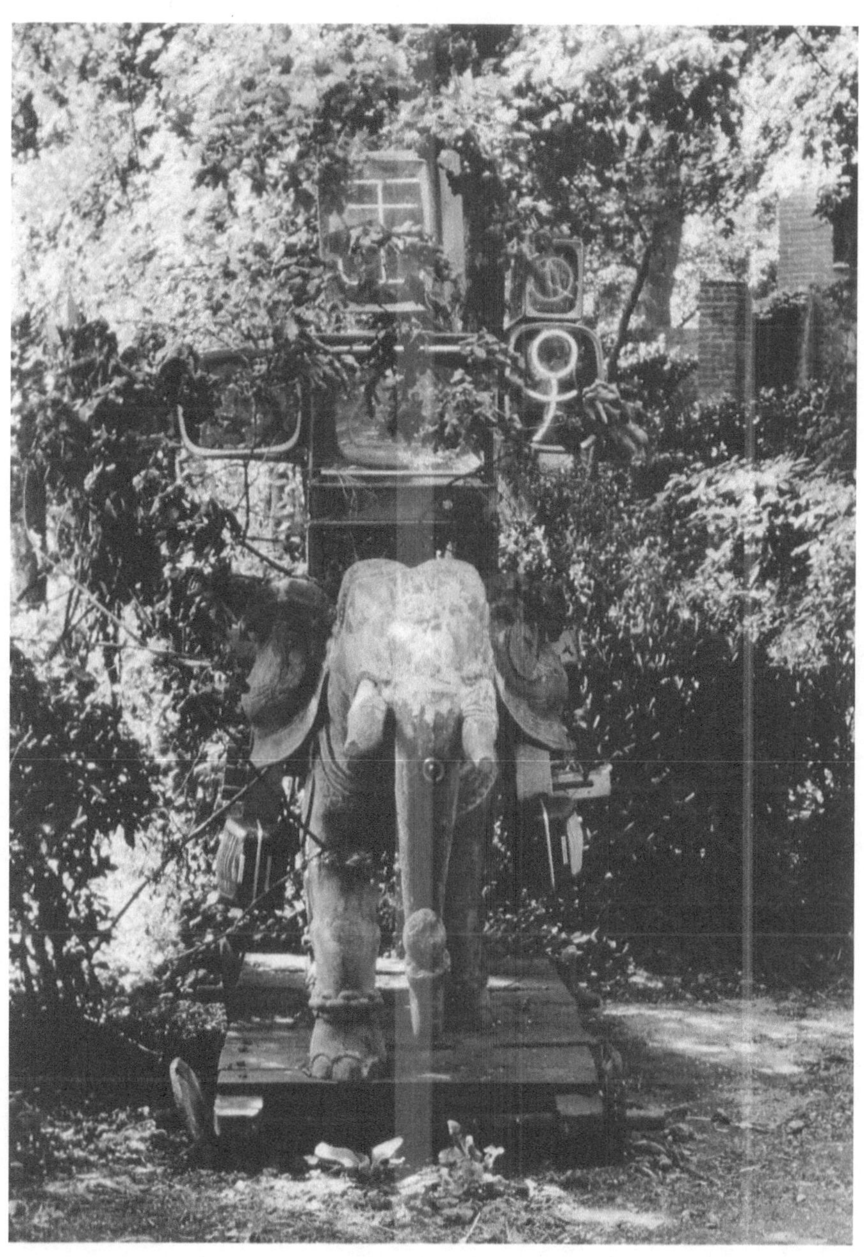

18. Nam June Paik, *Electronic Super-Highway*, Venice Biennial, 1993.

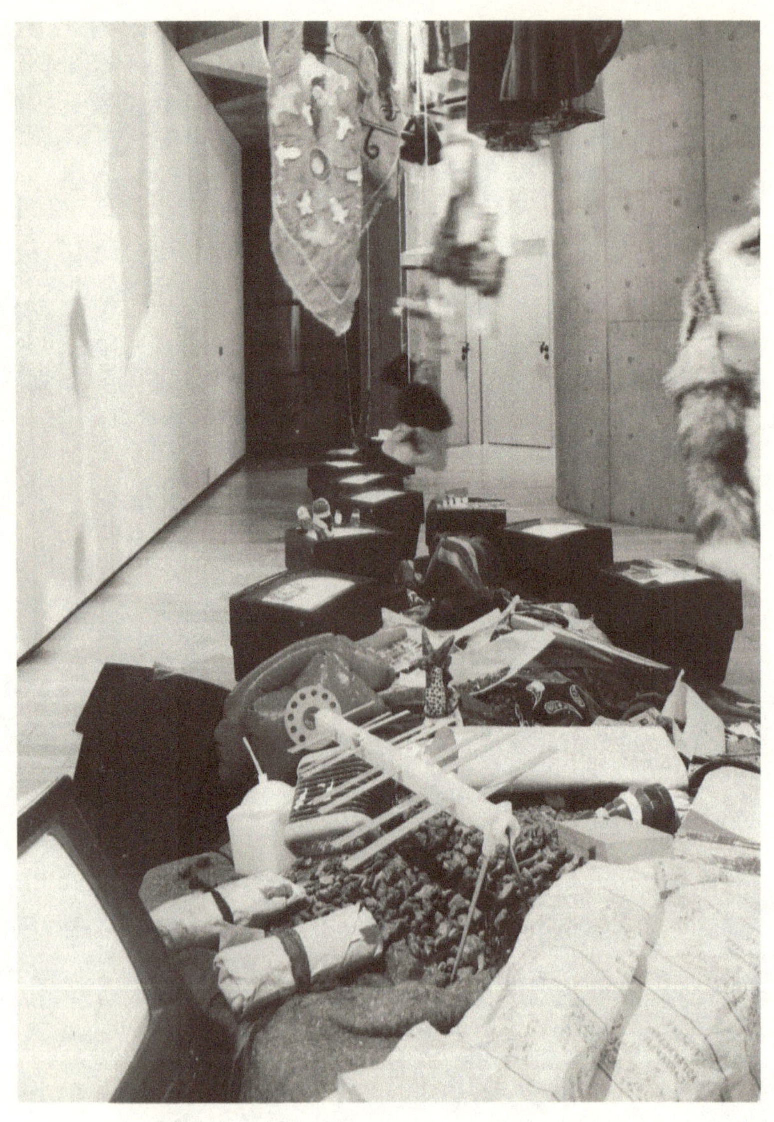

19. Nam June Paik, *Eurasian Way*, Watari-Um Gallery, Tokyo, 1993.

Today's world is a diaspora, as we read in the moving *First Diasporist Manifesto* written in 1989 by the Jewish artist Ronald B. Kitaj, who was born of immigrant parents in America and today lives mostly in England. A diaspora means extraterritorial living and the fruitless search for one's identity. As we know, among the Jews of ancient times, the ban on producing visual images was relaxed in the diaspora, so that Jewish art could be produced only in exile. Soon all Jews lived in the diaspora, at least until the state of Israel was founded, and they found in their art a medium of identity that was always connected with their religion. Today, the diaspora is no longer a Jewish fate, as Kitaj assures us, but applies to all who do not "feel at home in the world" and who therefore seek to join a group with common convictions. "Diaspora art," the term that Kitaj plays with in melancholy irony, is the opposite of so-called world art, and it usurps or replaces the old perception of identity that was for so long linked to the history of art in the West.

9 The Mirror of Mass Culture: Art's Revolt against Art History

Postwar modernism soon finds itself again at the old divide between "art" and "life," where it turns against the respective attitude of prewar modernism. It is no longer the intention to seize control of "life" in the name of art and on behalf of design and architecture. In Europe, even where the surveillance of the United States does not reach, artists want to surrender autonomous or "cultural art" (in Jean Dubuffet's phrase) to "life" and to follow the lead of the mass media. It is the debate on "high" and "low" culture that soon determines the course of art in an interchange with the everyday world. The same topic reveals an impulse against the dictates of art history. High modernism still wanted to make art history, in other words, to continue its linear progression into the future. "Postwar" art, on the other hand, soon left the guidance of art history in order to meet, in its own time, whatever the outcome would be in redefining its goals. As soon as the artists adopted the style of contemporaneous society, they had to break with art history's inner logic, at least the logic valid until then.

The Paris art scene, the Mecca of elitist abstract art that in the late 1940s just slowly replaced the equally elite surrealism, became the foremost place for that subversion that the new realists would develop ten years later. In 1949, Jean Dubuffet exhibited in the Galerie Drouin his collection of "art brut," by which he meant an art that was to be "untouched by cultural art." The exhibition in half showed the work of "patients in psychiatric clinics" who, in his opinion, had been spared the mechanisms of conformism. The declared enemy was the "officially recognized art in museums," which he also attacked as "artificial art," art for the intelligentsia.

Two years later, in December 1951, Dubuffet attacked culture in the speech "Anticultural Positions," which he delivered before the Arts Club of Chicago. Paradoxically enough, as often happens in culture when it is attacked, a facsimile of the handwritten manuscript was published in the guise of a work of art twenty years later on the occasion of an exhibition in the Feigen Gallery in New York. In his speech, Dubuffet exposes culture as "a dead language that no longer has anything in common with the language spoken on the street. It is increasingly alien to our real life" and is degenerating into a "mandarin culture." This is why Dubuffet wanted to convoke the testimony of the "so-called Primitives" and mobilize rapture against cerebral art. The world he cared for was not civilization with its technology but nature and unspoiled sentiment.

Again in Paris, as early as 1947, the young English artist Eduardo Paolozzi was spending his time cutting up glossy American magazines—with their new printing technology and their surrogate aesthetics of commerce —and turning them into collages. From a European standpoint, these everyday myths appeared as the faraway dream of a glittering consumer world and certainly not yet as stereotypes of one's own environment. Advertising used these illustrated magazines as a medium that took over from public posters, and in which the comic strip, the second root of "popular culture," was at home. With these modest exercises, Paolozzi, who was acquainted with Francis Picabia and the ex-dadaist Tristan Tzara, was delivering the program of an empathetic "art of the ordinary."

The piece *I Was a Rich Man's Plaything* of 1947 (fig. 20) reassembles the stereotypes of collective dreams as if in a mail-order catalog, no longer for the purpose of advertising but for analysis and with a good pinch of formal humor. The mistress's public intimacy is like the trademark of a world of clichés in which even Coca-Cola publicity has its place. The comic pistol, ironically aimed at the glamour girl's head, shoots a pop with the word "Pop," like a verbal echo. Paolozzi's strategy evokes a world in which it is no longer nature (human nature included) that matters but the happy consumption of mass media, which provide the hidden promise in this otherwise meaningless potpourri.

In the 1950s, Paolozzi became a member of the small Independent Group that heralded English pop art. In the winter of 1952, he introduced the group to his Bunk collages, which he understood as a beacon of resistance to high art and art history. In 1953, it was the exhibition *Parallel of Life and Art* in which the group declared war on museum art and revolted against the exhibition *Growth and Form*, where the celebrated art critic Herbert Read once again had propagated the ideals of autonomous art and the maxims of art history. But not until 1956 did the hoped-for scandal occur. The exhibition *This Is Tomorrow*, in fact, turned the leading program of the avant-garde—the proclamation of the future—into a farewell to art history. It was no longer the intention to guide art history into a yet unknown future but to give up the notion that art history still was to go on altogether.

The symbol of the new anti-art became the famous collage by Richard Hamilton, whose reproduction in the catalog and on the exhibition poster immediately turned it into the icon of "new brutalism." Even the

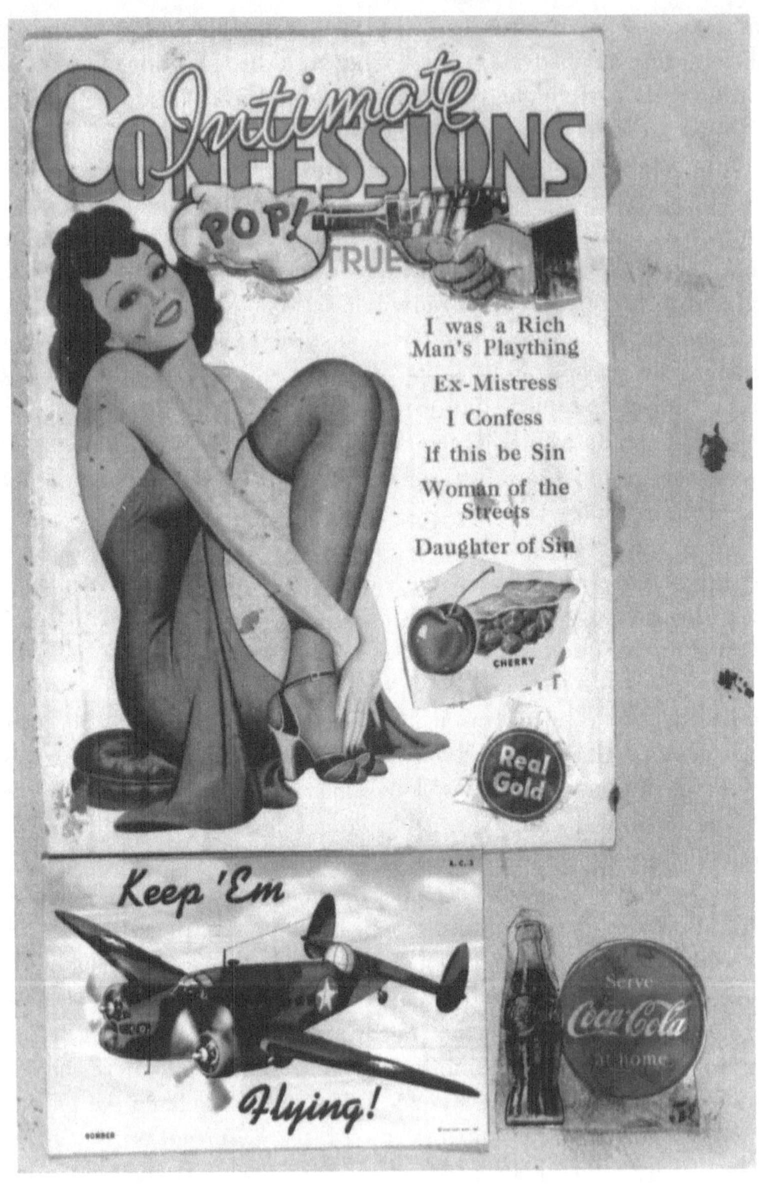

20. Eduardo Paolozzi, collage from *I Was a Rich Man's Plaything*, 1947. Tate Gallery, London. © 2002 Artists Rights Society (ARS), New York / DACS, London.

very question the title poses is the parody of a title, "Just what is it that makes today's homes so different, so appealing?" (fig. 21). The trophies of banality have turned "home, sweet home" into a public spectacle of consumerism. The body-building man with the "pop" racket poses in the center of the room as if in an advertisement for sports and fitness training, faceless and anonymous as a consumer idol. The point, however, is that this is a new type of collage. It stages not only a pseudosetting but also a pseudoscene that is also pure illusion and allows the conclusion that the world of consumerism has meanwhile penetrated the living space.

Events like these today are remembered as events of art history, although they were meant to undermine the validity of the latter as a frame in which to discuss art. The mere appearance of Hamilton's collage poses a problem, since it looks like a parody of what the artist hails in his texts as his new artistic ideal. It also raises the question of the future of an art that intended to abandon art history and enter the "real world" while simultaneously remaining art. Since it is neither advertisement nor commodity, it cannot be anything but art (in other words, a cultural commodity). Richard Hamilton and Lawrence Alloway, the speakers of this group, rejected all symbolic language and even abandoned the idea of an autonomous aesthetic in favor of "everyday experience." They sought to fuse the "fine arts" with "popular culture." This meant, in effect, that art, as an approach to everyday life, should be perceived in the same way as the latter. To solve this contradiction, the artists resorted to a *new* aesthetic instead of renunciating aesthetics per se, and this shifted the debate to another level.

The relationship between art and advertisement became an unexpected issue that undermined the old notion of the artistic idea. Reproduction was being reintroduced as a new type of commentary on the world, just as production, that is, the work of art, had served the artist's self-expression. Such contradictions in which art embroiled its audience, also sabotaged the narrative of art history, which could not carry on its accustomed pattern—even if this did happen in practice. The tense of art history was absorbed into the tense of the media world, which art reflects, criticizes, and comments upon. Art assimilated the style of its current society, which became its theme, and avoided its former tasks without solving its own problems. Such observations are not intended to criticize what happened but to serve to reveal the problems of describing art's new roles.

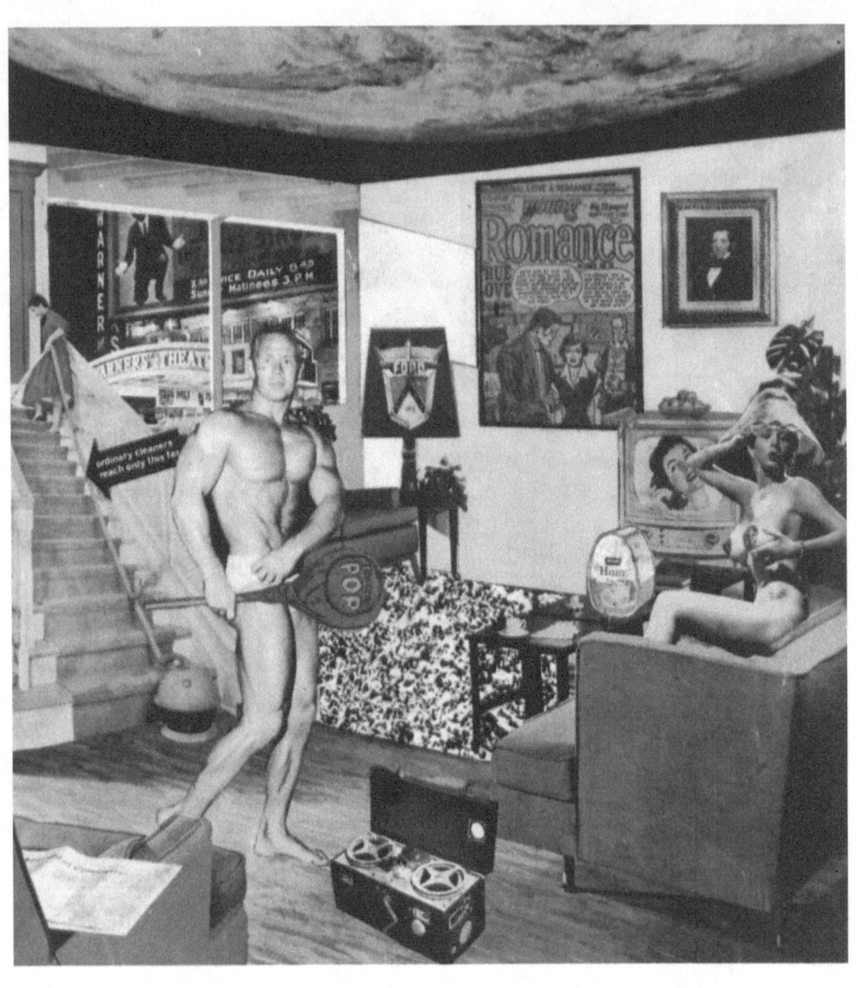

21. Richard Hamilton, *Just What Is It That Makes Today's Houses So Different, So Appealing?* Paper collage, 1956. Kunsthalle, Tübingen. Collection of Georg Zundel. © 2002 Artists Rights Society (ARS), New York / DACS, London.

Art had taken different attitudes toward advertisement over the years and already flirted with the public media of "Publicité moderne," as Lucien Boucher called it in his 1927 photomontage in *L'art vivant.* But the hope that such publicity would be given over to artists soon came to nothing, leaving artists only the role of subversion or of counterfeit. The triumph of design and the domination of the media were both achieved without them. We are meanwhile fascinated by virtual worlds in which art only will survive if it is *less artificial* than the new technologies of illusion and reminds us of forgotten realities. Today, visual advertising has become a commodity in its own right, and with a quasi-autonomous aesthetic: it sells itself; the market success of Calvin Klein proves this sufficiently. As a mass product, advertising blinds the consumer's eye to the thing itself and hides the illusion, its true nature, behind the ostensible effect of the product it touts. In this trompe l'oeil, it has become an unwelcome rival of art. By aestheticizing our environment, it is seizing control of some of art's public realms. In this interchange, art retains only the role of exposing and revealing the illusion inherent in the advertising products. Thus, mass culture is not merely a topic for art's new iconography but has become a challenge for art to such a degree that we may ask how this transformation still can be coped with by traditional art history.

Media studies have taken the lead in describing technological inventions and commercial data, which are, however, increasingly reflected in art. Mass culture has also become a topic within the humanities ever since literary and philosophical culture no longer were fixed on the testimony of text sources. The question is to what extent the idea of art was dependent on the paradigms of historical culture from whose dissolution it would be threatened, like literature and the book—in other words, whether mass culture will grant art a domain of its own. Here, again, we are confronting problems for continuing the practiced narrative of art history.

If we however consult recent studies on this topic, everything looks astonishingly simple. In the catalog of the 1991 exhibition *High and Low* in New York's Museum of Modern Art, curators Kirk Vanedoe and Adam Gopnik, by tracing the topic back to the nineteenth century and dividing it into genres, create a déjà vu effect. They identify the iconography of everyday life, including the mass media, as the leitmotif in modern art, by which the latter was able to revitalize and update itself. Anything with a long history lends itself easily to an impressive narrative, and thus the exhibition assured its public that art had not given up its life in the process but has, rather, found the strength for ever new kinds of resistance. We learn from such projects how easily art history can be rephrased, if only one believes in art. In the above-mentioned exhibition modern art appeared as a veteran in staying alive despite its permanent struggles with "low culture." But if traced back to the nineteenth century, "low culture" had the same origin in the bourgeois culture of metropolitan Paris that produced, on the one hand, the art of the salon but also, on the other hand, the *Petit journal pour rire*, whose lithographs anticipate the comic strip.

The concept of mass culture, however, in contemporary usage must be restricted to the postwar period and tied to the U.S. profile. Already, Clement Greenberg, in his early combative essay of 1939, identified kitsch with the mass culture as opposed to the avant-garde. "Kitsch" is dependent on a diagnosis of culture it involuntarily parodies. "Kitsch" as a term presupposes the possibility of keeping a safe position in culture and also the belief in the existence of an art that is to be distinguished. But what if art plays with kitsch and introduces the latter into art history? In that case, the old distinctions with their implied value systems crumble. Greenberg defined kitsch as imitating art without being art. Today, the reverse seems to be true when art (apparently) imitates kitsch in order to undermine (or to overcome) kitsch: a daring maneuver that poses certain problems on the part of the art critic.

The issue of kitsch is not restricted to the influence of "low" art on "high." Any art that paid attention to mass culture seemed to attack the idea of culture as such, to which art is intimately connected—so intimately that it attacks itself when it declares war on culture. But the militant impulse that characterized the art of the 1950s is long since exhausted. It lost its focus through constant repetition, and even the elite culture it originally attacked has since sunk into a gray zone where its present condition is not clear. Only the narrative of art history—like the art market and the museum—has kept itself firmly in the saddle by simply continuing its narrative where there is so much to narrate, thus keeping a cultural practice alive, however doubtful their object of attention may look in the meantime. But artists who still believed in art were more affected by this change of things than are those who merely comment on it. Thus some neo-abstract artists who revived the former gesture of abstraction in their works, introduced extra space for a distancing reflection or a kind of commentary with which they accepted their new situation. Other artists confronted abstraction and their own everyday environment in one and the same work, giving weight to both and questioning banal and aesthetic forms together. Where artists permitted personal statements, each brush stroke becomes an applied theory, as with the art of Sigmar Polke and Gerhard Richter.

An art that still stands by its cultural meaning has a choice between either withdrawing into its own myths or transforming the banal symbols of mass culture into motifs of protest or of sublimation. In its usual appearance art is found in constant self-doubt and keeps the periphery of its former existence. In the process, it must continually take new risks if it wants to remain true to itself. Its changes of role are a tactic to keep the game going, while the retrospective of its own history serves to recapture a significance which is not of the present. Usually, such observations are accompanied by the question whether art has not simply exhausted itself and is now conducting only rearguard actions. But the topic of high and low needs more consideration in this debate and raises the question whether art will survive when it is dissociated from what we called high culture and whether the latter still survives without "art" in the accepted sense. Art wins or loses in the name of historical culture, which took the contours familiar to us in the bourgeois age.

Art was always connected to the idea of the creative act that we identify in the work of art, and it has also participated in art history in a sequence of personal inventions. The early days of modernism reinforced the ethos of the creative act by placing all its bets on the immediacy of pure form and appealing to a vision that reveals the essence of nature: a vision that the viewer was intended to share. Paul Klee and his friends insisted, therefore, on the union of art and nature. Even the collectivist currents of his time that advocated the anonymous "style" did not touch the ideal of artistic creation. In the age of the digital media and the reproducibility of the world (not of art, as Walter Benjamin stated), this earlier creed has been lost. Mass culture replaces the authentic with stereotypes and repetition. It therefore compels art to share the new game in which art participates both by questioning (dissimulating) and also by reasserting itself. The viewer, who perceives, as it were, his or her own perception, expects art to embark also in the mediated vision of today's technologies in which we trust more than in our own eyes. We no longer believe in immediacy when we experience the world, as the subject claimed it for him- or herself, but we demand the presence of technological props in order to communicate with the visible world and therefore need to redefine the artist's part.

Seen in this light, the silk-screen pictures in which Robert Rauschenberg played out the ritual of technical reproduction, adopt a more general meaning in our case. Photos reproduced from prints and transferred to silk-screen were altered by the artist such as to enter the new contest of his composition. Motifs like John F. Kennedy and the space rocket returned, in any case, as stereotypes from the news, whose print pattern Rauschenberg used as a distinguishing mark. His motifs were thus readymade pictures that he integrated in his work. They bear the trademark of the mass media and offer the viewer the familiar experience of public news. Their transformation in Rauschenberg's art endows them with a new aesthetic appeal. Reproduction has itself become part of the artistic product, and the latter now appropriates the world via topical images. In *Persimmon* (fig. 22), Rauschenberg combines reproductions from art history effortlessly with those from everyday life, and thus levels the one and the other by the gaze he offers us.

Rauschenberg entered the scene at a moment when the aesthetic of the readymade clashed with the claim of unmediated artistic creativity. Artists from then on had to prove their skill to overstep the boundaries of "high" and "low" in both directions, without finally settling on one or the other side and without distinguishing the "objet trouvé" from their own intervention. Artists can use everyday found objects straight or interpret and alienate them aesthetically. By this strategy of playing art and nonart off against one another, they could reveal the remaining difference between the two and thus claim the right to continue making art. The found objects, whether taken from the waste bin or from an art catalog, were forced into the framework of their discourse, which was not textbound but visual, a visual treatise on art and life. This kind of discourse placed the perception of the world in the cultural framework shared by the artist and his audience. It is clear, however, that this is no longer the framework called art history.

In the gray zone of production and reproduction, art has been exploring new ways to secure for itself the freedom of an individual act on which it depends. It seduces by interacting with a technical reproduction by an individual signature such as a brush stroke cutting a swath through the middle of a halftone. Walter Benjamin could not foresee that art in the era of technical reproduction would survive through

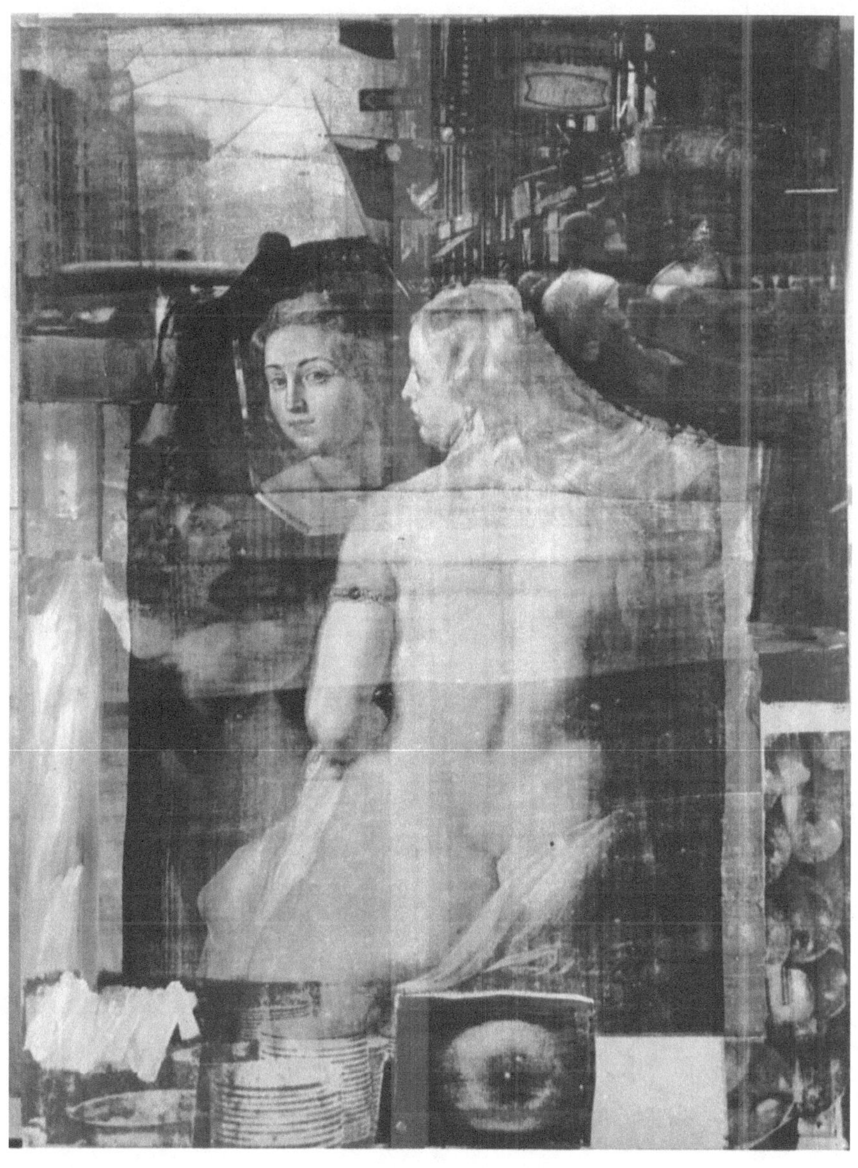

22. Robert Rauschenberg, *Persimmon*, silk-screen on canvas, 1964. Castelli Collection, New York. © Robert Rauchenberg / Licensed by VAGA, New York, NY.

such virtuoso acts of transformation In our context, everyday culture in the postwar generation was an antidote to art history from which art attempted to free itself. Today other boundaries have emerged where the distinction between "high" and "low" is more equivocal than it was in those times when it was turned into a program of resisting "high culture."

10 The Temporality of Video Art

When we now look at video and installation art, we find a somewhat different situation. Art history, as the chronicle of the art scene, has not yet come to terms with such art phenomena, even though their activity has spanned three decades and has a big share of the art scene. Although art criticism in this domain has become quite extensive, its results are not fully integrated in the established framework of art history. It is not the continuing debate whether products of this kind are to be considered art or not that has prevented its acceptance by art historians. Rather, it is the different working structure that has created resistance as to the method of dealing with art in technology. My intention is not to introduce media art as such but to review it in light of the obstacles it presents for the accepted methods of art history.

The notion of time offers itself for this discussion since the video artists have always been obsessed by it. But they precisely do not mean the official time called history in which artists have looked for their place so often. It is rather a quite different concept of time that has attracted them. First, there is the time of the medium itself, which, as with film, has to be performed in time. Furthermore, video is a transient medium and, as it is prone to accelerated decay, falls soon victim to time which already has led to an archeology of video art.

Video installations dramatize the problem of time, since they exist only for as long as they are actually on display. In contrast to videotape, which can be played anywhere, the video installation, like theater, is linked to a performance situation. But unlike theater, it has no text; and unlike film, no screenplay. Its picture sequence can be experienced only on the spot, that is, in a given space. It does not lend itself to be documented with photographs, nor does it offer itself for easy description. It can be captured only in its own medium, the video. As I have learned in my own experiments in Karlsruhe, there is as yet no satisfactory documentation of this genre. However swamped it may be with theories, media art is thus not present the same way painting is, which survives in a body of works. Precisely this seems to be the reason for an abundance of theories, which are born from autopsy but subsume the most disparate artists under the same heading.

At first glance, it does not seem at all difficult to place media art into the chronology of the arts, as it is, for sure, a creation of the 1960s. The remarkable book published in 1976 by Beryl Korot and Ira Schneider, *Video Art*, offers the most comprehensive insights into its early stages. Ira Schneider, himself a media artist, had already edited the journal *Radical Software*, which provided a forum for discussion. In the foreword to *Video Art*, he fondly recalls the 1960s, when the industry first made available a low-cost version of video for noncommercial purposes, giving artists modest possibilities. In the same volume, David Antin delivers a brilliant and less polite critique of television, speaking of a "theater of poverty" in which the economic laws of the mass media, controlled by big business, were repealed—although only on the playground of a small group of outsiders. Television, he writes, was disqualified as a medium for artists not only by its technology but also by its consumer-oriented practice.

Any history of media art is usually centered on the topic of its technological development, after the video synthesizer offered a wave of advanced digitalization promising unlimited control over images of every kind, whether old or new. The entire archive of images, as a technological memory, supports the invention of images, whose extensive use, contrary to all previous experience, does not exhaust the archive but merely enlarges it. The time barriers between present and past also collapse in the grip of this "digital magic," as the science fiction author A. C. Clarke calls it. In the grips of such technology, history is on the verge of being suspended in an inescapable present in which anything and everything is available and everything can be made and remade.

Before I embark on the subject of the temporality of video art, the relationship between art and technology needs to be briefly considered. The question whether technology is translatable into art is resolved by the successful application of that technology. Since it offers no useful information and serves equally poorly as entertainment, for which it is too "boring" and too "difficult," it could only be art. It is an unproven legend that it will have the power to change the face of technology, where inventions are far too expensive to be handled by artists. The problem of media art is not its qualification as art but rather its marginal position in relation to the electronic dream factories of California, whether Silicon Graphics or the studio Industrial Light and Magic (ILM), where George Lucas with *Star Wars* became a legend as early as 1977. The year 1993 marked the beginning of a new era when Steven Spielberg's film *Jurassic Park* introduced true-to-life dinosaurs. James Cameron's

Terminator 2: Judgment Day (1991) unleashed computer technology to create a pandemonium of hallucinatory images that triumph over all real experience. Digital technology ushered in a new era of film in which one could easily create a fantasy world. In comparison, media art does not impress by technological excellence. It is more like an elitist enclave within the media world and therefore dependent on success in the art scene. It even made its entrance with the intention of questioning the exhausted genres of the art market.

This brings us back to my topic. The time of video art, which is different from time *in* video art, has already lasted several decades, but it has been difficult to write its history or to describe its development as an artistic genre according to the established pattern of a linear course of events. Temporality can be established only in the work of single artists, but in the evolution as a whole its origin can only be traced back to the context of Fluxus and Body Art when video artists shared a common critique of the art market. Seen in this light, the video artist originally was another type of a performing artist. Like the latter, he or she, in the course of a personal entrance, involved the public in the work. In Fluxus, the artist used his own body to conquer the territory normally occupied by the work of art whose commercial and physical presence were replaced by the artist's ephemeral self-presentation. In video art, the same type of artist used the new medium—certainly not invented for personal expression—as a mirror or attracts the attention of the public with the help of a kind of mirror. This introduces slow contemplation in the face of semantic complexity into a fast-paced medium, which otherwise serves only blind consumerism; interpretation, as an open-minded exercise, takes the place of communication or information.

This inverse situation encourages self-reflection, which gives us access to the concept of time we are heading for. Self-reflection opens up to an "inner time" and in so doing turns away from the pattern of real time. It is the experience of the "self" that many video artists have almost conjured up, much as this experience is put in doubt today. At first it seems strange that they serve this goal by "editing," that is, the reprocessing of the videotape, expanding, condensing, or interrupting the film sequence in a seemingly arbitrary way. Such a time collage loses real time as it was in the recording and rejects any illusion of narrated time, as film or TV have it to bring a story to an end. The artist retains control over his material in order to initiate a dialogue with the viewer in a personal "language." In this process, the time collage intended to represent the "internal time" of the brain explains the purpose of editing in our context.

Nam June Paik, when contributing to the anthology *Video Art,* entitles his own essay "*input time and output time,*" by which he means recording time and transmitting time. In this respect, he criticizes some video artists who, in order "to counter the CBS-type entertainment . . . , refuse to edit or to change the time-structure of performances or happenstance." He therefore insists that in our consciousness, "input-time can be extended or compressed in output-time at will . . . and this metamorphosis is the very function of our brain. The painstaking process of editing is nothing but the simulation of this brain function." Video art, he continues, "imitates nature, not in its appearance or mass, but in its intimate time-structure," which is not a category of real time but represents "the process of aging (a certain kind of irreversibility)."

The analogy with the brain, which freely replays what it has stored, flashes up in the ironic aphorism, "Once on videotape, you are not allowed to die . . . in a sense." He played himself with the feedback structure of the video when he honored John Cage with a tape from his life on the latter's sixtieth birthday or when he replayed, as it were, Marcel Duchamp after his death in mnemonic situations that via rewinding reversed the flow of real time. When he recorded a famous concerto in which Cage had acted in silent time, Paik attempted to reduce his videotape to a similar zero performance whose images he commented on with the written slogan "This Is Zen for TV." The time loop, with its simultaneous effect on sound, text, and image, is meant as a metaphor for a personal time experience outside of real time.

In his essay, Paik makes the puzzling reference to "boring art," that is, time-exempt art that avoids the narrative sequence of linear time. The argument is taken up by David Antin, who in the same volume of collected essays distinguishes "video pieces and TV in relation to time." The fact that videotapes are *boring* or *long* "has nothing to do with their actual length" but with the attitude inherent in their use. While TV lives from its total control over "commercial time" as its hidden commodity, the artist's video embarks "on a serious critique" of TV culture by its inversed handling of time. It uses time "as an inner unit, that is, as the quantity of time required by a given theme."

Nam June Paik celebrated this inversion as the "boredom" necessary for contemplation when he exhibited in 1974 the installation *TV-Buddha* (fig. 23). Here, an old Japanese statue of Buddha he owned is sitting in front of a recent Japanese TV set that borrowed its design from an astronaut's helmet. The wooden sculpture imprints its own immobility on the monitor by the ever same mirror image, which arrests the speed of TV-time via the live transfer of the video camera's feedback. TV-time, the very distinguishing mark of the medium, seems to be suspended. The history dividing the old sculpture and the new medium likewise collapses in this simultaneity, which is an attack on the very narrative of art history. The video reprojects the Buddha's image with the immediacy of a mirror, as it is capable of both recording and transmitting at the same time, and thus also negates the time lag existing between the creation and the perception of the usual work of art. But the riddles inherent in this installation also include the hidden presence of the artist in the guise of the statue, which hints at a very different situation, the situation of the self and its mirror image.

It was therefore a telling gesture when Paik himself, in a performance at Cologne, occupied the place of the statue in front of the monitor. He also offered a similar replacement for the original installation when the latter was requested (but not granted) for the 1984 exhibition on *time as the fourth dimension of art* in Brussels (fig. 24). The two-headed *Hydra-Buddha,* in front of two screens, consists here of two masks, which were cast in bronze from Paik's own life mask while on the screens videotapes with a collage of Paik's works and his performances are played. The introspection of the artist implies the memory of time as it is stored both in the disembodied videos and in his bodily performances. The asymmetry inherent in the relation of input and output time (also in the replay of past works) represents the self in its time experience, which so markedly differs from the official time as narrated by art history and undermines the linear assurances of chronology.

It is the very mirror effect that Rosalind Krauss made the target of her critique of video art in a famous early essay in 1976 in which she claims that "the medium of video is narcissism," in other words, an "image of self-regard" in which the self of the artist is "cut off from history . . . as the source of meaning" for his work. The synchronous feedback presents this self as "split and doubled." The particular aesthetic, a "psychological rather than a physical condition," creates a "total difference" from the other visual arts. She therefore was not willing "to speak of a physical medium in relation to video," as the latter lacked the facticity of an "object-state, separate from the artist's own being." Apart from the political argument in the author's critique, her analysis also concerns my topic here, as it questions the qualifications of media art for the traditional narrative of art history as a chronicle recording events

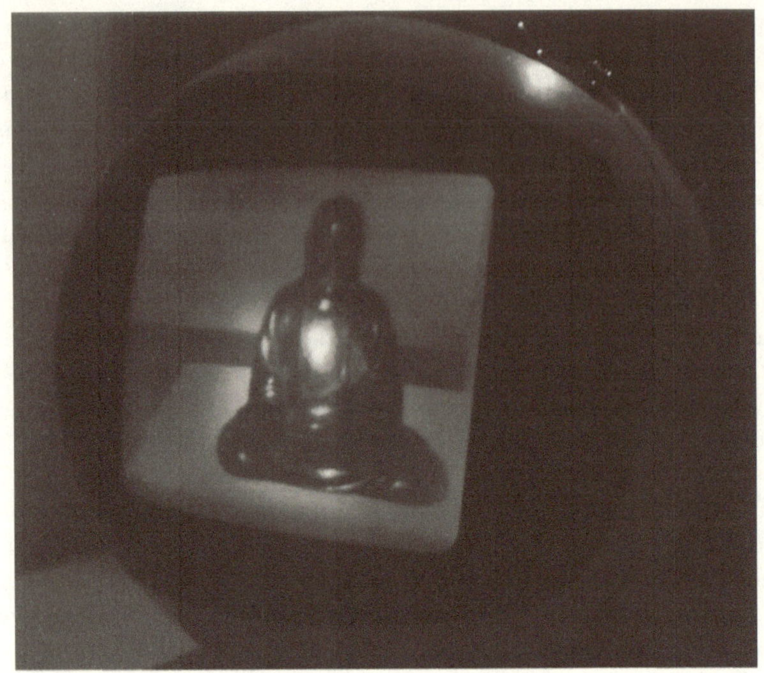

23. Nam June Paik, *TV-Buddha*, monitor image (detail), 1974. Stedelijk Museum, Amsterdam.

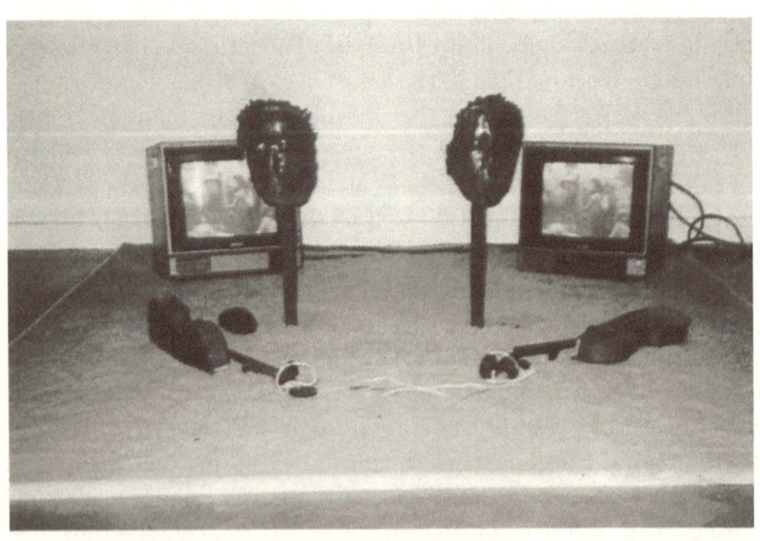

24. Nam June Paik, *Hydra-Buddha*, 1984.

and works within the framework of history and evolution (of the arts in general). Not only time, which is inherent in video art, but also the temporality in its public display is relevant for my argument.

Since then, video has developed in many different directions, but the mirror situation continues to spellbind. Renowned video artists such as Gary Hill and Bill Viola still appear with their body as a living medium, in which they enter a dialogue with the viewer. When Rosalind Krauss, in this respect, spoke of the loss of a text, she did not mean the loss of a specific text (such as a screenplay), nor the redundancy of text in video, but the loss of a hypertext controlling the social meaning and function of the work. In this way, even the text, which we call history, dissolves in individual consciousness as an uncertain site for communication.

Many video artists are aware of this danger and attempt to counteract it by a critical stance toward their medium, which tends to seduce a new art audience by the power of its photographic and filmlike images. I will select, for this purpose, two U.S. artists well-known enough to distinguish their use of video and video installation. Bill Viola and Gary Hill were both fascinated by the possibility of video to grant access to subjective time experience as distinct from the public time notion of history. In an interview from 1993, Hill called time "what is central to video, not linear time but a movement that is bound up in thinking—a topology of time that is accessible, . . . the works evolve from a self-reflexive practice that includes me as author/performer in the mise-en-scène."

Art history must reflect on the "rift" between video art and the former genres of the visual arts, to recall the term used by Krauss. The respective works are exhibited in the same museum or gallery space where other, familiar types of art are shown. This simultaneity calls for a reexamination of the discourse of art history in relation to this entirely new category of works that are so difficult to classify. Gary Hill, in the abovementioned interview, touches on two qualities of video art that in our context identify its different work structure. The paradoxical experience "of being intimate with time and estranged from it is what brought me to speech . . . the speaking voice acting as a kind of motor generating images. This puts one inside the time of speaking . . . suddenly words seemed quite spatial." The "speaking" installation, which introduces a voice in the exhibition space, alters the viewer's experience as much as the artist's strategy. Hill continues by saying that "Video embodies a reflexive space of difference through the simultaneous production of presence and distance . . . And yet, although my art is based on images, I am very much involved in the undermining of those images through language."

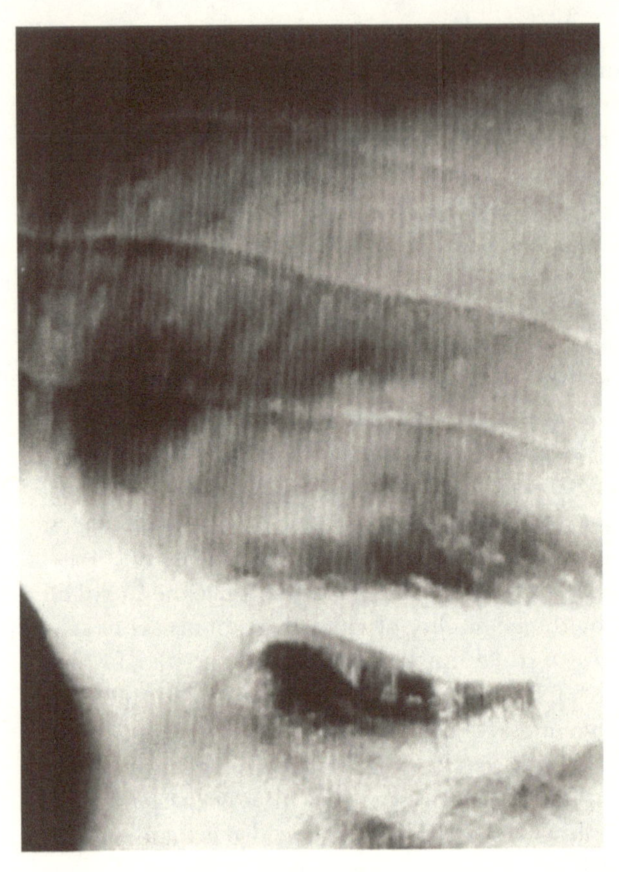

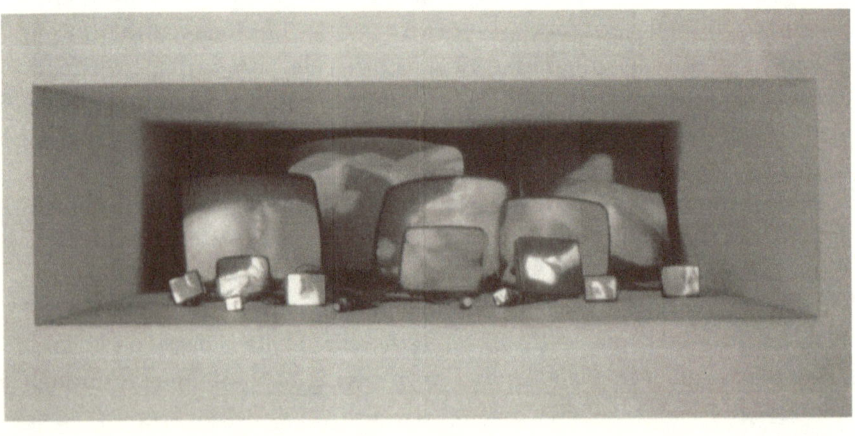

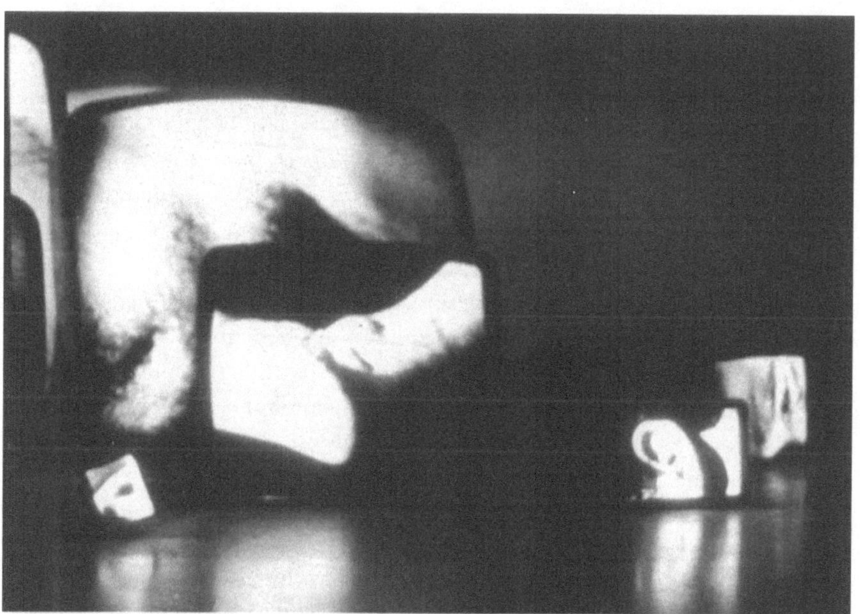

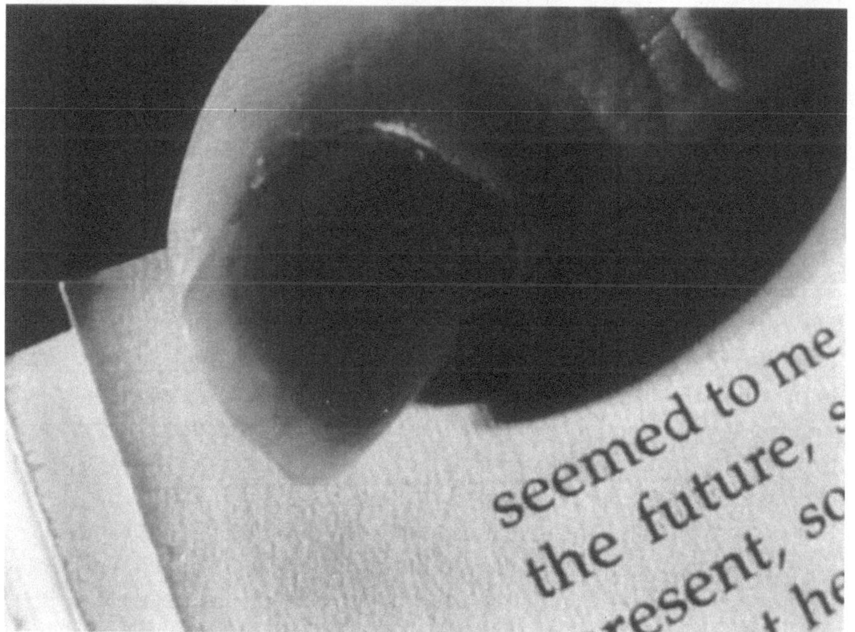

25a–25d. Gary Hill, *Inasmuch as It Is Always Already Taking Place,* video installation, 1990. The Metropolitan Museum of Art, New York. Details on monitor showing parts of face, feet, ear, stomach, and fingernail on printed page. Courtesy Donald Young Gallery, Chicago.

In a well-known installation that he exhibited in 1990, the artist decided to deconstruct the single image, which he distributed over sixteen monitors of changing size and to reconstruct, in a second step, the presence of a human body that "lives" between the partial views and speaks with his bodily voice. The title, *Inasmuch as It Is Always Already Taking Place* (figs. 25a–25d) seems to guide us toward the "epistemology of being," as he puts it ("being" as it is understood and as it experiences itself).

The installation refers to a picture whose painted space opens in the wall as a real space that shelters a kind of still life. Only the soundtrack encourages the visitor to search for the body that fills the niche (which, like a painting, we cannot enter). We are thus pulled between proximity and distance, as the single images remain behind the monitor surfaces at a cold distance even in the most intimate close-up. The work will never turn into a visible body. Even the incomprehensible sound—murmurings, groaning, a fingernail scratching a page of text—keeps us at the same distance but, nonetheless, bears witness to the presence of a living being whose presence no longer can be captured in an image, as it was offered by the equation of portrait and person for so long in history.

Individual parts of the body are captured in the videotapes, whose sequence differs between the respective screens. We identify these fragments as part of the same male body that is here taken apart into its separate "letters and words." The voice whispering, "I can't say," belongs to that body. The parts are like "picture syllables," which resist synchronization, and the single views on a skin that enclose an invisible self. One cannot dissect a living body, but one can do so most easily with visible monitors, which represent parts of an invisible body image. The incorporeal image and the apparatus together convey one unifying impression, which, so to speak, is born beyond what is actually shown The impression of a living body is enhanced by the analogy between the vibration of the video image and the breathing skin. Our perception fails to catch the invisible presence of a body, which nevertheless we experience as being "there."

This "turning into language," incidentally, also fulfills the purpose of "depriving the images of their power," as Hill says. This happens by restituting the human body with his voice, as it carries language. The image stands in a similar relation to the body as the body does to being: in a relation of difference. The search for a point of reference in the electronic flow of images guides us back to the body and its act of speech in physical time. The artist often refers to Maurice Blanchot, whose text *L'espace litteraire* (1955) he visualized in his installation *Beacon.* In this piece, too, he used the a strategy to relate language back to the body and thus to reconnect it with an embodied self. In the case of images, the strategy consists of opening a space for the invisible while remaining in the context of the visible and the representable.

Hill connects his concept of time with the concept of the body. "Vocalization was a way to physically mark the time with the body." When translated onto the body, sound is better equipped than the image to keep the presence of self. The artist sees language as a kind of "liberation" from the labyrinth of new images and their technological omnipotence. Here, the idea of narcissism is out of place, even when self-reflection so dominant in video art comes back into play. The analysis of the medium is brought about via the counteracting body, which still promises the notion of identity. After all, the medium itself cannot self-reflect. A kind of visual theory presents itself as an avant-garde position, since it reexamines the medium in order to subject it to a critique.

It is in the same context that the choice between video and spatial installation also plays a role. "A video work is not in the world in the way installation and sculpture intrinsically are, because they cannot enter a physical relationship with the viewer," as Hill remarks. The body experience, which Hill calls "visceral experience," is an important factor in the practice of the medium. The respective discourse is centered between the activity of the mind and body experience: the mind as a model of video editing, and corporeal sensation as the actor in spatial installation.

Hill, however, knows well that spatial installation is easily trapped by "an inevitable theatricality, which I try to minimalize." This is why he wants to deflect the viewer's riveted attention from the screen and its "never-ending images" with a performance use of images, instead of a performance *in* the image. It was not his intention to restore substance and illusion to images. Quite the contrary. The new images, "which are intrinsically immaterial, must lose even more of their false identity" by "having them glide over physical bodies and (simply and tracelessly) disappear in the depths of space." This vision comes as a surprise in the context of recent media art. Perhaps it will one day furnish a topic for historical discourse—at the beginning of a new history of art?

11 The Narrative of Art in the New Museum: The Search for a Profile

The site of the debate about art history will remain the museum of contemporary art, where any exhibition of new art also offers an occasion for discussing our idea of art history. But it has become questionable whether it is still possible to exhibit art history in the mirror of contemporary art. The current concepts of art raise the question whether they still agree on a common idea of art history. Simply to present works was not enough to bear witness to the course of art history and the state of art. We are still bound to an ever less comprehensible meaning of art that we still can identify within the context of its prior history, however that history may be understood.

As an institution, the museum, where artists and experts meet, has itself become a bone of contention. Pressure from the public, which expects to see in a museum everything that books no longer explain, has long since turned the question of content into an issue not only for the experts. Every debate on the subject of the museum also raises the question of what remains of the idea of art history. Where this idea has become uncertain, the exhibition space is being turned over to the most contradictory factions in order to rely on their credibility. Where any consensus is lacking, every type of art can demand access to the museum. Where no museum can meet the old expectations any longer, each museum allows exhibitions to let these incompatible demands have their say in a sequence of every imaginable conception.

The institution today thrives on the debates around its exhibition rooms. It thus continues to reenact the old play under every possible condition. When the Museum of Modern Art in New York opened the exhibition *High and Low* in 1990, it seemed to renounce the ideal of the exalted temple of high modernism and thus caused protests against the "desecration of the temple," where the vulgar design of advertising seemed to have moved in. As Arthur C. Danto explained on this occasion, the bourgeois concept of the museum as the *temple*, rather than the *school*, of art, was still retained even if modernism, of all things, became consecrated in this case. As late as 1958, Ad Reinhardt was still pleading vehemently for the museum as "shrine" rather than as a place of entertainment. Three years later, Claes Oldenburg turned the tables by exchanging the shrine for the shop when writing his "Store Manifesto."

The museum of today has not, for all that, become a department store, but it readily employs the techniques of advertising to stage a long-controversial art in the best possible light. An institution that increasingly resembles the theater by its changing repertoire favors the sensational mise-en-scène. It also tends to resemble a free trade zone, where the prize is recognition in the art scene. It is often questionable whether new art is begging for a stage in the museum or if the museum is hunting for new art. Without the museum, today's art would be not only homeless but also voiceless and even invisible. In turn, the museum, as barely prepared as it is for contemporary art, would give up itself if it closed its doors to new art. This enforced alliance effectively wipes out any alternative to the museum.

In the 1970s, it was still possible to speak of a "crisis of the museum" in the same way as one spoke of a "crisis of art." In the meantime, however, the former identity crisis has made way for the new museum boom, in which ambitious curators and the public so willingly accommodate, that questions of principle no longer matter. The new openness of the museum, so urgently called for, looks different than expected. Instead of serving a broader public with a more liberal selection of art, the museum finds itself in the hands of that public. The one time oasis for aesthetic experience has now become the stage for the public's self-experience, now that the latter has lost any other occasion for such desires.

In 1980, Douglas Crimp saw himself in a gleefully destructive vision sitting "On the Museum's Ruins," by which he understood the ruins of the powerful fiction to present art as a coherent system and art history as its ideal order. His criticism addressed the "moral and aesthetic autonomy" of modern art, which Crimp could not reconcile with his Marxist concept of representation and therefore wanted to force art into the political representation of society. He would have rather preferred an archaeology of the museum as the old refuge of a hermetically sealed art and therefore attacked the "neo-conservative use of the museum as a setting for the fine arts." On another occasion he called for resistance against a false postmodernism that rediscovers art's old genealogies and "returns to an unbroken continuum of museum art."

Since then, the so-called museum art has lost its "exclusivity" as criticized by Crimp, even if there are still enough attempts to keep the temple pure. As a result, the old controversies give way to the consumerism of a new era. Museum art no longer continues as a privileged and alternative species after the museum no longer resists the access of every possible art. Today, museum art can be anything, because anything can stand or hang in a museum. The museums are submissive even to the least suitable private collections, whose use is dictated by the sponsor.

At the same time, the new trend to topicality, as Siegfried Gohr remarks, seems to liken the museum to the annual "salon" of the nineteenth century. The close relation existing today between the museum and the art market reveals pressures from our society. Ever since our culture subscribed willingly to historicity as well as to the principle of marketing, it has ceased to classify the museum's difference from the market. The museum consecrates commodities that are simultaneously traded at the art fair. Institutions and events help in where art as such no longer appears to be convincing on its own terms. Enforced mediation is called for to support the former prestige of a weakened art. For a variety of reasons, society depends on a culture of privilege and is therefore determined to give art credit whether it deserves it or not.

Prices, as an index of prestige, often prevent a museum from purchasing a work that its own exhibition policy had promoted in the first place. Prices are subject to the laws of the market, of course, and thus make art resemble a mere commodity with which anybody may speculate. But the legendary prices paid for living artists must also be seen in another light. They are the visible symbols of an old myth of art and thus attract the aura that art itself is steadily losing. The prices cause an attention that art is frequently unable to trigger with its own means. In this sense, they offer themselves for a remythification of art, which as a result, thus seems to be protected from getting lost as a myth, the same way as we already lost religion.

Works in permanent collections, which no longer have a market value, are circulated within the museum's galleries so effectively that they constantly appear in an unexpected new light. The stage for contemporary exhibition techniques resembles that kind of theater that has prevailed in current museum architecture as a successful rival to the theater and the concert hall. The staging of art begins with the façade's inviting face and continues in the galleries, which are repeatedly redesigned for a new show. This type of staging is backed by the museum's education department, which has been addressing a new public for the last twenty years. It is no more geared toward opening up the temple than is the museum's theatrical setting, but reacts to a crisis of an "art religion" that strengthens the subjugation to a secularization of art.

This boom in museum construction is justified by a desire for the aesthetic of representation, which is gradually disappearing from all other public occasions, thus detaching itself from serving the museum's needs. Museum architecture was called in Germany the last project allowing "the practice of the art of building," to quote from an essay on the contemporary museum. Even more than the opera and the concert hall, with their schedule and ticket policy, and despite the paradox that we continue to revere bourgeois culture but are no longer a bourgeois society, the museum represents the cultural state or the cultural metropolis that can no longer do so by other means.

Once we today enter the theater of art, we are facing a great choice of exhibitions that skillfully meet two completely different demands: the need for information and the desire for surprise. The need for information reveals the lack of insight into what is happening in art today, which no one is in a position to survey anymore. Exhibitions have now replaced many other kinds of communication about the state of art and the course of art history. They always were meant to attract attention when a new movement was launched. But today they promise to offer knowledge that can no longer be satisfied other than with assertions—and with works intended to substantiate such claims.

The usual rituals of art, whose reasons no longer are obvious, gain all the more weight the less the public feels informed. These rituals surprise the public with the pleasure of an exhibition that replaces the uncertain pleasure in the exhibits. The new style of exhibiting answers the public's desire for spectacle with a type of entertainment, which the media are less capable of providing. People used to visit a museum to see something that their grandparents had seen on the same spot; today, people visit museums to see what has never been seen there before.

At the same time, museums invite their visitors in an audio-visual environment where they are shut off from the outside world and, in a dark, cell-like compartment, may experience the same intimacy as in front of the television at home. It is a kind of "screen environment" that we allow to capture our distracted gaze for a while. The museum, as a site for our imagination, has replaced the temple-like site of education it once embodied. Simultaneously, it aims at a disembodied space experience that is familiar from a television screen on which mere images pass in succession and cancel each other out. Thus, even when entering a museum we expect a telematic room quite foreign to the space of a museum.

The museum has become a railway station for the departing trains of the imagination instead of remaining the destination of a pilgrimage to the sanctuary of art. Installation art, too, creates alternative sites within the museum, denying the familiar museum setting by dislocating our visual imagination.

The museum was preferably the treasure house for a collection of unique pieces, unique in that they had only one place in the world. Here also, the power of the present was broken and exchanged for the time of history. Thus, the museum as showing items existing outside the visitors' lifetime and yet providing an experience of living space, inherited the situation in the temple or the church, where believers could physically experience the presence of a mythic time. The cult images in such religious sites were usually old yet present and visible as physical images, even as images to be seen only in a single place that you had to visit in person. The museum, as a symbol of a permanent place and of suspended time, thus is badly equipped for the ephemerality of today's exhibition practices. In a society that values data banks of information instead of a treasury of rare objects, a new mise-en-scène is required to despatialize and retemporalize the museum even within the museum and to exchange the "event" for the work.

The new energy in staging, however, finds its limits whenever premodern art, with its historical profile, is brought into place, in which case, prominent "visiting curators" for an episodic activity are given a freedom that the employees of the house themselves do not yet enjoy. In Rotterdam, Robert Wilson, the third in a row, succeeded in literally converting the museum galleries into stages on which the "performed" works from the permanent collections were hardly any longer recognizable (fig. 26). For a short time, the museum became a theater in the spirit of the baroque, which recycled art history as embodied in the old works, in a glittering "performance." The three art genres of "Portrait, Still Life, Landscape" (to quote the title of his exhibition) provided the repertoire for a mise-en-scène, which sometimes overdid the case when, for example, a Rodin bronze was displayed in an artificially illuminated autumnal forest as an example of "still life." It was a telling gesture to hand a museum over to actual scenography that transformed the museum into a stage with historical props.

In 1993, when Robert Wilson was playing theater in a museum, Peter Greenaway in another museum created a film situation without actually using film. The setting this time was the bizarre art collection of the former set-designer Mario Fortuny in Venice, a place where the film

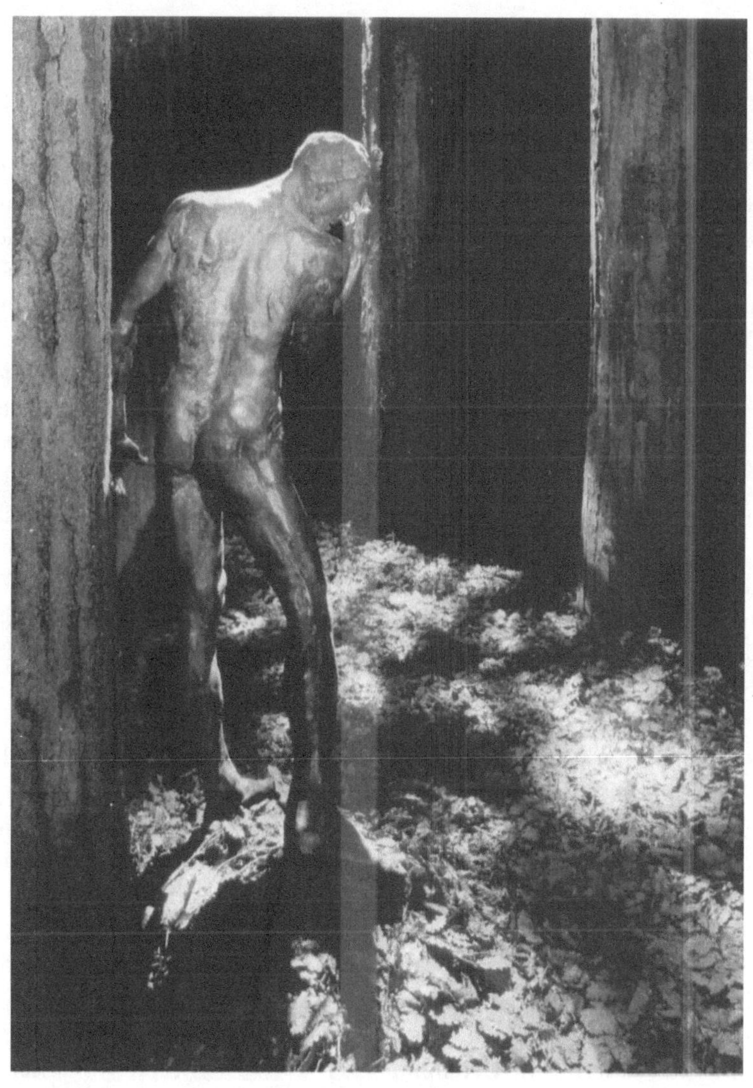

26. Robert Wilson, installation using a figure by Auguste Rodin, Rotterdam, 1993, room 3. Photograph from *Robert Wilson: Portrait, Still Life, Landscape*, exhibition catalog (Rotterdam, 1993).

director, on the occasion of the Venice Biennale, presented statues, masks, porcelain, and old fabric like props for an imaginary spectacle together with Fortuny's own paintings (fig. 27). Simultaneously, Greenaway used the same space for an exhibition titled *Watching Water* in which he displayed props from his own films. In the old collection, on occasion created for a ritual of memory, he installed spotlights that, in a hidden mise-en-scène, illuminated various items from the collection and, at an alternate pace, made the pictures stand out or recede into the dark. The viewer seemed to participate in a film in which the other actors waited for him or her to share the space on the stage.

Peter Greenaway, as he wrote in *Film Bulletin* in June 1994, intended in the long run to "overcome the cinema situation" and to return the cinema public to their own bodies in real space that they had lost in front of the surrogate of the screen. His projects, including a touring exhibition titled *100 Objects to Represent the World,* reached a certain climax in the exhibition *Stairs,* which turned the whole city of Geneva into a stage in 1994. From a hundred locations reached by stairs, the viewers would become the center of a cinematic situation themselves by looking through a frame in the guise of a cinema screen and thus experiencing world, art, and film fused into one and the same view or vision.

The scenographic transformation of the art exhibition meanwhile is increasingly entrusted to art historians who have not the experience for such a mise-en-scène and exhibit old and new works together in false or fanciful genealogies that seem to have been released from the laws of art history in favor of a newborn argument. Such experiments are still limited to temporary exhibitions in which, on the other hand, they tend to become models in general. In 1993, for the *Sonsbeek Exhibition* in Arnheim, Valerie Smith produced a hybrid between a wax museum and a fairground, in which the promiscuity of old and new, art and curio, was downright dizzying. The old curio cabinet, the predecessor of the museum, was reborn when contemporary works ingratiated themselves with stuffed animals and kitsch figures of saints from museum storerooms. In this atmosphere of dust and varnish, the memory of art history seemed to be left behind, since the show unleashed a chaotic stream of images and similes in which the contemporary exhibits appeared to have lost all their power to look like living art—as if they, too, already belonged in the repository of cultural memory.

The old forerunner of the museum, as Horst Bredekamp reminds us, makes a reappearance where art and the machine—whose separation gave birth to the art museum—are reunited in so-called media art. In the Kunsthalle in Vienna, which for a while occupied the Karlsplatz like

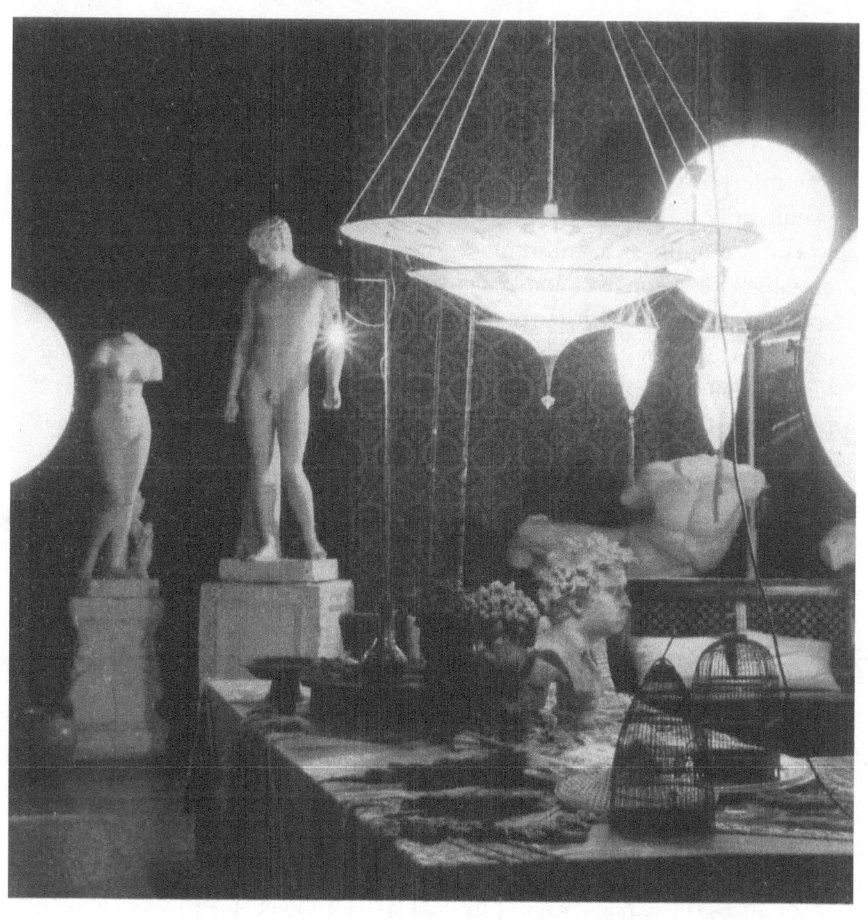

27. Peter Greenaway, *Watching Water*, installation in the Palazzo Fortuny, Venice, 1993. Photograph from *Peter Greenaway: Watching Water*, exhibition catalog (Milan, 1993), 23.

a forgotten container, an exhibition by Gary Hill demanded such complex technology that specialists spent weeks installing it. At the opening, however, the electronics were so well hidden—like the banks of machines behind a stage—that they allowed the illusion of a technology-free interplay of images that were technological. Such an exhibition is visible only as long as the electricity is switched on, since it is only the working monitors that illuminate the dark cubicles and fill them with moving video images. The real exhibition space fills with installation spaces that can be neither photographed nor described by texts, which is why exhibition catalogs no longer do justice to such works. The earlier presence of physical items, with their duration, here yields to the presence of a viewer, who enters the space and afterward brings his or her subjective impression home. The impression on the spot replaces the life of objects, and the exhibits are reduced to a sort of agency for the visitor. Art exhibited thus depends on the technology it contains, much as the transmission time of the videotape is regulated by computers.

As a post-technological tool of the imagination, the computer already has secret control over the old opposition between mind and machine. Its iconicity, which produces a digital (and *not* an analog) image on the screen, suspends the difference between the image and the sign in a hybrid between depiction and program. The computer, which challenges the received idea of creative art, moreover, as an archive of images, calls for a rethinking of the museum, because it behaves indifferently to museum pieces in their physical existence. Museum and computer technology thus in a way are rivals. The museum displays and symbolizes the experience of physical space (object space) as well as the experience of the time stored in the age of the objects. The computer, on the other hand, transforms images beyond place and time and into immaterial agents of information.

The museum's collection and the computer's database belong to different ages, although they coexist in the present. The collection principle in the art museum, moreover, lives from the condition of a selection that defined what we call art, while digital media aspire to the principle of completeness or totality of possible data. The selection, in turn, inaugurated the big gap within manmade pictures. Pictures inside the museum attained the status of art, while pictures that remained outside were forever distinguished as profane, banal, and artless. This very distinction, which justifies art history as a discipline, today loses its old and clear profile in the new media society.

Our concept of art is rooted in that of the Enlightenment age, which credited it with a timeless and universal significance transcending the specificity of individual works or genres: art was declared timeless and universal, much as human rights themselves were meant to apply to all people, however different they might be in race and origin. But this idea of art was tenable only when phrased in a general art history. The view of art history was needed to frame the individual time of the works since art history had a universal validity, while the individual works did not. That is why the art museum was to become the spatial equivalent of the time scheme of art history. It offered a place for everything capable of representing the logic of art history, which, when the Louvre first opened, was only old art, while new art first had to earn the status of museum art—it had to wait for it.

The nervous debate over the recognition of today's art proves clearly the degree to which we still cling to an idea not older than two hundred years—regardless of the age (or the youth) of the works of art to which we apply this idea. This idea of art history as still ongoing links us to the great tradition of historical culture, since we fear nothing more than art becoming a notion of the past. The definition even of contemporary art ultimately needs the horizon of its history, as it is this history that helps to explain what is, in essence, inexplicable. But art enjoys a privilege that mere ideas can never obtain: it materializes in "a work of art" that can be acquired by a museum and exhibited there as "art," that is, in a work that always possesses a place and a name. Even if it is a fiction, as Marcel Duchamp suspected, it is still a necessary fiction for the purpose of exhibiting culture, though market values seem to dominate as a result of present practices in art commerce. Even if the market insists on the purchase price and the museum proclaims art as its property, it is still only the symbolic value that can engage our fascination for art.

To clarify this symbolic value that was so visibly staged in the art museum, it seems reasonable to review once more the museum as the traditional site for contemplating history, at least in the bourgeois age. If history counts for anything, it is shared history in which a society seeks identity. But what about history in the art museum, where it seems to be contradicted by the fact that the old works have paid with the loss of their social use to enter the collections and thus become art? History thus lay not only in the evidence of individual works but more in the evidence of an institution whose collection was thought to represent history. The nation had long since taken the place of religion much as the national art museum had taken the place of the earlier cathedral, many of whose treasures the museum itself appropriated. Strangely enough, history acquired a new authority behind the same museum doors at which it appeared to cease, because the "immortal works" on display triumphed over time and celebrated the nation as living owner of these works. Once they attained their status in the museum, they were no longer subject to living time and instead became venerated in the name of a history as embodied in art.

The art museum was firmly integrated in the modern democracies where, in the name of the state, it visualized history, historical culture, and art that had become history. It appears to belong to all of us, and yet—or for that very reason—we have no right to take over the "temple of art," at whose entrance the state has placed its guards. Representation (art history) and the representing body (the nation-state) coincided in such a way as to be hardly distinguishable and therefore are subject to public protest, as was the case in 1994, when the National Gallery in Berlin, from its vast body of twentieth-century art, put on public display several paintings by such formerly established East German artists as Willi Sitte and Wolfgang Mattheuer. The public media accused the museum of having "smuggled" in pieces that insulted their feelings and violated the honor of the country. It is astonishing that emotions were still provoked by museum pictures when their exhibition on public walls seemed undeserved. The question of museum representation, as an official and public act, in fact concerned the institutions more than the individual artists.

Debates of this kind also occur in the former socialist countries, where there has been neither an unblemished museum tradition nor a democratic idea of the state. Since it had been the Party, in the name of the state, that had nationalized the churches' art treasures by transferring them to museums, the same churches are today requesting the return of these treasures, which would mean to dispossess public museums. Thus, Gothic altarpieces in Poland and old icons in Russia are being reclaimed from the national collections, because the churches see themselves as the true owners and as the genuine heirs of history. In Russia, the ownership of the ancient icon of the Virgin of Vladimir, which once carried the honorary title Patroness of the Country, has become the bone of contention between Church and state. President Boris Yeltsin in the end took the decision that the icon belonged to the state but could be used by the Church for acts of worship (fig. 28). This case is revealing, as it challenged not only the museums' ownership rights but also artistic value, as opposed to the more ancient ritual value. The opposite case is just as interesting. The monuments to Marx, Lenin, and other party leaders, who had always represented the official ideology and, therefore, the state, were sheltered—if they were not already destroyed—in hastily organized open-air museums, as if museums were places over which history no longer had any power (fig. 29). This is how images formerly in the service of religion were treated two hundred years ago when the Louvre was opened, but people then recontextualized their booty by declaring them works of art that deserved another look.

In the West, it is the museum of contemporary art that stirs doubts about its purpose when it, on the one hand, tries to follow close on the heels of the old museum, which it, on the other hand, no longer resembles. In order to be taken seriously, it assumes the appearance of familiar institutions, including the dubious claim to be exhibiting art history, although the art historical genealogy of the respective works is more than uncertain. The question is not whether there should be museums of contemporary art, but whether their representation is still suitable. Museums recently have become art fairs with current offerings and changing views on the atomized art scene, yet they suffer from the false compulsion to canonize their acquisitions as the latest state of the arts, while, in fact, serving the art market, which takes profit from this canonization.

The institutional crisis of the museum mirrors a new crisis of the public consensus as to its forum. Looking back today over the history of the museum, we see the enthusiasm of a bourgeois elite, composed of art collectors and curators, to celebrate a common ideal of art and art ownership. The same elite wanted to be represented by a single idea of art and art history and therefore favored the museum as a site of collective identity and as a stage for performing a common history, the history of national art schools and the art of mankind. After our attitude toward history has changed, as has our perception of the public sphere, the role of the art museum no longer is the same. The common notion of culture is as much in doubt as is our consensus on how to represent the several groups in society that, at the most, still allows for tolerance. Finally, in the TV age the experience of the public space, which one more often experiences on the screen, has changed.

In the case of the museum, where individual collectors have always played a role, sponsors are increasingly requesting their own representation at the expense of the public realm, at least in Germany. The Museum Ludwig in Cologne, which was founded in the 1960s, is a case in point. The call for recognition raised by individual collectors reflected the experience that today's museum has become a stage for public activities, as a result of which it qualifies as a forum in its own way. It therefore falls easily victim to the competition of rivaling groups in society who no longer accept to be represented by a single ideal of art and

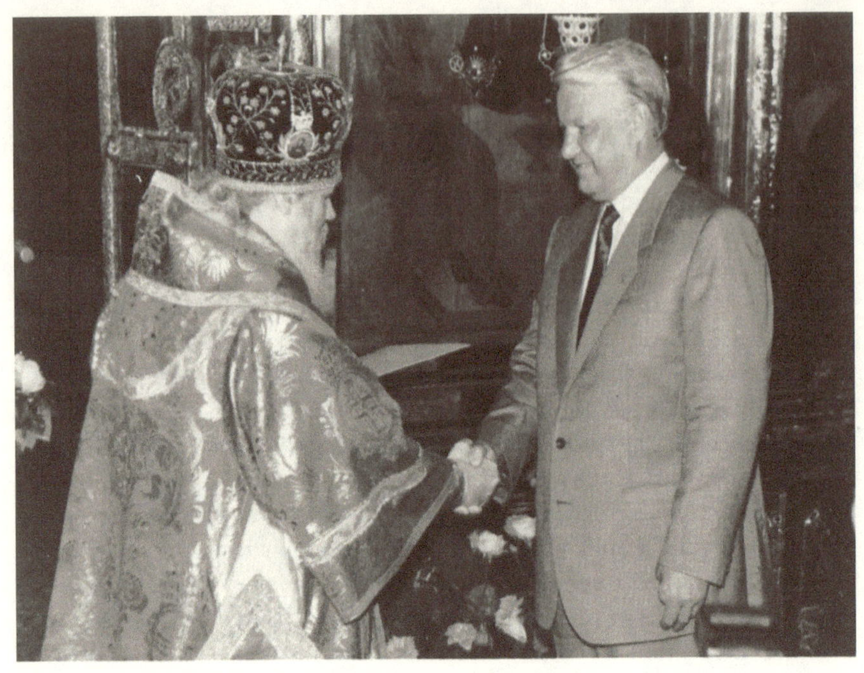

28. President Boris Yeltsin and Patriarch Alexei II in the Convent of Saint Sergei of the Trinity, near Moscow, in front of a replica of Rublev's icon of the Holy Trinity, 1992. Photo by Deutsche Presseagentur.

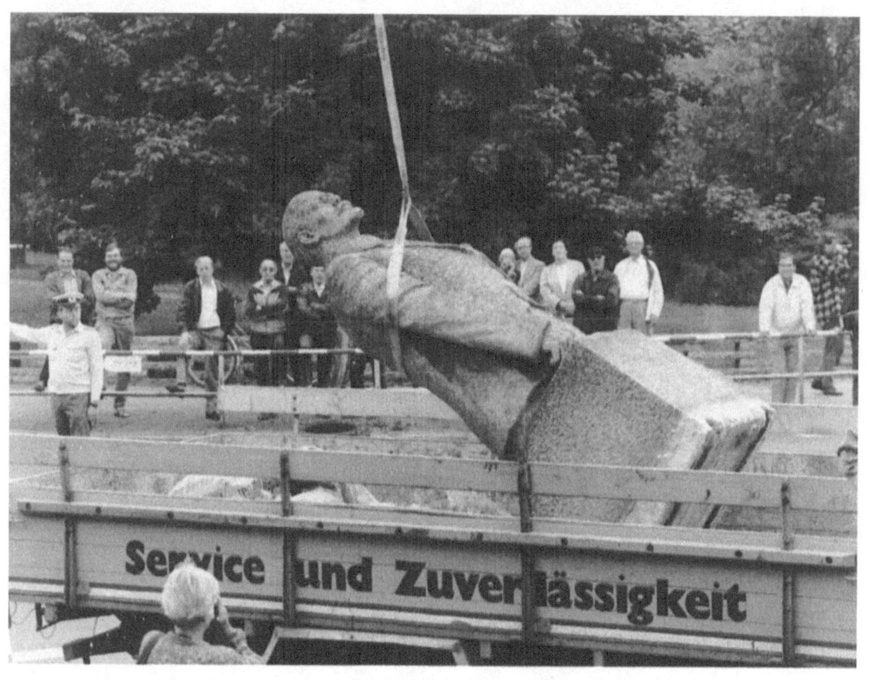

29. Dismantling the Lenin memorial in Stendal, East Germany, September, 1991. Photo by Deutsche Presseagentur.

history. The museum in addition is expected to guarantee the type of cultural representation for which we no longer have valid symbols. We want to experience the present tense, much as other generations wanted to view a coherent art history, and thus tend to be easily disappointed when the museum fails to succeed in what needs to be represented in cultural terms.

The desire for information, at the same time, is a temptation to politicize the museum. The museum has always been a political issue, however neutral and apolitical it acted. Today's form of politicization, however, comes from interest groups operating in international circles and masked by the harmless-sounding catch phrase of "cultural exchange." They wage a silent battle for the mutual recognition of "views of history" when represented by "commissars" who decide what profile should be given to an international exhibition. Instances of disputed cultural policy are the exhibitions in which the tortured and tortuous art history of Central and Eastern Europe is presented as a glowing "Century of the Avant-Garde," in which the single nations have a differing share.

In the future, other symbols may emerge with the label "art," symbols with less emphasis on historical culture as was customary for art up to now. Official culture was for so long obeying a dominant discourse and at the same time serving economic interests that it ceases to keep the authority of an obliging ideal. A widespread claim for creativity questions the artist's monopoly on self-expression, while the artists in turn are increasingly engaged in setting up and running "artists' museums" in which they can escape the art market, as is the case in Lodz. Regional and societal interests of small groups demand the access to symbols that are no longer measured against a recognized style (and market) of art. In art literature, too, there are new narratives that refuse to bend to a single overriding history of art. The explosive diversity of our world mirrors in the diversity of views and concepts—which, however, are controlled by a monopolized media culture. This explains the increasing tendency toward an unofficial culture in which the art concept is as uncertain (or insignificant) as the belief in the system of a single art history.

In New York, the Museum of Modern Art served "modernists" like a church in which the believers gathered to declare their creed. Its opponents, including Douglas Crimp, reacted vehemently against its claim "to tell the story of modern art," as he objected in 1984 on behalf of all unbelievers. The museum's belief in the "essence" of autonomous art, as

Clement Greenberg formulated it, suddenly seemed like a barefaced lie that no longer represented the reality of art production and its contradictions; in other words, the museum lived on the faith of its adherents. Arthur C. Danto, who had shared this faith, now felt compelled to conclude that the "history of art" of modernism "has come to an end," since it had fulfilled its aim. The "end of modernism" in Greenberg's sense was, strictly speaking, "the end of a theory that explains *why art is high when it is high.* What has come to an end is a specific concept of art history."

It may seem like chasing ephemera if we try today to capture the image of art history that I am discussing here. Why do we need a certain concept for it, if all artists, past and present, prove to be unarguably real—as real as history—and if their works exist as palpably as solid objects? One can only reply that fictions have also made history and that they, too, have been reified. Art is a historical fiction, as Marcel Duchamp proved long ago, and art history is fiction as well—as André Malraux discovered, against his will, when he wrote about a "museum without walls." It is thus a question of institutions, not of content and certainly not of method, when we ask whether and how art and art history will survive in the future. Even the cathedrals survived the foundation of the museums. Why shouldn't today's museums experience the foundation of other institutions where art history no longer belongs or where it looks entirely different?

PART II

The End of Art History?

12 Art and the Crisis of Modernism

Arthur C. Danto, in the preface to his Mellon lectures, marks a difference dividing contemporary from modern art. The difference, he explains, is the result of a deep crisis that modernism suffered in the 1960s. "The great master narratives . . . have not only come to an end . . . Contemporary art no longer allows itself to be represented by master narratives at all." The history of art, which always had framed what happened in art, was a master narrative of this kind and also applied to modernist art, as the latter followed the lines of evolution and progress. The crisis of modernism therefore also affects the practice of writing art history and the confidence in an unbroken continuity of art. It is not sufficient to reserve this practice for the past including modernism since art is continuing and therefore needs continuous description. It thus poses the question whether it still can be viewed in historical terms. After these terms became obsolete, they also appeared questionable in retrospect. The easy solution to invent an art history for contemporary art is no solution at all when any narrative is contradicted by what artists are doing and how they are thinking.

But what actually was the crisis of modernism and how does it relate to the topic of a book that does not deal with art in the first place? "Only when it became clear that anything could be a work of art could one think, philosophically, about art. What of art after the end of art where, by 'after the end of art,' I mean 'after the ascent to philosophical self-reflection'? When an art work . . . [raised] the question 'Why am I a work of art?' . . . The history of modernism was over." Though it is not my aim to discuss modernism at this point, its connection to art history as a narrative with a logic of its own is obvious. Can we apply this narrative with the same confidence when we have to argue against living art and when the concept of history has been doubted in favor of the notion of posthistory? Danto's philosophical discussion remains his own answer and thus cannot be applied to my topic as such. Yet he had an acute eye for what happened when "modernism was over" and thus touched on the very roots of art historical practice.

"Artists, liberated from the burden of history, were free to make art in whatever way they wished . . . In contrast with modernism, there is no such thing as a contemporary *style*." Whatever his conclusions are, he is describing not a mere episode in the history of art. The new self-doubt inherent in the production of such works as had always illustrated continuity and change also weakens the confidence in a historical sequence when its main witness, the work of art, collapsed as a norm. But how can artists liberate themselves "from the burden of history" when history is still a concern in their polemics? Danto reminds us that artists had located themselves within history and regarded their true mission to "make history" even in the avant-garde type of the game.

The conscience of history, after the end of modernism, was not over, but it suffered a deep change once that history was no longer obliging. There were enough artists who no longer cared for "pressing the limits of art or extending the history of art." They "had the whole inheritance of art history to work with, including the history of the avant-garde." But they did so now in the mood of retrospection. When believing that the old art history "was over," they also could dispense with the need to "overcome it." We will inspect examples of this postmodernist attitude below. They are guided by the experience of a gap separating artists from their modernist forerunners. But this new attitude does not only reflect a loss. It also reveals a freedom that formerly had not been permissible. It will be useful to discuss this new type of conscience (or non-conscience) of history in the context of my topic before discussing further the practice of the art discourse in our time.

In my book on the end of the history of art (1987), I discussed the performance of the French artist Hervé Fischer who, in 1979, solemnly had announced "that the history of art has ended" when appearing in the Centre Pompidou. The "linear extension" of that history would be a mere illusion after the "posthistorical emergence" of what he called "meta-art" had happened. In his book *L'histoire de l'art est terminée*, he comments that artists no longer were expected to devise an "as yet unwritten future of art" after they lost the confidence in the New for its own sake. "It is not art which died. It is its history as progress to the New that has ended." Fischer not only questioned an internal logic of arts evolution but also doubted the validity of history from the position of "posthistoire." Fischer's own escape from this dilemma was his belief in the social act since he regarded society as the only reality left also in art.

Others had searched for a different escape and had done so much earlier. The history of conceptual art appears in a different light when the latter is not understood as a single artistic current or episode but as the symptom of a crisis that no longer allowed art to materialize in the coinage of formal works (or concrete exhibits) and no longer would confirm the institutional logic of the art market and the museum. The farewell to the reality of the work as the witness in a historical sequence also meant to part from art's ritual to be embodied (others would say, reified) in objects with a symbolical aura. The loss of the faith in the production of works also implied the loss of safe examples for discussing the history of art.

The discussion can be summarized with the views of the conceptual artist Joseph Kosuth, whose essays were the secret counterpart of Danto's writings. Kosuth's essay "Art after Philosophy" (1969) opened a debate to which Danto contributed a complementary argument by speaking of "[t]he transfiguration of the common place," as his book written in 1981 was called. However their arguments differed, the two authors seemed to share the notion that art had become a mere concept and thus needed a new discourse. But what about the history of art when art was tantamount to a concept and thus to a definition difficult to narrate in historical terms? Kosuth's solution as an artist was to escape into language in order to do art. Art was to become a "critical practice" questioning the nature of art and thereby eliminating the old ritual of producing merely new art. The artist, Kosuth concluded, had to become an anthropologist who however had to turn to his own culture in order to analyze its institutions and to rediscover the new meaning of art. In the respective text, written in 1975, he criticized the implicit teleology of autonomous art embedded in its own history or, even worse, the timeless objectivity of formal art. In the same year, Kosuth took his farewell from exhibiting in the Leo Castelli Gallery with a written statement in which he calls history "manmade" and therefore subject to constant reevaluation. "Historiography is our own mythology and . . . art an extension of it." His own exhibits were an attempt to "overcome my historical baggage."

In an essay with the blunt title "1975" Kosuth recalls the late sixties, when "the Greenberg gang was attempting to initiate an Official History gestalt" that left little room for artists "that didn't happen to fit into the prescribed historical continuum." In the last battle of modernism as usually recorded, it was not only modernism but also modernism's claim of autonomous art, with an explicit history of its own, that the partisans defended. In the practice of art historiography in general, we may be reminded, autonomy had been the very precondition for distinguishing art history from social history or cultural history of a general type.

But the description of the art scene in the seventies is not yet complete. Artists who did not share Kosuth's beliefs nevertheless took a new stand in the face of past art history when they made it the topic of their work and thus offered a distorted mirror in which historical art (including modernist art) suddenly looked like an ambiguous memory. There was also nostalgia implied, when one regretted the parting from lost ideals and staged the regret by quoting prototypes no longer obliging except for a memorial service. The rendezvous with the myth of art history, as something like a memory, first culminated in the year of Picasso's death, 1973, since Picasso, in retrospect, seemed to represent an innocent type of creation that was lost forever. What mattered was the feeling of distance that dominated artists mourning not only the death of a great master but also the death of that belief in the history of art that Picasso, despite his avant-gardism, had so beautifully represented.

Renato Guttuso, the Marxist realist from Palermo, for this occasion found a particularly original type of iconography when he painted Picasso in the company of the great masters of the past—from Dürer and Rembrandt to Courbet and Cézanne—at a roundtable in a series of memorial pictures that he first exhibited in the Frankfurt Kunstverein in 1975 (fig. 30). This was an assembly of the dead in which Picasso already had found his place and in which he represented an artist of equal stance and equal belief in a continuing or live history of art. It may be remembered that Picasso indeed had reenacted past masterpieces in his late series after Velázquez and others. In one of Guttuso's pictures, even art seems to participate at this symposium, since two of Picasso's models join the group at the table. The life of art, as embodied in great artists of the past, takes on an ambiguous effect, as Picasso appears to be the last in the sequence. The memory of Picasso, thus, seems to amount to a memory when art still lived in the frame of an unbroken art history.

In the same year, Richard Hamilton, who had inaugurated pop art in England, placed Picasso before a canvas by Diego Velázquez, the painter of painters as Manet had called him (figs. 31, 32). As in the case of Guttuso, this is not presented as a fully developed easel painting but is being introduced in the open form of a study or sketch and thus differs from the ultimate model to which the title refers, also in technique. The title, *Picasso's Meniñas,* sounds paradoxical as it was Velázquez who did *Las Meniñas.* But the title offers a memory (and memory may be synonymous with art history) of the series of fifty-nine reinventions of the *Meniñas* that Picasso did in the autumn of 1957. Even then they had been studies, though studies not for a work but studies after a work and thus paradoxical paraphrases whose working concept was already uncertain. André Malraux had discussed them in his book *La tête d'obsidienne,* which he also wrote a year after Picasso's death. Hamilton, in a strange repetition, had restaged the ritual of memory that Picasso had

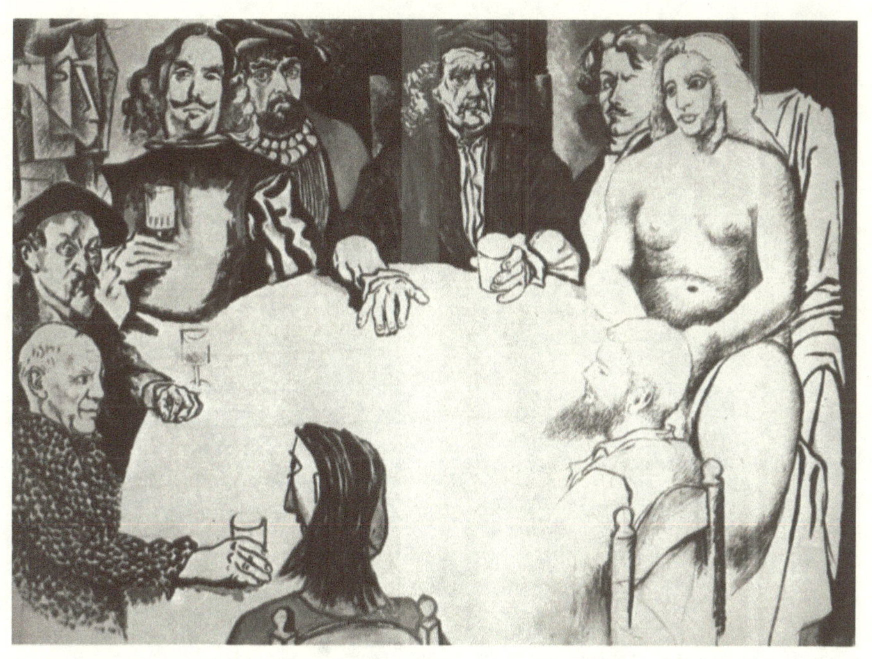

30. Renato Guttoso, *The Artists' Symposium,* acrylic and mixed media on paper, 1973. Grafis Arte, Livorno (1975). © 2002 Artists Rights Society (ARS), New York / SIAE, Rome.

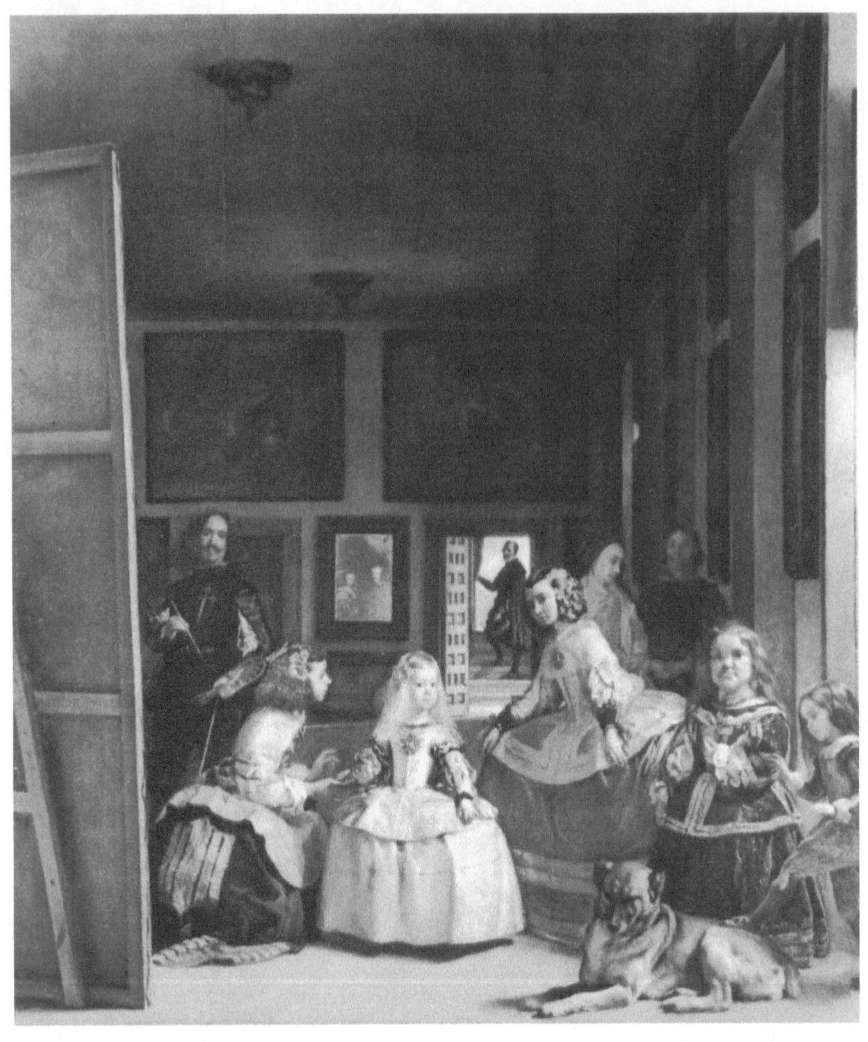

31. Diego Velázquez, *Las Meniñas*, oil on canvas, 1656. Museo del Prado, Madrid.

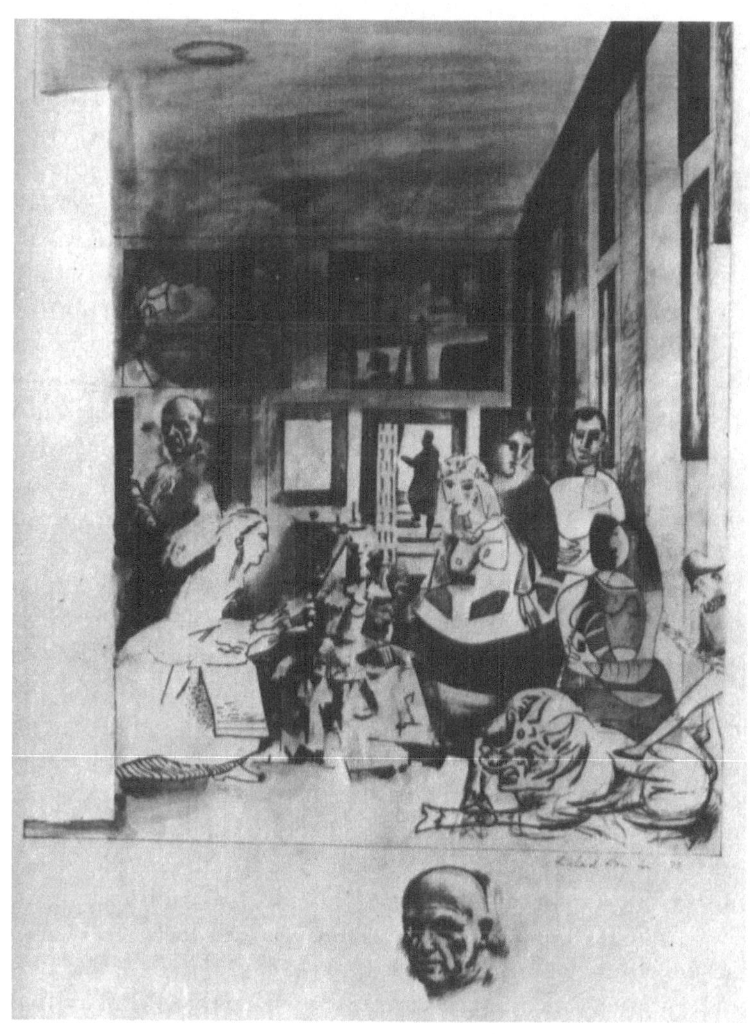

32. Richard Hamilton, *Picasso's Meniñas,* study 3, pencil and ink-wash on paper, 1973. Collection of Rita Donagh, North End. © 2002 Artists Rights Society (ARS), New York / DACS, London.

already had followed when doing "his own *Meniñas.*" But the repetition was acted out in quite a different spirit, as if Hamilton was visiting a lost era in the history of art. In his gouache, Picasso occupies the same place that Velázquez had taken in his picture and thus simply replaces the position of the old artist while the other figures are all transformed into figures known from Picasso's own work. The metamorphosis is ambivalent when we admit that Hamilton was mourning not only Picasso but also a closed tradition of living art history.

The same type of encounter with art history appears in a silk-screen print by Robert Rauschenberg in which the artist collages a random selection of museum pieces that all belong to the Metropolitan Museum of Art in New York for whose centenary celebration, in 1969, the silk-screen print was edited (fig. 33). It would have been absolutely impossible for an old member of the avant-garde to deal with a museum of past art in that manner. But the impression that Rauschenberg "returns" to the past would be equally misleading since he only displays a new freedom in front of something that is already closed and does no longer threaten his own situation as an artist. The print, with its solemn dedication and the signatures of the museum officials, to be sure, was a commission, but Rauschenberg was not affected by the ambiguity of the situation. His print offers a nostalgic mirror of art history as contained in a museum that did not collect modern art at all, with the exception of Picasso's portrait of Gertrude Stein, which is the most recent element in this ensemble. Rauschenberg surely also captures the sterility of a museum space that seems to mirror the space of past art history.

The print thus appears in a striking contrast to earlier works by Rauschenberg, like *Crocus* and also *Persimmon* (see fig. 22 above), a silk-screen print with paint on canvas in which old works of art appear in the midst of scanned pictures from everyday life and thus mix with contemporary reality of the media and their reproductive nature. Photographic prints of two Venuses, one by Velázquez and the other by Rubens, gaze into a mirror, which may be interpreted as an allegory in different ways. The works themselves are a new mirror of consciousness reflecting a diffusely experienced world. The printing procedure, which in this case is a technique predating scanning, appears like a metaphor for the simultaneity of images in our memory, which may be called a collection of a different kind. "Objects also have history," as Rauschenberg maintained, and to him they seemed more real than "ideas" but the things are here mere reproductions and thus assimilate to the reproductions of the art works on a similar level. Art history as exhibited in the

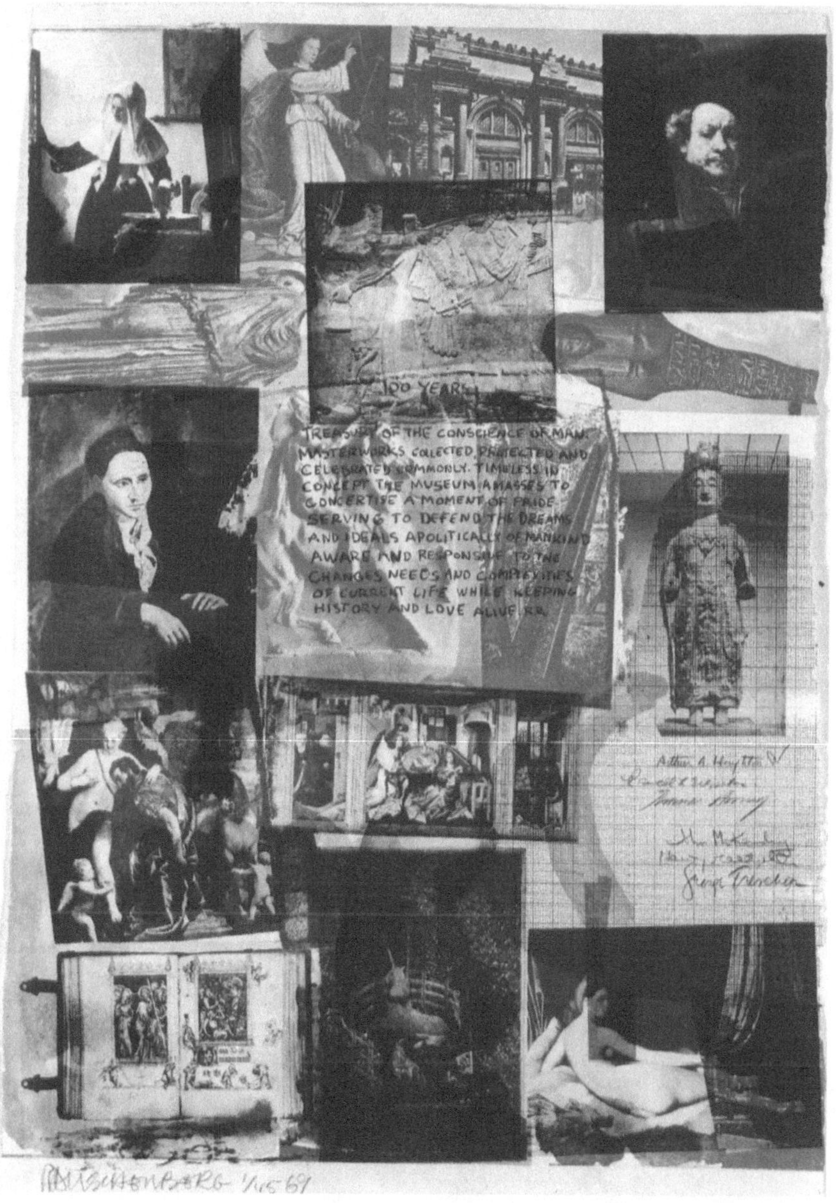

33. Robert Rauschenberg, *Centennial Certificate, MMA*, color lithograph, 1969. The Metropolitan Museum of Art, New York. Florence and Joseph Singer Collection. © Robert Rauchenberg / Licensed by VAGA, New York, NY.

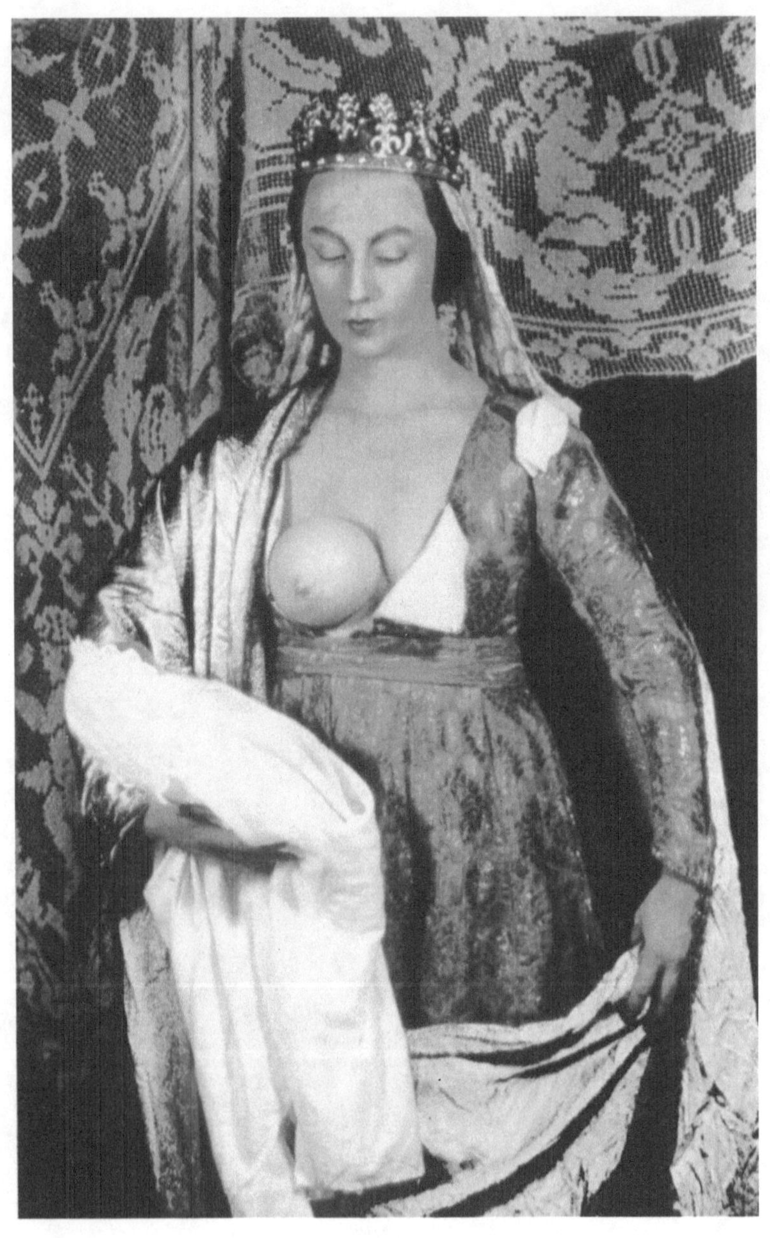

34. Cindy Sherman, *Untitled 216*, photomontage, 1989. Courtesy Cindy Sherman and Metro Pictures.

museum and as written in academic practice or surviving in our memory in Rauschenberg's work finds a strangely appealing allegory.

Twenty years later, Cindy Sherman borrowed readymade images as they are collected in the memory of art history in her series History Portraits. In *Untitled 216* (1989), she chose the mask of a historical picture, which allowed her to replay a Madonna with child and yet to remain herself in the photograph (fig. 34). Mask and body, pose and actor fuse as she performs art history with her own body but with the help of a false breast and of borrowed costumes. The light for the shot repeats the original light in the painted model like a stage direction. The artist plays again the artist from a lost history of art, but in this case she takes the place of the model and thus quotes the role of being artist from her archetype. While staging art history, she creates an image in which photography blends with the medium of painting. The choice of a pose has always been her main concern. Already in her earlier work she was doing performance art, as Danto has described. This time, however, she performs art history in order to create art again. In so doing, she enters a stage that the former model of the old artist, as her double, has just left. The performance of art history leaves us with the disturbing impression of a déjà vu that would have been the breaking of a taboo in modernist art. Art history is strangely encapsulated in the History Portraits much as film history is deconstructed and replayed in the "film stills" of the seventies. In a way, the artist confronts us with a kind of readymade which only can be reused but not reinvented. While museums introduce us into art which they have not even sponsored, Cindy Sherman in a new type of "Art after Art" musealizes the art production and makes us feel that art history has become memory for whatever use.

13 Art Historiography as Tradition

The story that Hervé Fischer thought was over in the artists' circles had begun with the art history written by Giorgio Vasari, Florentine by choice, in his *Lives of the Most Eminent Painters, Sculptors and Architects,* first published in 1550. In his introduction to part two of the book, he bravely remarks that he never wanted simply to produce a table of artists and works but intended to explain the course of things to the reader, since history was "the true mirror of human life" and as such also able to reveal human intentions and actions in the course of art. He therefore intended to present the artistic legacy by separating "the good from the better, and the better from the best." Above all, he intended to "discover the causes and the roots of each style and reveal the arts both in their ascent and in their decay."

Ever since Vasari wrote these enviably self-confident words, his successors have felt similarly obliged to present an outline of art history that would set the standard against which all individual works could be measured and that would provide a framework in which everything would find its proper place. But a history of this readability had to be first invented as a coherent scheme, while the works that it was to accommodate by contrast existed as a tangible reality. Initially, the enterprise took the form of straightforward narrative, which the author could carefully steer so that all went according to plan. But when later writers found it increasingly difficult to fit the growing material into Vasari's model, an official and universal narrative was demanded. In our case, the model had to answer a double question, since art history combined two concepts that did not share our meaning until the nineteenth century. Strictly defined, art was an idea embodied in works, while history was the meaning behind events. A clarification of the two terms was necessary before any attempt to describe art in the framework of its own history would make sense.

In 1764, when Johann Joachim Winckelmann published his *Geschichte der Kunst des Altertums* (History of classical art) in Dresden (fig. 35), he caused a sensation, as he was for the first time applying history in a strict sense to art. In his foreword, with the words of Cicero's *Orator* he stated that he was "using the term history in the broader

Johann Winckelmanns,

Präsidentens der Alterthümer zu Rom, und Scrittore der Vaticanischen Bibliothek,
Mitglieds der Königl. Englischen Societät der Alterthümer zu London, der Maleracademie
von St. Luca zu Rom, und der Hetrurischen zu Cortona,

Geschichte der Kunst des Alterthums.

Erster Theil.

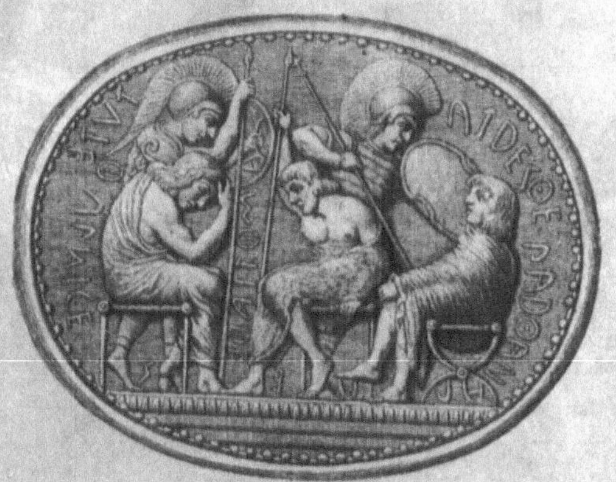

Mit Königl. Pohlnisch- und Churfürstl. Sächs. allergnädigsten Privilegio.

Dresden, 1764.
In der Waltherischen Hof-Buchhandlung.

35. Title page, Johann Joachim Winckelmann, *History of Classical Art* (Dresden, 1764).

sense" that it "had in Greek." His aim was neither the "mere narration of events in chronological order" nor the usual kind of artist's biography. Rather, he intended to "attempt an edifice of knowledge" and to extract "the very nature of art . . . from the works themselves" instead of merely discussing the "external circumstances" that is, to qualify art solely in the context of general history. His predecessors, he maintained, had however not penetrated "into art's essence and innermost being" and thus told mere stories about artists.

Winckelmann found Cicero's comments opportune, since despite his own life in Rome, to which art lovers were streaming from all over Europe, it was not Roman art but Greek classical art, even without any Greek originals at hand, that he was searching for. With Greek art, he was thus focusing on a subject that was imaginary in both method and object. Ancient Greece, for the author, with its free society represented the ideal condition for art to enter history. But Winckelmann handled the subject with such method (he called it his "system") that art history has been modeled upon his approach ever since, and that art in its truest, most genuine form would be described as an object of its own history.

Art was not merely a general denotation but a concept in its own right—which in the end did not even need to be illustrated by works of art and could even testify against the available stock of works if they proved unsatisfactory. It was therefore paradoxically possible to speak of art's absence in history whenever existing or living art production contradicted it. As a conception, art was either absolute (in the eighteenth century) or retrospective (in the nineteenth). Still, the accepted narrative was the historical one which became the descriptive matrix for organizing the discourse. The entity of what was called art was deduced from the universal scheme called art history. Inversely, everything that entered this framework by necessity had to be a born work of art whether or not it carried the modern notion of art with it from its origin. The Viennese school of art history, which dominated the field since the late nineteenth century, conceived everything (from the late Roman period to modernism) as part of a single art history that confirmed the unity in world art conceived as Western art. This self-confident universalism was possibly nourished by the ambitions inherent in the imperial Austrian hegemony, whose eastern expansion, after all, had reached beyond Austria's own cultural borders.

Initially, however, art history as taught at the Academy in Louis XIV's France—for the purpose of being practiced by the young painters—covered an astonishingly small ground, being divided into a "classical" section and one for "more recent art." This was still the case in 1793 and then again in 1803 when the Louvre was opened to the public. The ground floor was reserved for ancient sculpture, the upper floor for Italian Renaissance and French painting up to the seventeenth century, modestly flanked by the Flemish and Spanish "schools." For periods that had had no art in this limited sense, there was no need to involve the attention of art history. The so-called primitives, at the time a blanket term for any art earlier than the Renaissance, caused at this point still a certain embarrassment on the museums walls, as they could not be included in the "age of art." Of course, the "primitives" were seen in constantly shifting boundaries and finally, about 1900, were found in "prehistoric" art, which no one ever had wanted to incorporate in the materials of art history. Abbé Luigi Lanzi, who published his *History of Italian Painting* in 1792, justified his enterprise with the changed interests of the public, which was no longer satisfied with the usual travel literature or with the traditional artist's biography and its anecdotal narrative. He therefore intended "not to write the history of painters but the history of art itself," since "the philosophical spirit of the age demanded a system" for understanding how and why the arts, like literature and the history of nations, developed and declined. He aimed to educate the dilettanti or amateurs of the fine arts, whose "taste" for quality he wanted to promote, while the artists themselves already received their training in academies and museums. In essence, Lanzi was using Winckelmann's model for narrating the history of "more recent" art in Italy.

Soon after, things came to a head when Napoleon's art booty induced the Louvre to constitute a first panorama of European art, totally omitting medieval art which only much later became the concern of a kind of national archaeology. As late as 1814, Louvre catalogs would apologize for exhibiting the Italian "primitives" antedating the "splendid century of modern painting," as viewers might be put off by their "austerity." Other visitors, it was hoped, however, would seize the opportunity to study the exhibits " illustrating the course of art" that, in turn, would mirror "the development of the human spirit."

In Germany, too, at the time, art history gradually stirred the ambitions of the younger generation as an ambitious task of writing history. Johann David Passavant, who had begun as a Nazarene painter before taking over the newly founded municipal art museum at Frankfurt, in 1820 published his *Ansichten über die bildenden Künste und Darstellung des Ganges derselben in Toscana* (Views on the Visual Arts and a Description of the Same in Tuscany) in which he wanted to "present a clear and general description of the course of the visual arts, from their ascent to their decline." But he restricted his materials to the example of Tuscany, "since the art of this region had developed in a superb way and, thanks to the excellent volume by Vasari, has become generally known." Even at this point, Vasari's *Lives* served as a guide and thus reduced the possible area of investigation. Nonetheless, the author generalizes his project when he proclaims, "There are, of necessity, three periods in the art of every people whose art has reached its prime." This reservation betrays his belief in a secret norm of art—which Passavant simply took for granted. Art history could be narrated only where art had reached its proper destiny in the course of history and thus had manifested its definition (or its proper destination) in universal terms.

The reciprocity between historical narratives and axiomatic conceptions of art was already established in an early manner when the rhetoricians of antiquity devised evolutionary models that even surpassed the narrative methods used for conventional history. Narrating the genesis or decadence of style in literature and in the visual arts was always a rewarding strategy to put forward a norm or ideal for art. In this discourse, the single work constituted a mere station in the development toward the unfolding of a norm of art. Even if complete in itself, a given work remained open-ended in relation to the evolution of that norm. It seems paradoxical that, of all things, a norm (as the aim of future fulfillment) should render each result (each single work) achieved along this path incomplete and thus make it dependant on an overall historical process. The concept of style served to define the individual phases of the process and to locate them within a cycle where it would become visible in its truth and destination. The historical description of art thus began as applied art theory and consequently was in trouble as soon as the latter became out of fashion.

Renaissance art historiography already had erected a canon of ideal or classical beauty that culminated at a given stage in history and was lacking in all other periods. This teleological approach was rooted in the biological model of growth, maturity and decay that Vasari wanted to transfer from the life of nature to the life of history. The repeatability of this cycle provided the formula of rebirth or renaissance. The equation of an ancient and a modern cycle in art was pure fiction, yet it seemed to furnish the *historical* evidence that the artistic norm had already been discovered in classical times and could therefore now be *re*discovered. The classic, then, was the visible realization of an aesthetic norm that was no longer derivative but absolute. If art in the future would no longer fulfill the norm, so much the worse for art. Thus, history could not contradict but only confirm the historian unless the truths were no longer recognized, which then would confirm his fears. Vasari was thus writing the history of an idea as much as he was basing his history on an idea.

The rigid framework of this art historiography was as practical as it was impractical for Vasari's successors. Winckelmann, however, no longer wrote the history of contemporary art but chose ancient art for applying the same model of an internal cycle of style. Although this history was now situated in the context of Greek politics, it retained the appearance of an autonomous cycle. Winckelmann's neglect of the art of his own age in favor of the art of a lost and distant past for which he could claim an absolute truth was a telling choice. From the distance of pure contemplation, Winckelmann devised the fiction of an "authentic antiquity," which he nonetheless sought to establish as a model for *imitation* in the living arts. He thought to have rediscovered the cycle in the surviving Greek sculptures as a visible trace of time, as it was mirrored in the biological cycle, the apex of which by necessity had to be the classical.

The modern departure from an applied theory of art, which art history had been at an early stage, was achieved at high cost. After losing its function as training for artists, the new historiography of art depended on models from other fields of social research while liberating itself from philosophical aesthetics, which viewed art as a pure principle and thus detached it from any empirical context. This was the moment when, in the words of Hans Robert Jauss, "historical and aesthetic contemplation" parted ways: "blind positivist empiricism opposed 'aesthetic metaphysics'" after the latter declared its allegiance to a "semblance of autonomy" in art, which, in turn, necessitated Marxism to develop arguments for contradiction. The new art history profited much from Hegel's system of writing history and his historicist revision of former aesthetic discourses. Hegel's *Aesthetics,* first and foremost, provided a philosophical support for writing the history of art—the art of all peoples and of all ages. "Art invites us to intellectual consideration, and that not for the purpose of creating art again, but for knowing philosophically what art is." The art connoisseur, who regarded "imitation" as the meaning and driving force of art history, is replaced by the philosopher, for whom art incorporates a past stage in the history of "mind." Since, as Hegel maintains, art no longer offers "total satisfaction," the "science of art" serves to answer the new "need" for defining the role of art, a role already exhausted. The new "science of art" looks at art in a bird's eye view from where its history is seen spatially, that is, as a panorama of a universal "evolution." Art is simply the raw material for "the thought of contemplation," which knows more than art itself has ever known. In fact, Hegel attempted to disenfranchise all artists' aesthetics and all applied art criticism in favor of a new variant of global history.

Art, as a visible symbol of Weltanschauung, in Hegel's view had no autonomous meaning but represented "the essential worldviews inherent in its concept." Hegel's revision of the function of art in human society, which often was disparaged as "the aesthetics of content," had however a lasting effect on subsequent writing on art even after parting with Hegel's "system." "It is the effect and the progression of art itself" in which the latter finds its world historical task. By making visible whatever ideas were topical in a given society, art "at every stage of its progress helps to free itself from the content it has incorporated." Once "the content is exhausted" and the respective symbols have been fully established, it loses its "absolute interest." Thus, art ever so often "gets rid of its content" and thereby, to compensate for this loss, releases a new creative activity. But in modern times, Hegel claims, art is no longer bound to "a particular content" and therefore loses the authority to act as a medium of representation. All that is left to the individual artist is to reflect a personal view of art. "It is no help to appropriate past worldviews" as the Nazarene painters had done in converting to Roman Catholicism. For Hegel the very essence of art had already exhausted itself in history, which, for him, made possible the writing of art's history a posteriori.

Since the classical already had taken place, imitation ceases to make sense from a distance that is fixed forever. But it is not only the classical in art but also art itself that has already taken place in history. As the visible revelation of the mind, its function in a universal history can only be seen in retrospect. From now on, art was understood as an activity of the past when measured against "its highest destiny," in a famous phrase by Hegel. Since it lost "its earlier necessity in the real world," it has been displaced "more to our imagination." Hegel adds that, "drawn into aesthetic presence, the work of art no longer keeps the religious and historical context" in which it was born. "It emerges as an artwork which makes it autonomous" and, as a result, allows its new life in the museum's enclave or its qualification for the discourse of aesthetics.

That is why art can be viewed without the distractions of subject matter or symbolism. If the viewer is a historian rather than a contemporary, he meets art in the archive of culture. Hegel's aesthetics coincide with the rise of bourgeois culture, in which reflection on art for the first time became the concern of a newly born academic discipline. Hegel provided a philosophical model for this discipline in which art shifted from a living practice to a topic of memory in the guise of history. Whatever efforts are made to renew Hegel's discourse, they cannot compensate for his erroneous belief to judge history from an independent position, that is, from a position outside (or after) history.

That is why the so-called "death of art," as Gianni Vattimo discussed the term in his essay "The End of Modernity," must be translated in our own experience where it requires comment. When Vattimo speaks of the "utopia of a society in which art no longer exists as a specific phenomenon: (and where), in the Hegelian sense, it has been suspended in a general aestheticization of existence," the term "art" needs reconsideration. The "explosion of aesthetics outside its traditional boundaries" may be a contemporary experience, but it can scarcely be derived from Hegel who, as a representative of his own age, offered a kind of ontology of art (even when applying it only in retrospect) and thus also, in principle, delivered arguments for the creation of the new art museum, in which the historization of art found its institutional counterpart.

Quatremère de Quincy (1755–1849), the "French Winckelmann," took a stance against the claim of the new museum to become the site of "visible art history" and, in 1815, wrote a critique of this institution in his book *Considérations morales sur la destination des ouvrages de l'art* (Moral Considerations on the Destiny of Works of Art). The foundation of museums was an irrevocable turning point after which most of the experience of art was directed toward the past. But what bothered Quatremère most was the interest in an art that, once placed in a museum, had lost its place in life *(emploi)*. Advocates of the new institution were ready with answers. Like history, as whose shiny mirror it was exhibited, art provided a powerful "image of the progress of the human mind," as Joseph Lavallée wrote in 1804 in the first volume of his *Galerie du Musée Napoléon*. The Louvre catalogs from the very beginning were eager to provide a "course in history" that would instruct the reader about "the origin and progress [*marche progressive*] of the arts," to use another phrase of Lavallée's.

Quatremère, the critic of Napoleon's museum projects, was not prepared to accept art's confinement within history and contradicted the loss of the authority it had possessed in moral education. He therefore insisted on "mimesis" not in the artist's sense but in the sense of enlightening the general audience. An art that withdrew from life into the museum ceased to be a "school for good taste" where beauty had been an ethical ideal. Quatremère thus accused the new art historians and museum experts of "abusing the museum and abusing criticism." He accused the new art history for its support of the unfortunate pseudopresence of art in a museum, where it was "restricted to a passive role" and only satisfied an indifferent curiosity (Hegel's "Interesse"). "Since they (the works of art) lost their effect, they lost their raison d'être. Turning the exhibition into a practical course in modern chronology amounts to killing art in order to turn it into history"—"C'est tuer l'art pour en faire histoire."

After the Romantics invoked historical art as a model for contemporary art—the last time such an attempt went unchallenged—art historians and artists parted ways, and soon art history emerged as an independent academic discipline. Art historians did not care any longer for the art of their own time, since only the past seemed to have produced art worthy of that name. Conversely, artists no longer searched for models in the past but headed with the same energy for the future, over which the past would have no power. Both parties were concerned with the past, but in the opposite sense: the one took it as an ideal either to be recovered in living practice; the other, as a burden from which to be freed.

The telling term "avant-garde," used in the visions both directed to a new society and to a new art, has never shaken off its military sense, but now it has become history. Rather than an army, that is guided by a small vanguard, the avant-garde scouts out the paths to where the battle is to be fought and won. In the visions of artists and social utopians, the avant-garde was guiding the rest of society into the future where the latter would follow. Progress, which epitomizes the linear concept of history, is the task of an elite who would define it for themselves while believing that history was at their side. It was an elite composed of revolutionaries who succeeded the former elites of power and education. Although stigmatized as dreamers who would fail to recognize reality, vanguardism believed it would anticipate the fulfillment of history in the future. The art historians, if they paid attention to recent art at all, soon felt at variance with an evolution that they could not measure with their established paradigms—until the avant-garde's success forced them to take over its model of history *en gros*.

Since it was first used by Saint-Simon, the term "avant-garde" became a catchword in the socialist camp where it would justify the visions of a new society. In the artists' camp, it was the battle cry of the *refusés* who broke with the art of the salon and flexed their creative muscle against academic conventions. In the early dreams of utopia, social thinkers and artists were united by the same sentiments in which the renewal of art was also seen as a promise of social renewal. In historical practice, however, the harmony between the two camps, between art's autonomy and social engagement, soon ended in conflicts that would flare up repeatedly in modernity. Art's history, it was soon conceded, was different from social or political history, however close they approached one another.

The avant-garde finally represented modern art so triumphantly that the latter seemed synonymous with the history of the avant-garde—and was exhibited as such, whereby progress was recorded as departure toward new artistic creeds. It thus caused irritation when, around 1960, the linear direction of progress became uncertain and the received model of progress—as if there were no alternative—collapsed. Commenting on "the death of the avant-garde," art critics consoled themselves by making a complete turn and speaking of the "myth of the avant-garde," as if the latter had been a mere phantom. Others who resisted the loss of a cherished paradigm would proclaim the emergence of a "neo avant-garde" or even "transavant-garde" in order to save the continuity of modernism. By a strange about-face, the avant-garde had become the more important tradition just as the conservatives had previously held onto theirs.

Significantly, the crisis of the avant-garde was a fruit of its success. Suddenly even the general audience was waiting for an ever new avant-garde much as it had formerly resisted the avant-garde and thus offered the desired identity as the eternal enemy. In recent modernism, the avant-garde, despite or because of its threatening gesture of revolution, had found public acceptance which had deprived it of its necessary opponents. Art's desired power over life in the end resulted in its confinement in the art scene where, much as in sport, the general audience expected to applaud the latest world record. An unwelcome side effect of the avant-garde's success was its appropriation by the "art of advertising," where its creative ideas were forged into consistent practice of design. This launched a rivalry with what had hitherto been the avant-garde, until advertising for the avant-garde could no longer be distinguished from the avant-garde of advertising. In his book *The Tradition of the New,* the American art critic Harold Rosenberg in 1962 analyzed the paradox of exalting the avant-garde to an undisputed tradition. In an exhibition in the Guggenheim Museum in 1994, the formula was resurrected, but now, in a strange oblivion of what it had meant before, it became reused for the title for a show of "postwar masterpieces" from the museum's collections that were to confirm the unbroken power of an avant-garde whose identity could no longer be defined. When the sociologist Diana Crane summarized New York art from 1940 to 1945 under the heading of a *Transformation of the Avant-Garde,* as she called her book, she unwillingly demonstrated how easily concepts, once they become detached from their original sense, become fetishes and as such reclaim the role of timeless definitions.

Art criticism, which left its traces in art historiography, successfully entertained the fiction of an infinitely elastic avant-garde. Whether the latter was—against better judgment—still defended as a living force or criticized as absent, its paradigm did not suffer much damage. It seemed that in losing the avant-garde, one would lose the very meaning of modern art and its forward energy. The avant-garde had slowly degenerated to a matter of style and as such, that is, as an elitist phenomenon, was losing ground to "low culture." The few critics who contradicted the ideology of avant-gardism came mostly from the Marxist camp and therefore lamented contemporary art's lack of political engagement; but they were no exception in defining and redefining the same idea.

It is a telling coincidence that at the same time when the avant-garde lost ground, the monopoly of a linear evolution of style suddenly appeared an old-fashioned topic in art history writing. It may be objected that this is an analogy of very different areas: on the one hand, cultural discourse; on the other, a single discipline's favored method. All the same, the analogy cannot be ignored, since both the belief in a progressing avant-garde and the belief in the meaningful progress of style evoked an autonomous history that followed its own laws. If the progress of art was avant-garde's business and if this progress could be measured in terms of style, then the fiction of the true history of art affected both topics. Their analogy was their mutual vow to maintain art's autonomy—an autonomy guaranteed by works of a certain kind: in the case of the avant-garde, by works representing innovation; in the case of art historiography, by works representing a given style most convincingly. It is thus the autonomy of art that also preconditioned the formalist approach in the historiography of style and therefore remained a heritage of modernism in general. The doubts of the continuing existence of the avant-garde that characterize the 1960s may have been caused by avant-gardes with a different or with a lacking concept of the working process by which they seemed to disprove themselves as avant-garde. The work, as an entity of its own, had delivered the same paradigm that also attracted the attention of the historians of style. Subsequently, it was rather the context of art that in both cases gained unprecedented attention, as it was in the context rather than in the creative act that a new definition of art was expected.

14 Methods and Games of an Academic Discipline

Art history, as a discipline, profited in its own way from the general crisis of the old idea that art was synonymous with a timeless and universal idea (which it, to be sure, never was, however strong that fiction worked as long as "classical" education mattered). The crisis was felt in Romanticism, but it also was enforced by the museum age in which no axiomatic doctrine of art could be upheld any longer. The new axiom of history as an explanatory paradigm allowed the exercise to contemplate art as a privileged manifestation of history and to understand the changes in art as an index of the temporality of history. The respective discipline, as a latecomer within the humanities, was expected to demonstrate the course of history in the mirror of art. This intention implied the isolation of art's form as "style" and the analysis of the individual work as a mere item of style in the collective sense while anything else that also distinguishes art definitely received less attention. Soon, biographies of single artists also had to prove the style pattern in the version of "individual style." The monographic treatment of a single work, as a rich "text" or cosmos of its own, therefore had an astonishingly late entrance into the scholarly practice because the topic would have contradicted the obsession with the anonymous "law" of style and its evolution.

I must insist on these roots of a discipline since that worship of history, as it became idealized in the retrospective dreams of bourgeois society, no longer is ours. Michael Podro, in his book *The Critical Historians of Art*, has enough to say in this respect when he discusses this topic under the heading of the motivation of change. Heinrich Wölfflin, who contributed most to the promotion of art history as an independent field of research, in his *Principles of Art History*, published in London almost twenty years after the German edition in 1932, even entertained "an art history without names" in order to describe the autonomous but forceful evolution of art under the law of history. "One day," he writes, "an art history must come in which the genesis of the modern way of seeing can be followed step by step." Then, "the history of styles will be described as an uninterrupted sequence," a breathtaking time movement of an abstract beauty and logic.

This view not only was based on a concept of art's autonomy but, in addition, implied the history of style as an autonomous process. Philosophical aesthetics, however different their aims were, involuntarily backed this position by confirming the autonomy of art. Even Theodor W. Adorno, still in the tradition of the age of Enlightenment, insisted on the function of art to have no function. In its early phases, art history, as a discipline, identified style as the unity among the diversity of historical art. The methods that supported this topic and that changed when style lost its former fascination allow for a brief survey that will help us to identify the intentions that were behind the traditions of the discipline.

In a celebrated elaboration on the narrative of style, the Viennese art historian Alois Riegl developed the theory of *Kunstwollen* (the will to art) as a magic formula for grasping the secret motor in art's development. The theory was rooted in the climate of historicism, which intended to justify every manifestation of history as an end in itself and to avoid judging it according to standards not born in the same time. If "artistic capacity" was limited in a given time, the implication was to consider these limits as its very intention, its "Kunstwollen." In this way, archaic art as well as decadent art could be measured against its own ambitions and not against an axiomatic viewpoint be it classical or not. Thus, art history acquired an almost unlimited competence for embracing the art of all times. It was in the line of historicism that, in the end, world history turned into a phenomenon of style. When styles in art were equated with styles of thinking or styles of life, the analysis of art's historical shape was celebrated as an all-explaining manner of narrating history. The spirit of an age seemed to be synonymous with the style of an age or vice versa. The *Zeitgeist* explained the *Zeitstil,* which, in turn, was followed by the next one in the interminable course of history. Art history, thus, appeared as a master narrative for explaining history as well.

Henri Focillon propagated a self-explaining law inherent in *La vie des formes* (The Life of Forms), which was expanded and updated by George Kubler in his fascinating study *The Shape of Time.* Like the old model of the cycle (in nature, society, and culture), this model of history claims that art everywhere went through similar cycles, which are not subject to chronological time but to an altogether different time pattern of change ranging from an early stage via a stage of maturity to a late stage. The explanation of the individual phases, as solutions destined for given problems, had developed in other disciplines from which it was applied to an autonomous history or style. The sequences in this cycle appeared as finite quantities, since during any given stage, a topical problem suddenly could take another direction and thus give rise to a new sequence based on the given level reached by the development. The actual date of a work mattered less than its age within the course of a cycle. Any two works could belong to the same period but represent an altogether different stage in their respective cycles: one could reflect an early phase while the other, despite the same date, could represent a late phase in another cycle.

In such a view, "chronological time" (to use Siegfried Kracauer's expression) is exchanged against structural time, which as a stylistic cycle or morphological sequence could undergo a duration and a tempo that were not to be measured in years or decades. This view is rooted in biological models based on slow or fast growth of species and races. But what was it that caused art to "develop"? As we know, works of art do not grow, nor is art a confined entity; it forms a general concept. The respective problem was solved by selecting single traits in art's physiognomy that permitted the disclosure of a trajectory of style. Scholarship was eager to single out successful developments from others that failed to make history. It thus not only relied on the density of its material but also employed an intentional selection, which worked best where a minimum of characteristics applied to a maximum of examples.

Such methods, despite their uncertain paradigms for explaining the direction of evolution, matured in the soil of a connoisseurship that emerged in the discipline. As a consequence, art history even today seems to fall into two categories; the results of the one compel museums to amend the current labels of their exhibits while the results of the other have no direct impact on the barren descriptive facts on a label, the data of a work. Connoisseurship was oriented toward the single work, whereas history became restricted to the sum of the works in which it was embodied. Today we are faced with a new connoisseurship that, with the help of the sciences, explores the technical structures in a given work rather than the work itself. This development toward technology threatens to become an end in itself. In this way, this method seems to practice the end of art history when it dissolves works into technical data and reduces the artist's personality to anonymous techniques.

In their appropriation of the paradigm of style, Bernhard Berenson (1865–1959) and Heinrich Wölfflin (1864–1945) represent a revealing contrast. Berenson was so successful in advising museums and collectors, for whom he identified their acquisitions, that he was able to acquire the villa I Tatti near Florence where, in a photograph (fig. 36), he poses as the proud possessor of a masterpiece. Mere "historical meaning," as he noted in *Florentine Painters*, was nothing compared with

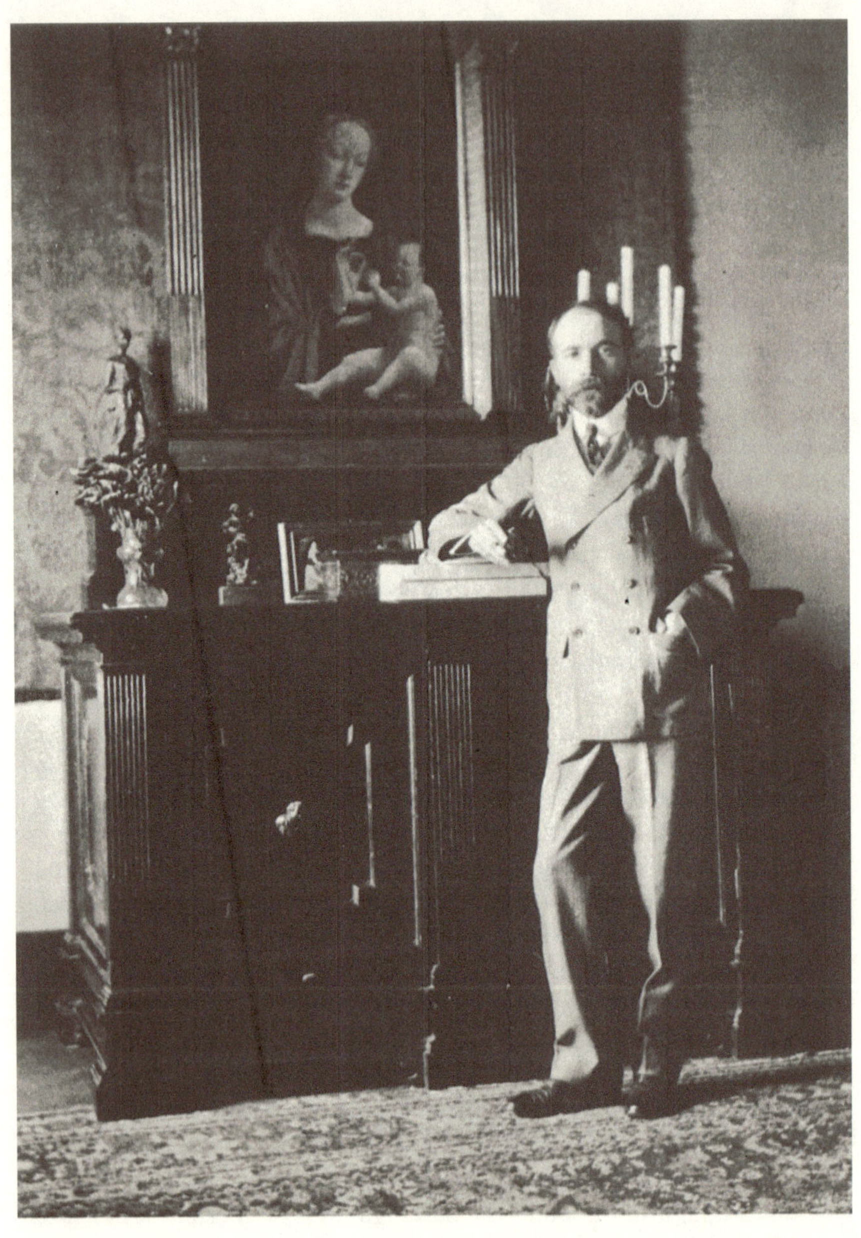

36. Bernhard Berenson in the villa I Tatti, Florence, 1903. From David A. Brown, *Berenson and the Connoisseurship of Italian Painting* (Washington, D.C., 1979).

"pictorial meaning." In brilliant prose, he wrote a new type of artist's biography and assembled in his writings an imaginary museum of Italian Renaissance painting: indeed, he so much assimilated the mentality of the Renaissance age that modern art mostly remained alien to him, a position he shared with his friends, the collectors. Hence, the writing of a continuing history of art did not matter much to him as a discourse of general significance.

Wölfflin, too, chose an ideal of the Italian Renaissance as a subject of his book *Die klassische Kunst* (The classical art), but he had a university career that helped him to establish the professional profile of the discipline and liberate the latter from the shadows of cultural history as practiced by Jakob Burckhardt. His way of "looking at art" rather than examining single works satisfied the cultural ideals of the educated elite more than collectors' interests. He justified his preoccupation with the formal aspect of art by referring to a book written by the artist Adolf Hildebrand, *Problem der Form* (Problem of form), which in his early days had "fallen like refreshing rain on parched ground. At last here was a new way of getting hold of art" and a new approach for making "art's essence" the theme of art history. Soon he reduced any single work so much to an example of style that the pendulum swung back in the opposite direction. The new battle cry was iconology, as Erwin Panofsky (1892–1968) turned it into the most successful method in art history of its time.

Iconology was an old term when Panofsky reused it in 1939 in order to introduce a new discourse in art history, no longer a discourse of style but one directed to a "history of types" that was to study the "tendencies of the human mind" as it materialized "in certain themes and ideas." Thus the history of art in the sense of a formal entity was to be transcribed into a history of "cultural symptoms" or of "symbolic forms" in the sense the philosopher Ernst Cassirer had defined them. Iconology was called upon to retrieve "the true meaning" of art from documents and texts drawn from the same tradition in which the artists had lived, and thus to recover the cultural knowledge as stored in the production of historical art. In the introduction to his *Studies in Iconology*, Panofsky placed much emphasis on the acceptance of art history among the established fields of the humanities and thus presented his field as a true "humanistic discipline." Iconology helped in this respect since it made use of the same texts that the classicists and the historians celebrated as their sources. It is important to rediscover the importance of this topical logic that was addressed to the other members of the Institute for Advanced Study in Princeton. The American context in general mattered in this respect. The appellation of the "true" method of art history was, for reasons easy to explain, restricted to Renaissance art, which proved to be the most rewarding realm for discussing humanist thought also in art. The relation of text and image, for the first time, became a familiar topic in art history though there was no satisfactory theory as yet in reach for dealing with the problem in general terms.

Today, the question arises whether this type of iconology can be updated for contemporary concerns or whether an altogether new type of iconology has to be developed for a comprehensive study of images, which the term, when taken literally, implies. It is obvious that the study of Renaissance art, even when extended to other periods, cannot be the only purpose of a general discourse of the nature of images. The sole application to art has had its merits and may still be continued along the same lines in the practice of the discipline, but it is no longer qualified for the general discourse on images, most of which today are to be found outside the limits of art properly speaking. Ernst Gombrich, in several of his books, has already anticipated a broader use of iconology in the sense of the visual heritage and the internal logic of images versus texts. But it has been W. J. T. Mitchell, originally a literary critic, who in his *Iconology*, a study of "image, text and ideology," as its subtitle says, in 1986 has opened access to a redefinition of what the term may imply in the future.

But already in its original, Panofskyan variant, iconology has inborn structural problems and even deficits that Georges Didi Huberman thoroughly addressed in his *Devant l'image: Question posée aux fins d'une histoire de l'árt* (1990), to whose analysis I refer with no further comment. Initially, the method made rather ambivalent use of discussing ideas and ideals for their own sake without paying much attention to their social and even ideological functions. At times, the respective practice seemed to revive a parlor game in the age of the old humanists (or rather, their patrons and sponsors), who flattered themselves (or were flattered by the artists) by decoding textual sources or literary, philosophical, and other messages in the pictures. At that time, the perception of art was guided by encoded messages that seemed more obvious to the layman than the creative potentials of the formalist composition as such. It makes sense to rediscover these riddles and metaphors today after our culture has lost them, but this hermeneutic activity, in its restricted aims, cannot claim to be the master discourse in art history and also has no visible connection to the earlier attempts to write a history of art properly speaking, that is, to explain what this history was and how it may be described in retrospect. When studying contents of works rather than works themselves, iconology also lost the very entities that made up a history in the proper sense and thereby approached what had been called *Geistesgeschichte* in art history, a term that is not easily translatable. The relation between art as such and the visual heritage has generated ever new problems whenever art history has attempted to limit their materials to art. At times, art historians such as Alois Riegl wanted to escape such boundaries by applying the concept of style to everything visual, such as fashion and objects in ordinary use. Riegl's view in a way harmonized with the aestheticization of life by the art nouveau, which would bring about a new era of design. All such attempts reveal the problems that an art history properly speaking generated when isolated from any other aspect of society.

Iconology, in its more developed ambitions, in turn was based on a tradition of philosophical hermeneutics that had made the nature of historical perception their theme and thus delivered the terms for empirical art criticism. Wherever such an approach overcame "the positivist naiveté that lies in the concept of the given by reflecting the conditions of interpreting," to quote a remark by Hans Georg Gadamer, it developed into a critique of positivism and invited a reflection on its own premises. Interpretation did not amount to simply "reproducing the original production" of meaning and form. In the case of aesthetics any such experience is necessarily preanalytic and yet is forced into the subject of a methodical analysis. In addition, we have to remind ourselves that in the days of German idealism a normative aesthetic transcended the realm of the art production of today. The concept of art in its older sense eventually was transferred to a concept of the work that attracted the former attention directed to art. Thus, the aura of the single work inherited the ideal beauty inherent in the older doctrine of art. This view of a work, therefore, as a philosophical problem, must not be confused with the work studied by empirical research.

The problem at hand soon lost its object or changed its direction when interpretation as the question of truth in a scientific sense, to quote Wilhelm Dilthey, became the real target. But the dialogue between the one who interprets and the work to be interpreted carries the danger that the former will only celebrate his or her approach if need be at the cost of the work. The hermeneutic mind that is left alone is easily tempted to reproduce his own exegesis. Art history borrowed from this type of hermeneutics the belief in the possibility of guaranties or rules for approaching its objects, that is, the works in question. Hans Sedlmayr established norms for interpreting art that his school had to follow faithfully. He even did not hesitate to distinguish the "work" as a self-referential item of interpretation from the mere "Kunstding" (we could also call it "objet d'art"), which the interpreting mind encounters before the hermeneutic procedure awakens or recreates it as a work of art. Historical research in this context was relegated to a minor function, which made a "second art history" possible. This description, though it only may serve to memorize a certain moment in the history of the discipline, still may remind us of the conflicts that by necessity broke out wherever the given history of art was transformed into a model for looking at art. This is why establishing universal rules for the study of art is a contradiction in terms since they have to be rethought by each successive generation. Since the process of systematic interpretation also involves the interpreting mind, the hermeneutics of art can never lead to a permanent solution.

A particular problem already defines the early work of Heinrich Wölfflin when he wanted to establish ideal notions of art as ideal norms in human perception. Wölfflin's famous "principles of art history" offer a catalog of general "laws" that appear intrinsic to art and supposedly belong to physiological and even psychological norms of perception. Thus, Wölfflin classified the classical era (Renaissance) and the Baroque era in terms of style with inborn "categories of perception" such as the "open" and the "closed" forms, to which he accorded significance as universal as his humanistic education would allow him. But the problem has much broader implications. Our perception of art is linked to contemporary conventions or, in other words, to the "period eye," which has to be explained in cultural and not in biological terms. What Wölfflin assumed to be permanent norms in fact is subjected to cultural and social changes, which in turn filter our perception. This is a received truth nowadays but was not accessible yet to Wölfflin, who aspired to the authority of an "absolute eye" overlooking all art in its history. It is, in fact, the other way around. The historical styles mirror historical modes of perception that we can reconstruct today with their help.

Having gone this far, we may be tempted to leave the decoding of art to psychology or, at any rate, to look for such guidance. But pertinent attempts have been usually confined to a psychology of perception Gombrich relied upon when he wrote *Art and Illusion* as a "psychology of stylistic change." Any style, much like taste and fashion, answers conventions of perception that are applied to conventions of representation or vice versa. Thus, styles of art and styles of perception coincide in generating a constant learning process in which any mimetic strategy becomes "a lasting event in the theory of perception." The danger in

Gombrich's method is the temptation to reduce anything in art to the game of perception. The implied axiom of illusion, however, embraces a simplified notion of visible reality that was to be matched by pictorial illusion. Today it is rather the notion of fiction, both as an aim and as a strategy in art, that attracts our attention. So it is appropriate to digress briefly on the possible meaning of the interplay of fiction and reality for describing art history. Illusion was a mimetic goal that sometimes employed scientific aids such as central perspective but whose intentions had already reached a saturation point in the nineteenth century, bringing all representational art of this kind into disrepute. Thereafter, the effort of an ever more perfect reproduction of nature came to an end and with it ended the hope of perfecting art along the lines of imitation.

Most different concepts of reality applied to nature are given to society as the constructed environment. Reality, understood in the latter sense, rejects precisely the safe reference for improving art, since, in contrast to natural history, social and cultural history have changed at greater speed than even art could change. Their reality has always been a *historical* reality, which in turn became the topic of ever changing interpretations in the various humanities. Wherever art represents the sociocultural world, the naïve game of mimesis of the visible yields to a new game whose rules are determined by the politics of communication. The definition of reality proved to be a constant source of controversy among the various interest groups in society, wherever they had access to representation. In the art of the twentieth century, abstraction and realism have long contradicted each other in their respective concept of reality: abstraction has entertained an almost mystical effort in discovering the invisible behind the world of appearances, while the various realisms either questioned social reality or, as state art, produced ideological counterfeits of social reality. The reproduction of reality has always been guided by the aim of either affirming or negating it.

Not even photography, which claimed to own an indexicality of reality, has kept its former promise. In the words of Susan Sontag, it developed into an "elegiac art" that meanwhile "tends to aestheticize the world." There are as many photographic ways of reproducing the world as there were in painting before the advent of photography. In this sense, the short history of photography presents us with a model case that may elucidate the problems in the long history of art. For quite some time, the history of photography seemed to coincide with a history of photographic techniques, according to the motto "One always does what one *can* do." But why is it that, despite the camera and its given technology, we recognize the great photographers by their personal style? The choice of their own style even extends to the choice of a particular technique which was to shape a personal perspective.

Man Ray and surrealist photography paved the way to use fiction as a means to overcome photography's inherent indexicality. "Subjective photography," whether in photocollage, multiple exposure, or other techniques, was turned into "autonomous photography" long ago, for fiction also serves the self-presentation of any medium. When representation triumphs over its motif, fiction uses a technology for a personal mise-enscène. As a result of its technique, photography had an immediate mastery of reproduction, which favored its liberation from standard tasks.

Fiction, too, in its own terms, is a statement about the world, and perhaps the history of art could be described as the history of fiction. After today's technological environment has displayed the natural environment and after the various worldviews have competed with each other, reality has become increasingly opaque—and thus a new topic for dissent. Already the old realism, in Gustave Courbet's sense, was too polemically charged to lend longevity to an art on the edge of society. As soon as art began to embrace reality, it became entangled in endless contradictions. As soon as artists began to compete with each other in defining reality, they compromised each other with their conflicting results. The desire thus grew among artists for a final "truth," which they sought in a new definition of reality. In the early twentieth century, "style" became a grand utopia whenever it was enlisted to prepare a new model of society: "style" with an ultimate and universal authority was expected to become a rescue from all thematic and pictorial pluralism.

But abstract art, which was chosen as the expression of the new "style," was only a short rest along the way, while at the other end the program designed to combine "art and life" was defeated either by "life" or by its own illusions. Abstract art flourished in the private visions of individual artists and alienated itself even further from mass culture in its postwar variant, which the *nouveaux réalistes* sought once more to counteract around 1960. Conceptual artists soon denounced the reality of art as a cherished fiction, while photorealist painters lured the same viewer into a trap of perception. As art is inextricably entangled in its changing environment, it retrospectively discredits a "master narrative" that claims to describe it as an independent phenomenon.

In the meantime, the discipline of art history, to reach self-reflection of its methods, takes refuge in its own history and thus reveals that it has reached the Alexandrism of a late cultural situation. To gain a picture of the present state of things, one would have to inspect national variants and trace art history in countries like England, where art history does not have an old academic tradition, and the United States, where it was liberated from German émigrés long ago. It was there that the discipline welcomed specialists from other fields, due to the fact that the retrospective approach was less strictly canonical than in Germany. In France, philosophers such as Louis Marin, until his premature death, and in Italy, members of the Umberto Eco school such as Omar Calabrese taught the subject of art history in other ways of thinking. The "new criticism" in the United States and the aesthetics of reception and deconstruction had their own part in academic practice.

In the United States, Arthur C. Danto, from the philosopher's perspective, has reopened the discourse of art history and also has joined my argument about the "end of art history" (see chapter 2). In *Art History's History*, Vernon Hyde Minor, while surveying the different methods of the discipline, appends such an easy résumé of semiotics, gender studies, and deconstruction, as if a complete revision of the canon already had taken place. We are facing a decentralization in the games of the academic discipline which dissolves and contradicts the former unity of aims and means and which soon may well cause nostalgic feelings in remembering what art history once was and how sure it was of its own mission.

15 Work of Art or History of Art?

Whenever the historical explanation of art appeared to have been exhausted as a topic in its own right, the work of art, which at least had a tangible existence, attracted attention instead. The work of art has its own indisputable reality, which is why we would like to believe that it has always been the first and the most important concern of art historiography. But the situation is quite different when we inspect the literature on art: in the eighteenth century, the preferred way of speaking about art was as an ideal, for which individual works only served as examples; in the nineteenth century, the new concern for "art history" again reduced single works to proofs in the framework of style as useful witnesses of development. In both cases, the works ranked behind the primary themes of "art" or "art history." Only very late, perhaps not until the postwar period, when contemporary art already had begun to question the concept of the work, art scholarship recognized its own credibility due to the fact that it possessed works that visibly embodied such a time pattern.

The work of art represents a characteristic unit that requires an equally characteristic approach: interpretation. The latter is not a priori bound to a particular method, since a work is accessible to different methods and allows for all kind of questions. The game of interpretation needs simply a work and a person, the interpreter, who claims a right equal to the work itself. A given work requires to be understood, and its viewer wants to understand it. Even in the ancient world, poets attempted an adequate response to works of visual art, arguing that these were silent and thus needed an interpreter to make them speak. Sometimes they employed the technique of ekphrasis even for nonexistent works so convincingly that such works really did come alive in fictional description. The reinvention of the work in question on behalf of the interpreter has remained a temptation to this day: one is often ready to make the interpretation convincing by supplying what is necessary or desirable for it.

Marcel Duchamp undermined the reality of the work, as opposed to the fiction of a large-scale history of styles and ideas, by his symbolic act of converting ready-mades into works of art. He did not care so much for the distinction that ready-mades were functional objects and therefore a priori differed from "mades" in the sense of personal creations. Instead, he insisted on the recognition that the material aspect of the work, as a fabricated object, was not enough to turn it into a work of art. However solidly it may exist, the work of art only acquires its proper status by a symbolic transfer. This view not only conveys irony but also historical knowledge. It was never the reality of the object but the idea of "art" that decided the matter; the object was the vehicle of an idea, even if only that of "art history," that one wanted to read from it. The equation of work and idea emerged in a climactic moment of modernity.

But the frame of reference represented by the unit of the work of art is still not exhausted until the artist, traditionally the creator or author of its idea, is brought into play. A given *object* was the site of his *concept*, which he realized in a *percept* for a third party, the viewer. The artist communicated with the viewer only through the work, which was why he intended the work to speak for him- or herself. The relationship between the artist and his work is as difficult to define as is the relationship between art as an idea and the work as an object. The artist appears as independent creator, while the individual work is always one of a series of dependent creations, however finished and complete it may appear. He even could be right against his own product, if only because he would produce others that would express his ideas better and more comprehensively. The main interest of art scholarship was therefore to study an artist in his works and to view his personal development in their light, as a result of which art scholarship needed works as evidence for this project. The notion of an artist's oeuvre then served as a generic term embracing the individual production as a whole.

The constellation of artist, oeuvre, and work becomes manifest in a portrait photograph of the painter Fernand Léger published in the catalog of the first Documenta exhibition, which supports my argument (fig. 37). As a self-portrait, the scene appears to have been staged by Léger himself, even if he is also the subject. Two large pictures of his fill the viewing field such that they extend beyond the frame, thus revealing his oeuvre as an incomplete unit that ultimately exists only in his production as a whole. The artist's head and shoulders emerge in an empty corner and, so it seems, in an interval between the two pictures. Léger with this mise-en-scène referred to Nicolas Poussin's self-portrait of 1650 (fig. 38), which he admired as the representative of French classicism. In a text that he wrote on color he recommended that every foreigner

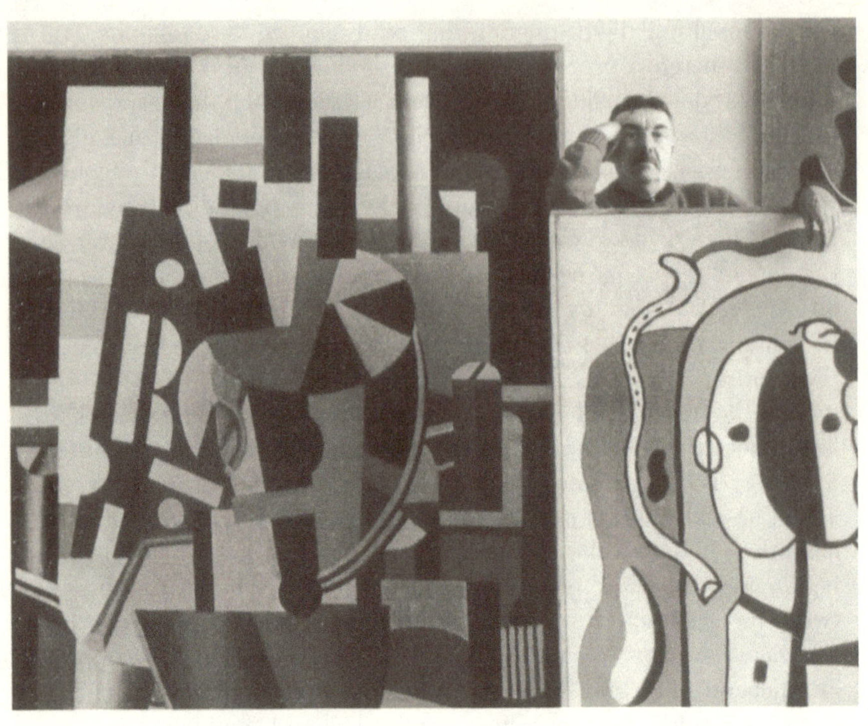

37. Fernand Léger in his studio, about 1950. Photograph in *Documenta I*, exhibition catalog (Kassel, 1955), section 4, plate 3. © 2002 Artists Rights Society (ARS), New York / ADAGP, Paris.

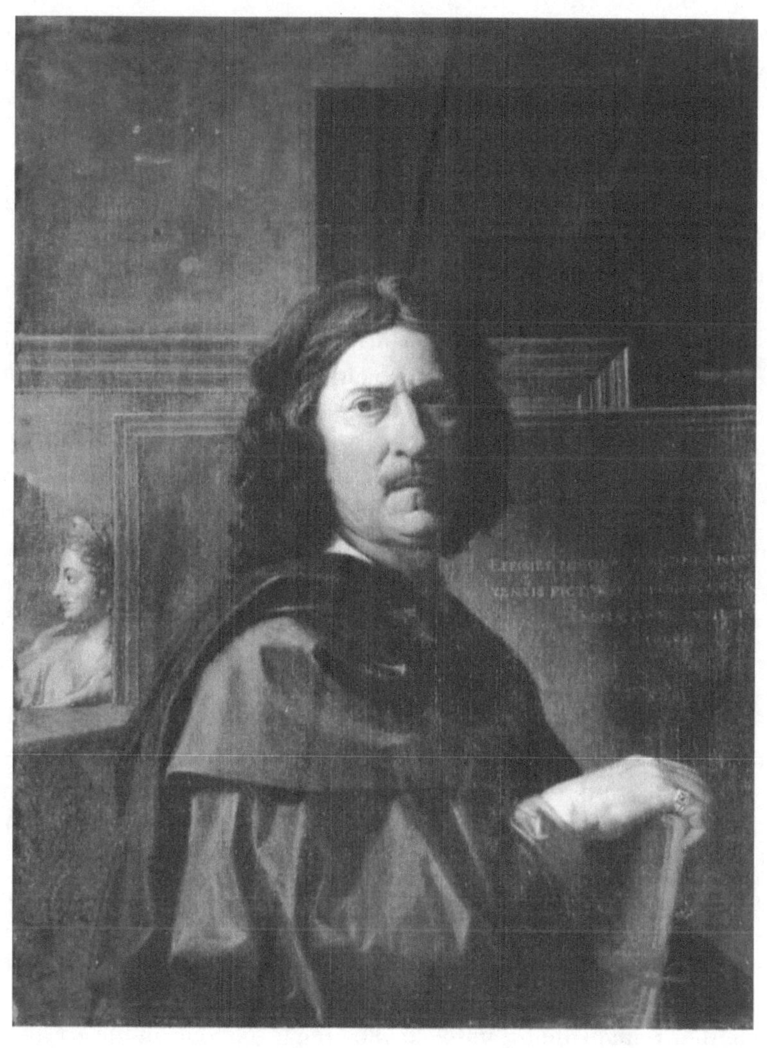

38. Nicolas Poussin, self-portrait, oil on canvas, 1650. Musée du Louvre, Paris.

should study France by first going to the Louvre where Poussin's painting hangs. In a 1945 essay, he refers to Poussin when describing the contrast between "objet" and "sujet." In modern art, in his view, the object in its lucidity was destined to triumph over the subject in its sentimentality. Taken further, the relationship between object and subject was to be extended to that between a work and its creator: the latter had to give priority to the work as witness of an objective, modern world instead of serving his self-expression.

For this reason Léger steps back behind pictures in which the human figure has already disappeared or decomposed, while Poussin with his own body covers his own works, which fill the background in a similar parallel arrangement. Poussin's self-portrait is a work in its own right, whereas Léger's photograph is not. The change of medium allows photography to capture the reality of Léger's person while simultaneously contrasting it with his works, which have their separate reality. Léger suffered from the painful ambivalence that his social ideas of art still depended on the old medium of easel-painting—Poussin's medium, whose limits he so urgently longed to make explode. Under such circumstances, the self-representation of the artist in the work, in the manner of Poussin, for Léger had become a major problem.

The work, which involuntarily retained its accepted status for Léger, testifies to history even when it no longer exists but can still be remembered because it did at one time physically exist. The history of art thus consists not so much of the eloquent texts it has engendered but of the silent works that it has handed down to us. Regardless of the history of their various reception, works allow us our own access that culminates in their physical encounter, whatever we may think of the "loss of the aura," in Walter Benjamin's sense. Works thus represent history in that they represent historical ideas of the world in historical embodiment. As such, they remain almost untouched by the turnabouts in the art historical discourse we are discussing here.

This is not true of the discourse of style that relied on the "pure form" as its own domain. The paradigm of style prompted Heinrich Wölfflin to speak of an "inner history" of art in which every form "continues to work procreatively." Since then, the discourse of style has generated other concepts, such as genre style or functional style, which threaten the unity of the old concept. It is only the single work that still today asserts its former position at the crossroads of all the determinants (artistic, iconographic, etc.) that have conditioned it. Works react with equal force to existing traditions and to contemporary experiences they reflect. They were neither conditioned exclusively by other art nor did they testify solely to art, which would be pointless to question. The conditions they have absorbed and the impacts they have left on later artists concentrate in the unit of a work in a paradoxical ease.

This notion of the work, which scholarship embraces more confidently than ever, however, has long been subject to strain, initially from the outside, until the art scene itself undermined the respective concept from the inside. Externally, the crisis came into the open already when André Malraux, reusing an early concept of style, published his *Musée imaginaire:* a fictional museum replacing works by purely formal qualities and notions of art where works of world art turned into photographic clips to serve merely as illustrations. The real museum with its limited number of works yields to a book whose potentially limitless illustrations and texts release an overall vision of the art of all ages and peoples. The literary *re-creation* together with the visual *reproduction* generated a new experience of art. A contemporary photograph shows us a bird's-eye view of Malraux's salon, where a panorama of art (but not a coherent panorama of art history) covers the floor in preparation for the art book (fig. 39). Georges Duthuit sharply attacked Malraux's concept in a two-volume critique of 1956, *Le Musée inimaginable,* where he accused the writer of reducing people and works of art to "fleeting fictions": "After the *roman de vie,* follows the *roman d'art,* and all direct experience of the work itself is repudiated" in favor of beautiful illustrations and the imagination that released them. But his critique was soon forgotten, and in his later role as minister of culture Malraux was able to test his project in new, spectacular happenings. I still remember Wolfgang Fritz Volbach warning students against reading Malraux because he would rob them of their belief in art history.

His book as surrogate of an art collection presents itself with a choice of surprising analogies in which "pure art" seeks the observer's gaze, freed entirely of all historical and thematic preconditions—indeed, even detached from the existence of the work's unit itself. Works are here no longer entities of their own nor do they refer to historical artists. They rather reemerge as vehicles of humanity's self-expression as an immortal species, which Malraux pursued in its most distant and inaccessible traces. In contradiction to Oswald Spengler's famous theories in his book *The Decline of the West* (1918–22), he wanted to celebrate human creativity as seen in the global mirror of its creations. He understood art as the "last coin of the Absolute and therefore as an immortal self-expression of mankind." Significantly, the photographic details that illustrate his comparative study are not described as such but as

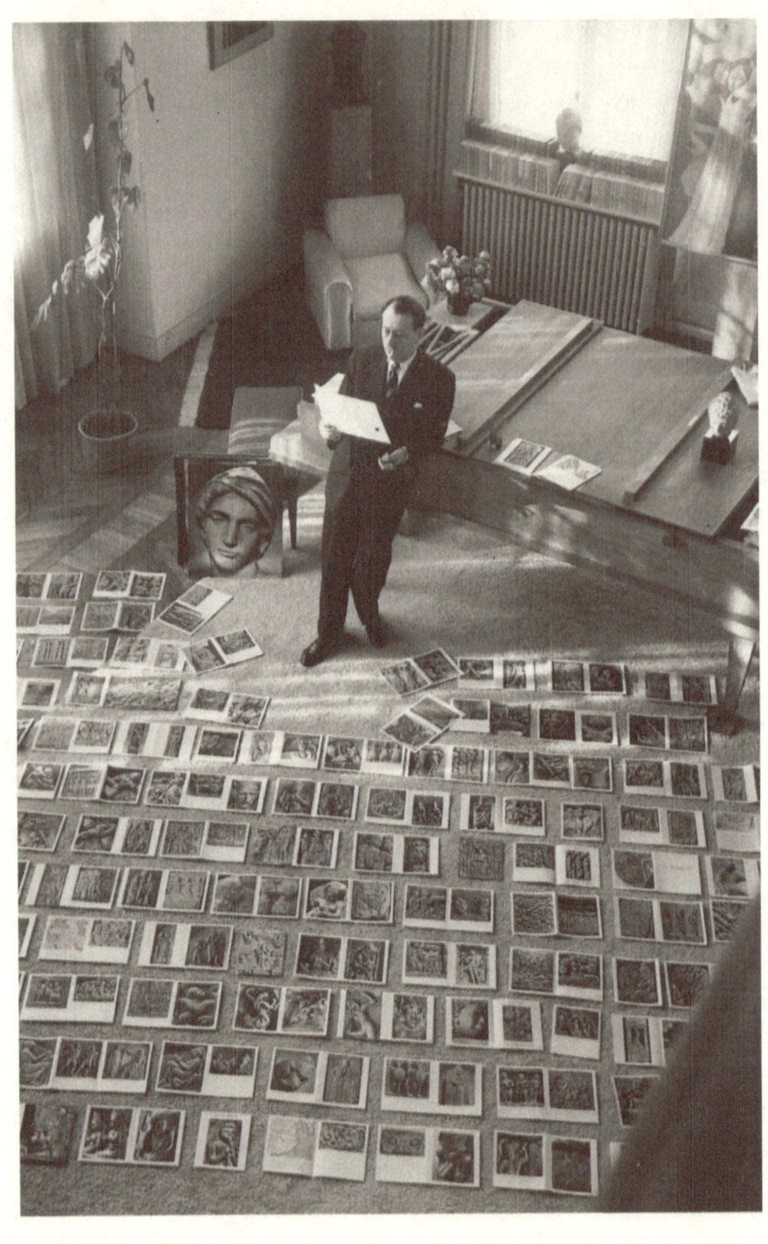

39. André Malraux with the illustrations for *Le Musée imaginaire.* Photograph taken about 1947.

"fragments," since Malraux saw each work as merely a fragment of an overall unity or of universal esthetics (fig. 40).

It is a strange coincide that, from the 1950s on, art historians who had never considered individual works as a topic of their own, now embraced a new hermeneutic endeavor whose contrast with Malraux's project was total. New monographs on individual *works* replaced the old monographs on individual *artists;* the biographical schema gave way to a hermeneutics in the manner of literary criticism. Charles de Tolnay, who initially had departed from Panofsky's iconology, published monographs on the *Mona Lisa* or Michelangelo's *Last Judgment,* and this inaugurated a work-oriented type of research whose methods were flexible enough to accommodate philosophical views and to live up to a work's originality. Each work was seen as embodying a complex net of ideas in need of an interpreter and thus offered an incentive to write a congenial text.

However, the most famous text that emerged during the controversy over the reevaluation of the work as the last stronghold of art history was a philosophical contribution. In 1966, Michel Foucault published *Les mots et les choses,* which he introduced with an interpretation of *Las Meniñas* (see fig. 31 above)—only eight years after old Picasso in a Paris gallery had exhibited fifty-seven studies based on this baroque masterpiece of Spanish painting. It was a French paradigm that prompted Foucault to investigate the "classical age" of the seventeenth century with the focus on a "theory of representation" in which the picture, along with language as the "tableau des choses," became the topic of an "archaeology of knowledge." In his painting, Velázquez already subtly distinguishes the work as material object, which we see in a rear view, from the work as an idea and a creative act in which the painter, the model, and the viewer are all involved. In Foucault's language, which always brilliantly is meant to fail in the face of the nonverbal structure of the work, the painting is a symbol of "représentation," which here becomes its own topic in a self-reflection of the creative act. As a result the painted work itself was recognized as the locus and impetus of theory.

Philosophical hermeneutics was followed in the 1970s by literary recreations of a painting. Thus, Peter Weiss chose Théodore Géricault's *The Raft of the Medusa,* the emblem of pre-Romantic salon painting, as a case study for his own views on art in his *Die Ästhetik des Widerstands* (The Aesthetic of Resistance). In the subsequent volumes, Weiss, a former painter, continued to recreate or restage works of the old masters, which runs oddly parallel to the simultaneous experience of the loss of

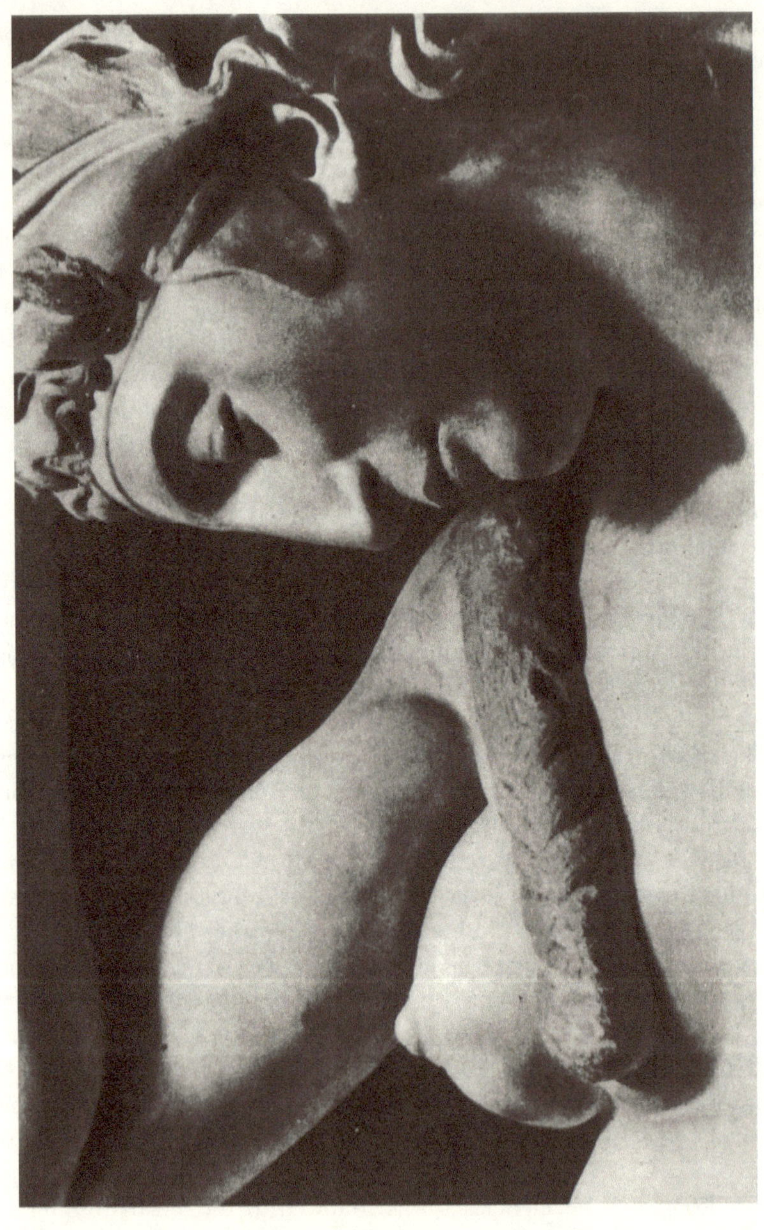

40. André Malraux, *Le Musée imaginaire*, part 1 (Paris, 1951), 62. Michelangelo's "Night." Explained as "fragment" in Malraux's book.

the "work" in contemporary art. There is meanwhile a full-fledged literary movement dedicated to the nostalgia for the former idea of a work, whose profile has been lost in literature as well. The only other example I will mention here is Julian Barnes, whose *History of the World in 10½ Chapters* returns to Géricault's painting. Filmmakers like Jean-Luc Godard and Jacques Rivette meanwhile also take successful part in this "archaeology of the work." In his 1983 film *Passion,* Godard has a Polish film director shoot scenes from great works of art—among them Rembrandt's *Night Watch* (fig. 41)—as a film set; but the director finally gives up this enterprise, saying he "does not have the right light" for it. The loss of convinced and convincing works in the visual arts of today's culture, which no longer bothers to invent or justify them, explains their return in literature, photography, or film where such memories do not conflict with literary practice.

By contrast, since the 1960s, visual artists have polyphonically proclaimed the "death" of the former concept of the work of art. They wanted to escape that concept in their search for an extended art practice. As a single statement, the work no longer would do when all they wanted was to make "proposals" in order to open the work's limits. Yves Klein, in his *Fire Pictures* and *Anthropometries,* by their utopian devices, liberated the artist from the traditional profile of the work, which he blamed for continuing the same old "spectacle." In his 1957 diary, he described his monochromatic "proposals" as "landscapes of liberty." When he came under attack in London from critics who demanded an explanation, he played a tape recording of human screams. "This gesture alone should have sufficed. The public had understood the abstract intention." Elsewhere, he noted with laconic ambiguity: "My pictures are the ashes of my art." He also wanted to free the theater from stage production. The void seemed to him the last refuge of the "Absolute," and therefore he inaugurated a non-show in an empty gallery.

Along the same lines, Klein soon was determined to transform the creative act into an independent event: the work of "performance." In his *Les Anthropométries de l'époque bleue* he used, in his own words, female nude bodies as "living paintbrushes," which, however, he did not touch himself, just as he did not directly lay a hand upon the work (fig. 42). Rather, the work was produced in the presence of an invited audience to the accompaniment of chamber music, with living models who transferred "pure pigment" of blue onto the canvas with their own bodies, under the direction of an artist dressed like an orchestra conductor performing the myth of artistic creation. We may ask ourselves whether,

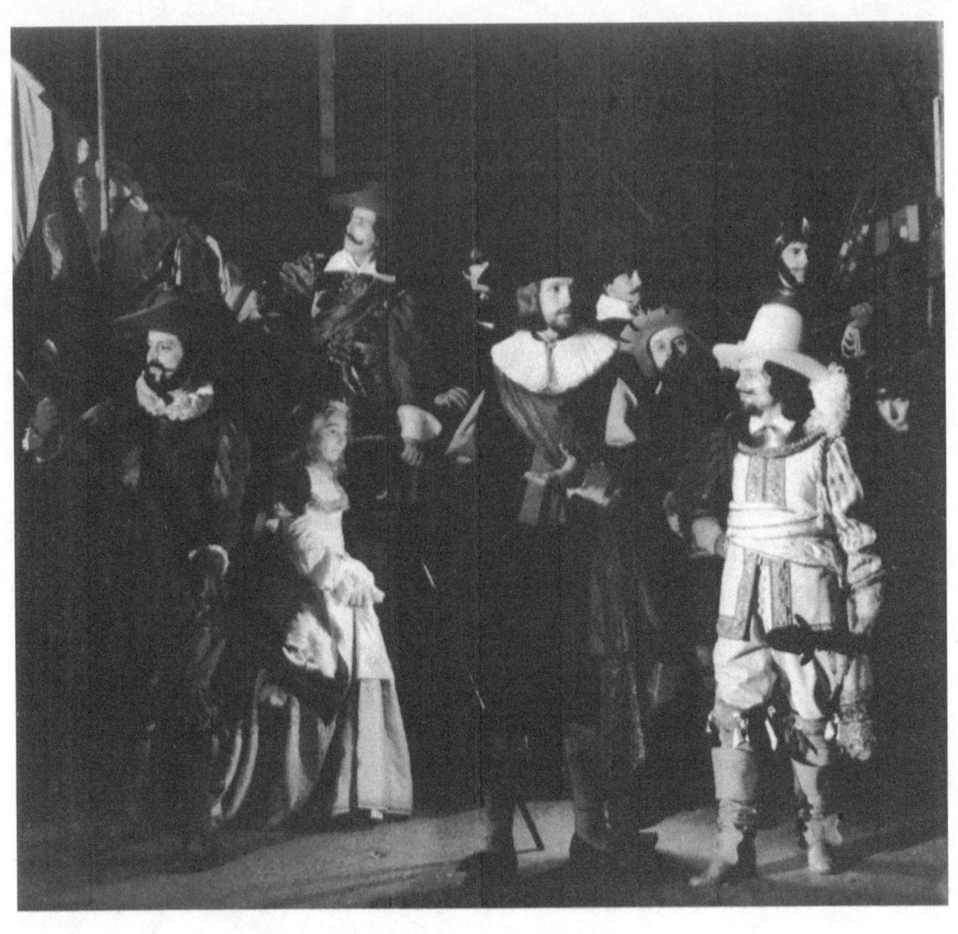

41. Jean-Luc Goddard, Rembrandt's *The Night Watch,* film still from *Passion* (1983), detail.

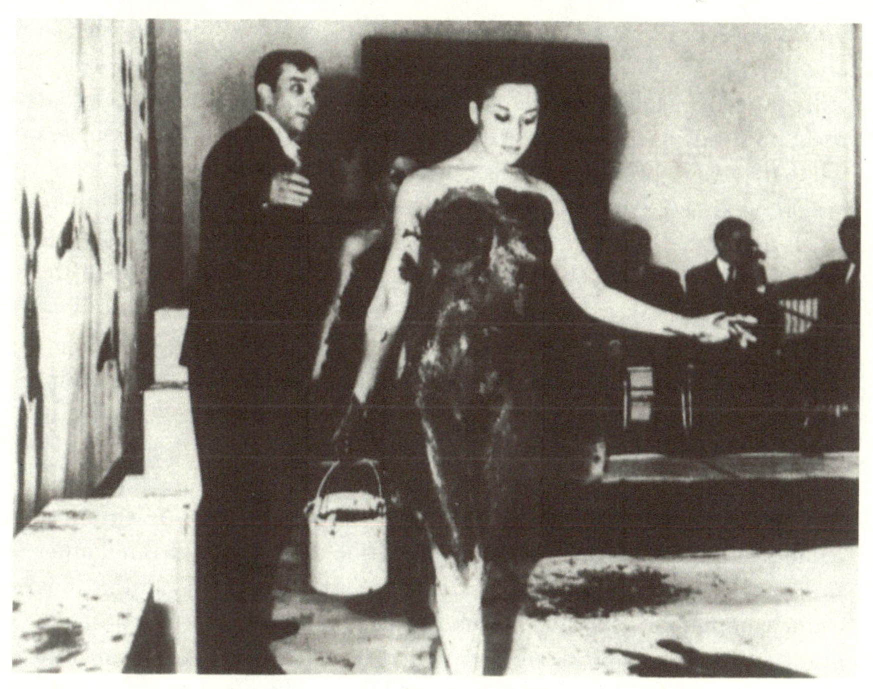

42. Yves Klein, action art titled *Les Anthropométries de l'époque bleue*, March 9, 1960. Galerie internationale de l'art contemporain, Paris.

after such reflexivity, the necessary innocence could still be regained in creating the usual works and whether a work that produces itself would still succeed in following the course of art history. It is doubtful that their position in art history was ever in the minds of the old masters while they were producing their greatest works. Nevertheless art scholarship remained fixated on the presence of works and rediscovered them when nothing else of substance seemed to endure. Even the enigmatic metamorphosis by which Yves Klein reached the utopian gesture of the play-acting artist-creator, did not discourage his interpreters to talk of "works."

The situation can be summarized as follows: Art history, as we know, investigates works that carry representation. But it is also engaged in self-representation when it uses a particular kind of discourse, the discourse of art history. The old procedure of explaining the world through its history in the meanwhile suffered the crisis of representation. Doubts about exclusive rights on explanation have also infiltrated other branches of scholarship. In the case of art, things seemed right as long as the commentary chose a role analogous to that of authorship and creation, in terms of representation, while retaining the same distance to the work as the work maintained toward the world in representing it. In other words, the respective text depicted the work much as the work depicted whatever it chose as its subject.

This familiar order was already disintegrating when, in the modern period, the presence of the work found its meaning in nothing but itself. In this process, the artistic form acquired the same authority that motif and content had formerly possessed and thus it guaranteed the complete autonomy of the working process. Today, this innocence in the creative act has gone lost, and the original forfeited its established meaning as a unique creation, unique in terms of its formal entity. If the roles of commentary and work were once kept strictly apart, this changed when art declared itself to be a text about art. Montage dissolved the former unity of representation as embodied in a work by replacing it with the work's self-reference. However much the work is still, in retrospect, a pièce de résistance, it may be questioned that its former position based on its coherence in structure and meaning, still can be upheld.

16 Art History versus Media Studies

Art history for a long time concentrated on the examination of phenomena of style and yet evoked the illusion that its approach was comprehensive enough to justify the claim that the term "history" implies. The more it opened up its field of research, the more difficulty it had to find a common denominator for the multiplicity of questions it was confronted with. Today, the models that once possessed the authority of the old academic discourse are exhausted. So we are compelled to pursue several art histories that secretly compete with each other or even exclude each other. For a certain time, it seemed as if it was possible to match the new questions by escaping into what was called a social history of art. But the hope for a new reigning discourse proved illusory, because the time of master narratives seems to have passed. Only the complexity of what a single work comprises in itself still continues to fascinate us. Whatever a work has to say is expressed in its visual structure or expression, even if we all too often tend to select what corresponds to a given discourse.

Individual meaning not only is implied in a work's production but extends into the history of its reception, as has been discussed in literary criticism. A given work did not only exist for its contemporaries for whom it was made but continued to impress later generations among which artists joined the ranks of its interpreters. Thus, production and reception in the case of the work of art are inseparably linked in the individual history of such a work, even if we keep them apart in our discussion. Any new work was seen against a horizon of expectation that constantly changed along with the coming and going of ever new ideas of art. Against this background any attempt of imitating or contradicting existing solutions in art production addressed an already initiated audience that would follow or resist it. Competition not only existed between living artists but also moved later artist to react to existing models. Seen in this perspective, the old view of a linear evolution of style loses the authority it once was given since its mechanism no longer can be upheld in the light of new discussions. People have always lived with single works rather than with styles, and the same works still today inspire our new questions. Works age less than the discourse we address to them.

Today, art history is practiced in an environment in which new technologies and visual medias have changed our ideas of reality and visibility. We value them mostly in light of the information they transmit or purport to transmit to us. This new experience explains why we are more and more inclined (or seduced) to understand historical art production with reference to their born messages as historical media (including the already historical media of the modern age like photography and film). Also picture painting appears as a medium of its own whose aesthetic and social function had its imprint on what the single work had to say or how it could say it. Images and language both served as systems for a symbolical communication with the world. Today, as nonverbal communication meets with growing interest, even the social sciences include visual media in their research.

Art history would gain a new authority, given the contemporary constellation among the humanities, if it would not fear to betray the autonomy of artistic images, that is, to lose sight of art among other visual territories. The choice cannot be between discussing art against nonartistic media or vice versa. It may however be that a topical dualism between art in the absolute or mass media outside the art world appears as an obstacle to open art history beyond its traditional boundaries. Such a dualism however does not give justice to historical periods when such boundaries were much more fluid. Today, our world is filling up with images and symbols in which the distinctions between medium and reality have become blurred, as Susan Sontag once described in her book *On Photography*. Contemporary artists, too, are prompted to reflect on signs and fictions in mass media, the way they reacted formerly to the experience of nature. Even in classical modernism, art production had given up the paradigm of nature as their exclusive reference. Contemporary art continues in this line by analyzing the fictions of mass media that have created their own type of reality by interfering with our gaze and the world.

There is a naive reductionism in play when art historians still leave any media theory to modern visual technologies like photography, film, and video while setting aside historical images as art properly speaking. It may be conceded that the beginnings of media theory have taken place in film studies and related fields. But this is no reason to leave things where they were. We may also add that current media theories long ago have consulted art theories, and even Marshall McLuhan confessed that he owed his inspiration to art criticism when he wrote his primer *The Mechanical Bride*. We also may be inclined to turn the question around when we discover the introduction of the art discourse wherever the boundaries of entertainment and information are left behind. The borderline of art runs straight through contemporary visual media and thus disregards the territorial claims of the several academic disciplines in question, even when the latter wish the world to be ordered according to their own concerns.

It is agreed upon that media studies and art history profoundly differ in their interests. It is therefore unthinkable that art history should become an expanded form of media studies, as also an annexation in the opposite direction would make no sense. But the coexistence of art and nonart images even in historical times invites a dialogue between the respective disciplines. So-called media art (like video installation) may be called the most advanced version of media theory and media criticism. Art history, though it is sometimes embarrassed to admit it, has long enough studied its usual topics in the sense of visual media as well. It therefore seems appropriate to sketch the relation between public media and art while bearing in mind that this relation has undergone constant change. There was a time when the visual arts belonged to the larger territory of public images and therefore served information as much as insisting on their aesthetic proprieties. Today such functions are distributed to separate realms, since information and communication only survive as a matter of technology and politics.

Media studies necessarily are restricted to questions of technology and communication (how do media function, for whom, and for what purpose?), which means that their scope differs from that of art history. Questions in media studies boil down to the following one: How does communication work? Nevertheless, communication today is opaque enough since it functions via anonymous channels and leaves the recipient with the ubiquitous TV screen, which produces the phantom of an absolute presence where there is only the transmission of illusion or pseudopresence. In addition, public media always know the answers and spare the recipients from asking their questions, as they never question themselves. Their power lies in their ability to overcome space and time while providing the illusion that the viewer participates in life events. I freely admit that I am consciously contrasting such public media with art as an individual expression or personal message. But artists who are working with "special effects" in advanced technology are confirmation enough that they see themselves in the very same conflict. Their installations attempt to restore a space for personal orientation and experience that contrasts with the public site of the TV monitor and allows the audience to become active again. It seems that the protagonists in this type of art scene today defuntionalize their technological tools in order to appropriate them for the scope of art that, in this case, means replacing rapid consumption by a hermeneutic effort allowing for uncertainties and open questions. Peter Sellers, in a talk he gave on the occasion of the Erasmus Prize at Amsterdam some years ago, called for an art which is slow, dark, and difficult. Art always lived from symbols more than from facts. The question of art is not one of technological tools but of conceptions and ideas.

Looking back at historical art, we are now in a position to rephrase the discourse in such areas as well. In any pragmatic study, new experiences generate new questions. It is clear that art history had entertained an all-too-naïve notion of art and thus generated a useless argument over whether a given work only belonged to the sphere of art or also served in terms of a public medium in society. This false argument, which meant art versus society or the other way around, turned up in the course of a development in which the discipline tended to claim everything in the past for being art, regardless of whether such items ever had been created with the notion of art. Today, the solution might be a new type of iconology (if I may use this term, not in Erwin Panofsky's sense but in the way W. J. T. Mitchell used it), which would integrate the art topic in a larger context. Such an approach will also do justice to visual media in general, whether they would or could be called art or not. If this view is accepted, then art could be called a historical and therefore changing phenomenon in the same way that we speak of the history of art collection or art theory which did not exist at any time. In my book *Likeness and Presence* I therefore distinguished the era of the image from the era of art, as I suggested in the subtitle of the book. This means that the notion of art, after antiquity, became again a driving force in the production of art from the Renaissance on. Since any discussion of this kind is still subject to doubts and controversy (medievalists are not concerned with placing their topics in such perspective, while modernists usually do not care for studying anything prior to modernity), I will illustrate the point with a few examples.

In a seventeenth-century catalog of works that testifies to the early history of art collections, David Teniers the Younger wrote of a "theater of painters" in which art was performed like on a stage: art as exhibited in an art collection. It is precisely this type of staging art whose continuity today causes endless discussions. While art still had to be introduced or justified as a topic of its own in the century of Teniers, today on the other hand it meets "the dilemma of its own existence," as Harold

Rosenberg had put it. In his view, "new media have taken over most of its former functions." In 1950, Jean Cassou called film "a perfect expression of the modern mind," which, as a medium, still dealt with contemporary reality that had been completely abandoned in painting of the abstract manner. Already in 1936 Walter Benjamin had declared photography and film to serve modern society better than painting, which still seemed infected with an aura rooted in its religious prehistory. Since then, the discussion has never ceased to touch the functions and the respective media branches of art while the discipline still resisted this opening of the discourse successfully. Cinema, too, has been taken over by the ubiquity of television whose accepted form as a medium already seems to be on the edge of a new era in which the public will select its own programs. The public sphere also lost its traditional meaning in the age of the Internet. Given such experiences, we may be prepared to agree on the view that, when all the perceptual media are in a constant flux of change, art alone cannot be kept apart from this condition of temporal aspects.

Contemporary art however has also found new ways of keeping its presence even in the era of mass culture. Ever since it allowed new kinds of realism (such as those of pop art) to enter its repertory, art restored figuration, which once had been declared dead, and thus regained new territories on both sides of the boundaries between what has been called "art and life." Where the arts were sent into a momentary exile, they returned with a new profile and an extended scope, even if their methods at first seemed unexpected and unfamiliar. They still are credited with an authority and freedom of which the entertainment and advertising areas only can dream. Their freedom, to be sure, lives at the expense of their limited importance in the sense of social and economic acceptance.

The discontinuity in art practice existing between the traditional and the present type favors the view that art, as we understand it today, was a phenomenon not present at all times and at all places and does not give the guarantee to exist forever. Instead of accepting its existence as a matter of fact, we may meanwhile ask ourselves how art entered certain periods and societies and in which sense it was possible to become accepted. As long as art was not put into question (which means in the period of museums, galleries, and the art market, which certainly is not over), it was sufficient to narrate this history with praise of its achievements or complaints about its decadence. But when art no longer is a matter of course or no longer is accepted as something given forever, we may again engage in a new way of tracing its history. Already Benjamin asked the question as to what art could mean in the era of mass media and how it was subject to change. The current discourse, which reiterates Benjamin's argument, tends to accept his view of the year 1936 like an article of faith while forgetting to ask Benjamin's question again under the present circumstances. He wanted to inquire into the changing cultural significance of art in its given environment. Such a question takes on a completely new meaning in our days where we experience the dawn of a world no longer Euro-centric and not even Western. Benjamin was a faithful advocate of high modernism with which he shared his enthusiasm and his innocence. We therefore need a new Benjamin who could explain our world to us today.

17 The Myth of Modernism in the Mirror of Art History

The rise of modernism in Europe produced two disparate reactions. The guardians of history feared the dawn of art, while the partisans declared modernism to be a logical continuation on the path of art. Seen from today's perspective, both reactions missed an important part and yet revealed a partial truth. Art did not come to an end but took a new and different course, the course of modernism. The farewell from traditional genres like painting implied the loss of an ideal such genres had long represented. Abstraction seemed to lose sight of the real world, Dada revolted against art as a concept, and Duchamp unmasked art as a bourgeois fiction. Such reactions not only distinguished progressives from conservatives but were ultimately concerned with a canon of art history, which was defended by the opponents and ignored by the advocates of modernism, for whom the new revealed a historical necessity. The rise of modernism inaugurated the debate whether art history could or even should continue to accompany a living history of art. Conservatives in the German universities such as Henry Thode and Hans Sedlmayr lamented the loss of a historical heritage in whose mirror modernism looked distorted. Progressive critics and writers such as Julius Meier-Graefe and Carl Einstein hailed modernism as a fulfilled promise of past traditions which from their viewpoint had prepared such a development.

Both medieval and even primitive art, which had no real stance in academic art history, were now cited by artists as distant and even true models, since they contradicted traditional art as much as modernism did. It does seem reasonable to establish new guidelines for writing art history and to create analogies which served both sides for their conflicting issues. The battle also involved the possession or loss of what art historians felt was threatened by the exodus of artists from common territory. The further course of art historical research immediately took a defensive direction. What had not become a standard of art history by then would not become one for long, since, in the face of continuously shifting boundaries between old and new, it seemed impossible to process all the materials that had not already become art history's property.

For some the problem seemed to coincide with the history of the avant-garde, which had engaged in a kind of alternative history of art beginning with the "zero hour" of the *refusés* and the Secessions. What for the one group seemed to signify a new era in art history, for the other group seemed to indicate the end of that history. From now on, the two positions took little notice of each other particularly since they served different ends and were practiced by different people. This situation changed in Europe after the big war, when art critics like Herbert Read in England and art historians like Werner Haftmann in Germany intensified their publications on modern art. But the early rift still survives in the present, where it may be observed in the embarrassment about non-avant-garde in and after modernism, which yet defies classification. In addition, media such as photography and film met with so little attention that art scholarship for a long time remained fixed on painting or sculpture, which alone seemed to deserve to be classified as art.

The inevitable historicization of the avant-garde created a problem of a particular kind. Suddenly it was no longer the history of the avant-garde but avant-garde as history, which mattered. The alleged "end of avant-gardism" became, similarly like the "death of art," an opportunity to rethink or even revise the writing of modern art. There was hostile resistance against consigning the avant-garde to the same kind of history which the avant-garde so long had assailed. The discourse in modernism revealed the fear that, by losing the avant-garde, the future would also be lost, leaving behind only a frivolous kind of art that no longer concerned itself with ideals of history. In addition, however, the avant-garde view of history became suspect, and looked itself questionable in retrospect, which meant that it depended on the faith of the believers and on the hostile resistance of the opponents. With the acceptance it found in modernism, the avant-garde in turn became a victim of history rather that a victor who would force his own laws upon history.

For a certain time, a third kind of art history, in terms of model and methods, makes its appearance, which has neither the authority of the old history of style nor the monopolistic claim of a history of innovations but which differs in its aims from both types of art history. Problems had emerged in the latter types when, for example, premodern art for the one party had become an irrefutable canon while it mattered for the other party only as a negligible kind of prehistory. For the modernists, modern art seemed to live from a permanent battle against tradition, as a result of which traditions that lived on in modern art did not become a topic in its own right. But since the "Tradition of the New," as Harold Rosenberg called the transformation of the avant-garde into a historical phenomenon, had been established, it also became possible to discuss the tradition existing *in* the new. If the same questions will be addressed to premodern and modern art, art history as a discourse will change. The modern culture of the two past centuries, after it has become possible to call it historical, invites for a new type of discourse, which, however, is not in sight, given the distance separating the modernists and the others.

The plea for a third type of art history provokes a question whether old and new art, so much divided by time and aim, can be integrated into a common narrative. So far, only textbooks on a more popular level have treated premodern and modern art together, in which case the best thing that could be said about them was their irreconcilable difference. We are still so much involved in an internal view on Western art that we have little interest in looking at it from the outside and treating it as a history more defined by a cultural space (the West) than by a dividing time pattern. Yet the new global situation encourages also art historians to rediscover a larger territory that can be explained by a common history that was not merely modern. Now that both old and new in Western art have matured into tradition it no longer makes sense to play them off against each other as different cultures. We no longer simply can claim to "possess" either one or the other now that they both have shifted into a distance that we once only felt in front of premodern art. Even the opposition against tradition, which dominated modernism, turned into a lost tradition that no longer applies to contemporary art.

What conclusions can be drawn from this turn in art history's situation? There is a possible conclusion that makes us rethink the aims of the discipline instead of hiding behind established methods that merely guarantee professional success. The more art history has accumulated positivist knowledge of its materials, the harder it becomes to navigate the discourse through this accumulated knowledge. The proven answers the discipline once gave itself become questionable in the light of our current experience in a picture-dominated world of mass media. The general audience increasingly becomes impatient and demand an answer for the surviving significance of art in our society. In this context, the myth of modernism requires a certain revision. It may be that modern art was more a continuation than a departure. It must be conceded, however, that art changed its status with the foundation of the museums as the only remaining public space. In the museum area, art was confined always to the destiny of receiving the consecration of the museum and thereby being recognized as art in the first place. The museum, which was created for the old masters, also changed the course of modern art, which needs no further comments. But it may be added that the coexistence of premodern, modern, and contemporary art in the same institution, even if that institution, the museum, often looks rather different, invites a similar synopsis in writing the history of Western art, at least as a unity in relation to the art of other cultures.

A difference between modernism and premodern art may be seen in the respective response to art's contemporary environment. The relationship with the world, intrinsic to all art, can never be reduced to any simple formula. As we have learned from research in the past decades, the old masters were not simply the exponents of a period style but reacted to their respective society in a number of ways. Thus, the supposed unity and wholeness of traditional art lends itself not to an easy opposition against art in modernism, since such an antithesis lived from an all-too-romantic and simplified view of premodern art. Scholarship has long refuted the petrified image we entertained of old art by revealing art's complex and even contradictory relation with its environment. But we usually hesitate to change this cliché since we lived so long with it and since it served the distance that modernists kept from such ancestors. Often art is cherished more for the beauty of our own retrospective ideas than for what it has been in its own times.

Another problem in dealing with art in modernism is the discrepancy between what we know and what we like to think in terms of the broad lines of what happened. The history of progress easily accommodated to a linear narrative in which individual artists, manifestos, or "movements" confirmed the success story of modernist art all too easily. In the meanwhile we may ask ourselves whether such a narrative still keeps its hermeneutic authority or whether it only serves its own purpose. Modernism did not only constitute a story of freedom but also entertained regression and defense. The various attempts to submit living art to political restraints have determined its past as also have the interests of the art market. But such insights did not cause the respective historians to rewrite what has happened. Perhaps a professional body departs only reluctantly from the boundaries of its discourse, because only within such bounds can it keep its authority.

Such descriptions are not intended to juxtapose the two traditions in question only in their deficiencies. Rather, they are meant to invite us to build bridges and analogies. After all, they both happened in the West, which means that what seems so completely distinct as a result of art history easily tends to coalesce when seen from the outside. Modernism, as a result, cannot claim to have been a separate and independent culture since it emerged from its own historical roots and also from cultural conditions only valid for the West. The debates that were conducted over art in modernism often were controversies over the inheritance that modernist art did appropriate or unsuccessfully refused to appropriate. I only mention the obsession with a firm concept of art, inherited via romanticism, that discouraged any attempt to leave it behind and instead generated the various efforts to twist it into the extremes of anti-art and pure high art

Usually it is forgotten that artists in modernism, whether they took a polemical stance or not, look back beyond the bounds of modernism in order to find their identity within long and convoluted history that deserves to be called polycentric history of art. To give just one example, Fernand Léger obsessively discussed in his writings the origin of painting or the lost function of mural painting, after art as a commodity on the art market since the nineteenth century had lost any public impact. In the photograph we have mentioned (fig. 37 above) he is posing between his canvases as if he would like to express his desire to become a modern Poussin while at the same time insisting on his decision to put tradition in its place. Ever since Nikolai Tarabukin in 1923 wanted art to take development "from the easel to the machine," to quote the title of his book, the escape from the canvas became an abiding utopia and thus was ill at ease with the critics' determination to continue their writing along the old lines, whether or not living art proclaimed irrevocably "the last picture." Painting neither began nor ended within the time limits of modernism, but its never-ending end became intrinsic to the myth of modernism, which was a myth of art.

Similar objections as to a linear narrative are raised by the crisis of subjective creativity, which was subject to collective ideas already in the 1920s and which culminated in the battles between what was called "art and life" where design had an easier part than free art. I would like to illustrate the old debate with the practice and conceptualization of what we call the "work of art." This topic, the subject of my recent book *The Invisible Masterpiece,* has not yet found the place which it deserves and which it needs in art historical discourse. All too often the critics and historians tended to iron smooth what produced in fact a continuous crisis of definition and redefinition among artists. Walter Benjamin, in his famous essay, obstructed further discussion by limiting the work of art to its aura in the romantic sense, without taking into consideration that a work which was restricted to become a lonely representative of an obsolete conception of art, by necessity had to be a difficult construction that never satisfied the needs for long. The uncertainty around the profile of

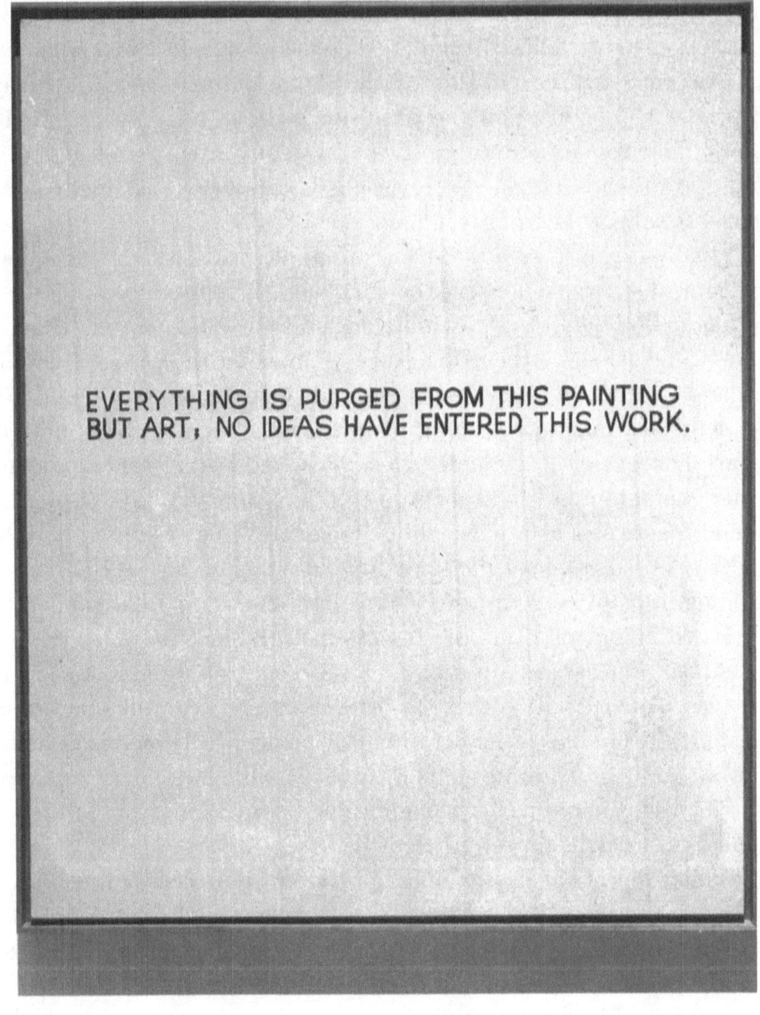

43. John Baldessari, blank canvas with epigram, "Everything is purged from this painting but art, no ideas have entered this work." Acrylic on canvas, 1966–1968. Gallery Sonnabend, New York. Courtesy of John Baldessari and Mariam Goodman Gallery, New York.

the work, culminating in the utopia of art absolute though incorporated in a single work would lend itself to another type of narrative dedicated to art in modernism and prior to modernism. Would one engage in such an alternative view of things, the crisis of art in early modernity would reveal a necessary heritage from what had happened before in European art. I also would like to remind the reader that modernism in Europe had happened under different conditions and in different time limits as regards the development in the United States, even if such a view may cause an uneasy response by American readers.

The coexistence of two types of modernism, which both have receded into history but still represent an inevitable dichotomy in retrospect, left its traces in such works that stage their own perspective on modernism. George Segal's portrait of Sidney Janis presenting an "icon" from Mondrian's early modernism is a case in point (see fig. 13 above). The gallerist, as a collector, seems to trace a mythical genealogy of art by pointing to a work that, in the given mise-en-scène, became integrated in George Segal's own work as a memory of another time that still lives on but no longer serves the guidelines of an obliging model. A picture by John Baldessari that appeared in the Guggenheim show *The Tradition of the New* offers itself for a last remark on modernism (fig. 43). The picture lends itself to be read rather than seen, large and white as it is and with a text like an epigram whose message looks like a last will. Even if the text across the center of the picture only refers to this very painting, the whole drama of modernism vibrates from within. "Everything is purged from this painting but art." The picture is transformed into an emblem that seems to propagate a mere idea of art. But the second part of the sentence discourages this view: " No ideas have entered this work." It is of course an idea to say that no ideas are involved. Innocence, irony, or deeper meaning? Only the work itself appears to survive in such a labyrinth where work, idea, and art conflict with each other.

18 Postmodernism or Posthistory?

When the sixties discussed the crisis or the end of modernism, soon thereafter another topic, the notion of history as a suddenly obsolete category for the narrative of art, became the target of the debate. Even modernism was not an easy matter of definition, as its meaning differed in European circles from those discussing the arts in the United States. The time span identified with modernism was much shorter in the United States, and the break with an accepted norm of culture or art, which had been canonized by writers such as Clement Greenberg, was felt as a dramatic event in the Unites States, where attempts of reaching consent about such matters then were still recent. Modernism may be called a project of becoming modern and creating symbols of modernity. But the age of modernity reaches further back and thus cannot be called synonymous with modernism but represents a space of history that, in the meanwhile, has become past history precluding the hope of saving the modern age from the fate of receding into history.

In the following pages, I want to connect the topic of *history* with the topic of *art* in the sense that art has been defined by and lived in a history of its own, which means that a safe notion of history was needed for establishing consent on the notion of art. Before 1960, every work that claimed to be art was to deliver the proof by marking a new stage in art's history. Thus, art was inevitably linked to art history, considered as its ever recurring law and temporal pattern. This former view soon conflicted with another position, which only accepted art as a successful fiction, backed by art institutions rather than by virtue of a particular history or individual success. For the same reason, it was soon impossible to speak of the end of art, since any end only can happen within an established framework of history. What therefore was believed to have ended was that very concept of history which allowed an end to happen. Where such a concept was missing, also any discourse of ends, maturity, or beginnings collapsed. Whereas Hegel envisaged a possible end in art while simultaneously establishing the discourse of art history on a new level, today we rather contemplate the end of a linear history of art, since art has meanwhile taken leave of the bounds of a history of its own.

In the sixties, artists like Donald Judd challenged traditional art genres by speaking of "specific objects," that is, objects, not sculptures: specific to these objects was their context in which they were presented as art. At the opposite end, but at the same time, the conceptual artists devised art by ideas rather than in palpable works, thus taking leave from the work as a safe entity in art's embodiment. Instead of producing works that always leave traces of a given moment in history, artists now were inclined to perform with their own body, which only permitted an ephemeral presence in an exhibition. Such activities not only dematerialized works in their traditional profile but dissolved the concept of history, at least in its born materials and testimonies. Events, or happenings, did not allow for the same objectivated kind of memory or trace of history, as did works of art in the old sense.

Allan Kaprow, who had earned his living by teaching art history in a college, forced all attention to the art environment which in a way took over (or replaced) the experience of art properly speaking: an environment that turned the former visitors of an exhibition into active participants. At the same time, he admonished artists to create the *context of art* rather than art in the old sense. Installation inaugurated a space where viewers became active themselves. Installations are ephemeral by definition and thus only survive in books that record past events instead of describing art history in the old sense, in the sense of a logic evident from surviving material evidence.

In his book *The Anxious Object,* Harold Rosenberg in 1964 describes the "aesthetics of impermanence" and discusses art's temporality while taking shape in transient materials. "The short-lived work of art, as dramatized by Tinguely in his self-destroying *Sculpture,* stages art as an event." And again, "The aesthetics of impermanence turned the work of art into an interval in the artist's life and in that of the viewer as well." Rosenberg then was still under the spell of the spectacle that Jean Tinguely performed on March 17, 1960, in the sculpture garden of the Museum of Modern Art in New York (fig. 44). A fantastic machine parody, composed of pieces of scrap metal, painted white, and titled *Homage to New York,* took half an hour to set itself on fire with an ear-splitting din and to disintegrate into meta-scrap, while two painting machines, called "Meta-Matics," went on producing paintings that were immediately consumed by the flames. The choicest remains were given to the museum, but the action itself, with its half-ironic, half-poetic, kinetic extravagance, survived only in photographs or in the personal memories of the participants. The happening denigrated the essence of the work of art and counteracted the working process by an inversed

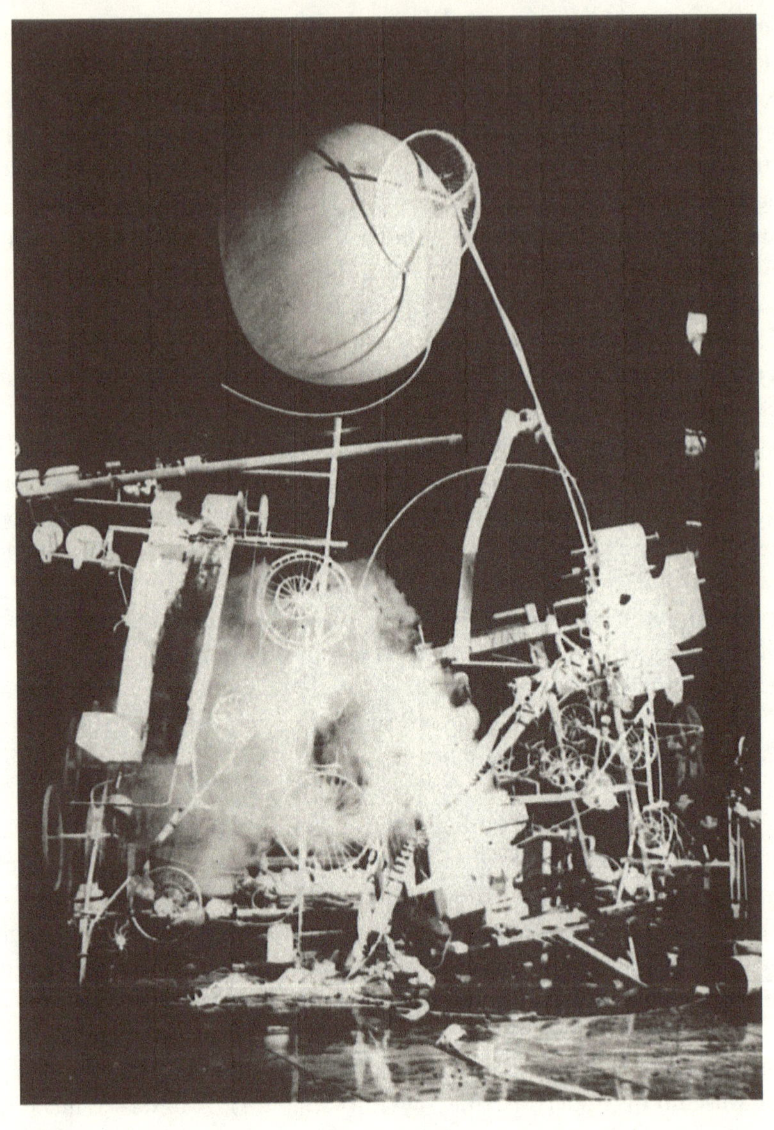

44. Jean Tinguely, *Homage to New York,* March 17, 1960. Museum of Modern Art, New York. © 2002 Artists Rights Society (ARS), New York / ADAGP, Paris.

symmetry. "L'art ephemère," as the battle cry went, invaded the venerable temple of modernist art as in a sudden attack.

Rosenberg may have wavered between fascination and doubt. But when he finally decided to criticize such phenomena, his clear-sighted observations did not receive the attention they deserved; for he noticed that visual art and metaphorical, quasi-verbal performance were approaching each other by an increasing interaction. This also demolished, as he said, the safe borderline between an art that plunges into actions and an art criticism that comments on these actions. "By circulating an event in art history, painting sheds its material body: it takes on an astral body ubiquitous in art books, in catalogues, TV, and films, as well as in the text of art writers . . . and which exists in accordance with the frequency of its public mention, that is, in dependence on time." This view allows me to proceed further in the discussion of what art history as a written genre can be after modernism when art no longer lives from works that have an independent existence (even if in dark storerooms) but rather casts an impermeable net of record and description over fleeting facts and data that only survive in texts. Temporality and textuality approach each other, after we no longer have access to works that remain present as reified symbols of their momentum in history.

In his essay "The Open Opus" (Opera aperta), Umberto Eco already in 1962 described the new situation of the work of art as moving into unpredictable directions that no longer offer us a firm viewing point. The work, whose existence he still took for granted, acquires "the ability to kaleidoscopically transform itself in the eye of the beholder," thus involving the viewer personally in creating aesthetic experience. With equal justification, we could meanwhile speak of an "open discourse" in which texts about art transmute into an art of texts. In this sense, Paola Fonticoli introduced Achille Bonito Oliva as the protagonist of a new art of criticism, "La critica d'arte come arte della critica," as her title says. The critic seems to adopt a role similar to the performer of music, in the sense that he or she now is the one making the music; yet, unlike the musician, the critic does not use a score but instead writes the score of how artists are to be presented and how they are to be understood. The critic also selects such works or artists that will illustrate his favored type of criticism. This is what Olivo did, when he hunted for artists of his own choice. First, he coined the term "neo-avant-garde," and, later, in 1980, the concept of the Italian "trans-avant-garde," in a book with the respective title. On the cover of his next book, entitled *The Dream of Art: Between Avant-garde and Trans-avant-garde*, he smiles out of his portrait by Sandro Chia as if staging not merely as the author but also as the hero of the book (fig. 6 above). The earlier book states that art has "finally" found its truest themes and "returned" to its true destiny, the labyrinth of imagination and myth, which also meant that social and moral issues no longer mattered. Oliva maintained that the "creative practice" had carried off the victory over all censorship and over a discourse dominated by the American media critics or guardians of art, thus permitting an intuitive painting of a new kind. It is with the confidence of a self-fulfilling prophecy that he describes and defines what matters in art.

For the same purpose he grandly dismisses the *Arte povera* of the Sixties as "repressive and masochistic," thus contradicting the position of Germano Celant, his opponent. Celant, in his famous catalog of *Art Povera* (*sic*), makes the confession of "not trying to be objective," since such intentions would be tantamount to "false consciousness." His concept for *Arte povera*, he declared, was just a "work among other works," as they were made by artists. As the chosen term was arbitrary and possibly marginal, he noted, he might exchange it any time for terms such as "concept art" or "anti-form," in which case he would, as early as tomorrow, write a new and different book about the same subject. The aphorisms that introduce the book in their poetic language not only are considered as being art in the first place but also claim to be free from the baggage of history, which means that the course of contemporary art could be rewritten at leisure and at any moment in any possible ways (fig. 5 above).

The coexistence of concepts of art that, in principle, are mutually exclusive, no longer is seen as an exception or even as a problem. In one current, works disappear behind ideas or else within "objects," while in another current works return with almost mythic ambitions. While a technological art tends to recede into what Paul Virilio calls the "aesthetics of vanishing," in another current the cult of the art material continues to be practiced with almost archaic confidence. Documenta exhibitions repeatedly aim to establish a main current of contemporary art but contradict themselves by their continuing free choice against all expectation to the contrary. It is not enough to describe the situation as pluralism, since even pluralism lived from the opposite experience of a preexisting and expected unity of art. What happens in the art world only makes sense after it is written about with the professional urge to provide a personel vision rather than information.

Western culture after modernism offers a sight similar to the experience of ethnic cultures that Claude Lévi-Strauss, in his *Tristes tropiques,* describes as the experience of being left alone with nothing but one's own view of something very alien. In the early seventies, the small, mainly French movement called *Spurensicherung* (securing traces) was characterized by Günther Metken in his synonymous book as the artists' search for "anthropology and self-discovery" (fig. 45). In their hands, the heritage of art history, which once had presented a canon for collective memory, changed into an occasion for a personal archaeology. Thus emerged "a multitude of personal museums, which taken together make up a new *Musée de l'Homme*—but a museum without history." Historical forms thus were transformed into fictions including the fiction that it was possible to appropriate everything by personal memory.

Where art history was exhausted as a continuing task or mission of living artists, it resurfaced as an ubiquitous hallucination providing an inexhaustible reservoir for reappropriation in a very personal way. The so called "Art after art"—movement in the Seventies was the main stage for *playing* or pretending art history without any longer *being* in art history. Old Picasso, who even ended up deconstructing his own former oeuvre, in a way anticipated this movement, which however only went public in 1971 with a Lugano exhibition titled *D'Après.* At the occasion of this show, Giancarlo Vigorelli asked the question whether we have to admit that "we have become ourselves a mere choice of copies, reprints, and imitates." The *D'Après* attitude did not mean producing copies after old art, but implied the intention to make art by the mere act of quoting art and by borrowing art's claim from acknowledged models where such a claim was guaranteed.

The 1978 Whitney exhibition *Art about Art* was hastily put in line in the catalog by Leo Steinberg. The author. as was to be expected, deliberately turns the tables and insists that artists at all times had copied, outdone, and corrected each other. He could even make use of the materials collected by K. E. Mason in his book, titled *Themes and Variations,* a rich choice of old paintings together with their old copies. This was temptation enough for a virtuoso like Steinberg to trace what has to be called an *epiphenomenon* back to an old *phenomenon* and thus to celebrate a totally coherent history of art in which even the old masters seem to have taken a postmodern position. But an objection may be raised. The quotation exercises in art after modernism operate from a position beyond art history and reveal the experience of a loss. Such art as they are quoting, appears as a "belle captive" that hides somewhere in the depth of history and only allows the nostalgic view of what

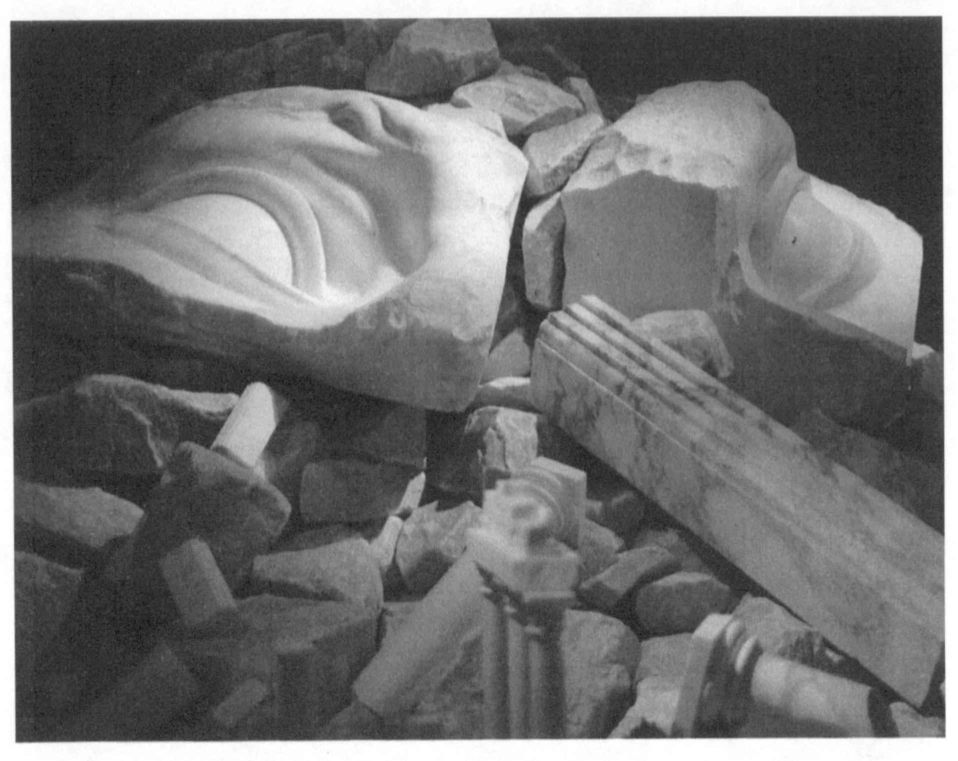

45. Anne and Patrick Poirer, *The Death of the Giant Enkclades*, assemblage, 1983. Venice Biennale, 1984. © 2002 Artists Rights Society (ARS), New York / ADAGP, Paris.

has been and is no longer. Art history comes here into play as a topic of memory and no longer as a task to be taken further. In such a mood, Arwed D. Gorella called a picture *The Geometry of Memory.*

The *D'Après* that appears in the title of the Lugano exhibition also makes a confession. Not only artists seem to live in a time after, which means in a time after art history in which art embarks on a posthistory of finite possibilities and reacts with infinite and sometimes arbitrary applications. It is not that I consider the so-called *quotation art* as the most important movement of its time, but it offers symptoms that relate to my argument. A few years earlier, such a movement would have appeared unacceptable because not understandable, while later the same movement did not appear any longer original, since its aims became commonplace. My argument also relates to the discussion of the continuity of painting, as painting most visibly represents a site either of memories or of changes. Even the Whitney exhibition mentioned above was intended to promote a "new image-painting," in which Philip Guston set the tone. Three years later, the Royal Academy in London housed the exhibition *New Spirit of Painting.* The suggestive title revealed the desire to discover a new power of painting and to promote neo-expressionism as the spirit of the age. But such attempts proved short-lived and also fell victim to the uncertainty of any concepts of history as concepts of time.

Some years later, Harald Szeemann mounted an exhibition not of painting but of monumental sculpture at the German site of the same exhibition that had migrated from London to Berlin. This time, the title was *Zeitlos* (Timeless), as if a block of stone in a quasi-sacred space could prove that all great art is timeless. The material favored an all-too-easy idea of art's autonomy in a poetic zone, and this against the evidence of video and video installations which at the same time had introduced a most ephemeral experience of art, an art representing the dynamism of a hypermodernity, as Marc Augé called the late twentieth century. But even such objections miss the point when they serve the hope that art will ever recover a position in which it defies change and doubt. Where there no longer appears anything never seen and radically new, there also nothing can really grow old and thus need to be replaced once and forever. The slogans surrounding the concept of time in the Eighties and Nineties appear like gestures of protest against the feeling of loss that took hold of the discourse of art history.

What books about art did not elucidate was instead entrusted to spectacular exhibitions, which, however, served other needs. The Amsterdam exhibition of 1984, borrowing its title *La grande parade* from a picture by Fernand Léger, presented "Highlights in Painting after 1940" in a panoramic view that did not intend to describe "an art-historical evolution." The aim, rather, was to deliver "a contrasting picture of sometimes irreconcilable attitudes of mind" and thus to "represent painterly imagination" regardless of the painters' position in history but with reference to the personal taste of Edy de Wilde, who as director of the Stedelijk Museum then went into retirement. In a similar spirit, Pontus Hulten mounted the 1992 exhibition in Bonn, whose title *Territorium Artis* indicated a kind of personal playground for the curator where he had assembled his favored "masterpieces" from modernism without any longer respecting the "calls for order" valid in modernism.

Such projects appear in open contradiction to the growing expectation of the general audience to receive information about the state of art in retrospective exhibitions rather than in books: in exhibitions that lived from unexpected discoveries but were expected to represent a truth more reliable than the personal view of an art historian as book author. In addition, works as they were shown in such exhibitions were not merely records of past events, leftovers that allowed memories of past modernism but were themselves "historical bodies" created by modernism. At any time they might cause us to change our view of what had happened and how it was to be seen. They seemed to embody a secret and not yet completely deciphered message or index of modernism, which defeated any rigid concept of art's "evolution" and therefore could be studied and restudied with a curiosity no longer dedicated to written texts with their inevitably past interpretation. This accounts for the ambivalence that lives in exhibitions of this kind, an ambivalence in repudiating and equally in confirming the pattern of history even in modernist art.

But the skepticism looms large in any retrospective view on modernism as soon as the latter appeared as something that ended forever. In this sense, art suffered the same crisis as history, understood as a binding authority and continuing model. The connection with the discourse of "posthistory" may help us to elucidate the peculiar situation that characterizes art history after modernism. This connection was made for the first time by Arnold Gehlen, who had introduced the discourse of "posthistory" in Germany. In his book titled *Zeitbilder* (Images of time), he predicted: "From now on there can be no longer any development in art that is art's own development. Any somehow meaningful art history is over and done with. What is to come, already has happened: the syncretism of a mess of all sorts of styles and possibilities—Posthistoire." In 1960, this was a daring statement, however prophetic it may seem in retrospect. For the left, who only felt disillusioned with history much later and who promptly discovered their own posthistoire, Gehlen's view came from a conservative and therefore unacceptable side. Wolf Lepenies however already in 1969 made use of an argument by Claude Lévi-Strauss who in his book *Le Pensée sauvage* from 1962 described tinkering *(bricolage)* as a model for posthistory. For the tinkerers, "the world of their means is limited, and the rules of their games tell them to manage with what is on hand."

Arnold Gehlen voiced similar views in favor of "cultural crystallization" in 1963. "I am venturing the prediction that the history of ideas is over." He therefore reminded his readers of Gottfried Benn's dictum that one should "count on the inventory." This is why Gehlen speaks of a world that no longer offers any surprise: "The alternatives are known, as they are in religion, and they are in any sense final." It may be, however, argued that "such an end to history is as an artifact of thought" when measured against real history, as Lutz Niethammer put it. It is a genuinely Western preoccupation to take refuge in a new idea that serves to compensate for the loss of an old idea such as progress. Even the loss generated a new law when it provided an occasion for contemplating history in a situation after history. "Posthistory" in turn depends on a basically modern concept of "history" which equally is or was an artifact of thought or a device for constructing identity.

One may even go so far as regarding "history" as a concept for compensating the loss of history in the old sense which the nineteenth century felt had irretrievably occurred with the French revolution. Much the same may be said about the contemplation of "art history" as a new type of discourse that goes back to the early days of the "museum age." It seems that, also in this respect, we have reached a situation of no return and thus must reconsider the rules of the game we call "art history" without necessarily rejecting the canon that is inscribed in the collected knowledge inherited from the practice of the respective discipline. And, finally, we must acknowledge the rights of other national or cultural traditions to change the unilateral view on one type, or chronology, of art in one frame of art history that too long deserves the privilege of a master discourse.

An experience of living after the end of history liberates the artists and fetters the historians, as the former respond to such an experience with new creative energy, while the latter can do nothing but memorize a lost game that they only may comment upon. The artists continue to make art, even if their work often may look as a ritual of memory, and thus perpetuate the old game, as they may feel free to expand their own concept of art beyond the one-time obsession with progress that moved the avant-garde. In retrospect, the assumption that traditional art always resulted in inventions and innovations looks like an undeserved myth. This is what caused the fear of being left with nothing but imitation, as if any link with tradition necessarily would end in epigonism. Progress, in turn, often was nothing but the dutiful repetition of the creative act which was a peculiar obedience to history. It thus ultimately contradicted the resistance against history which only served the impulse not to copy history. History, in the view of the avant-garde, seemed to take a linear course of continuous change and upheaval but not to allow any attempt to recreate or to redefine progress. Such a misconception also was responsible for reinventing the reason for art at any time, as if no art or only wrong art had existed before.

In this respect, the difference that today dominates thinking after modernism is obvious. The need for proclaiming yesterday's new to be today's old and exchanging it for anything yet newer has weakened. And there emerges the insight that art cannot be constantly reinvented the way any single work of art can be newly invented. On the contrary, it needs the concept of art for creating new works in the first place. Art has no independent truth unless we are talking of general aesthetics or metaphysical concerns which however reach beyond the bounds of art. Duchamp in his own days could afford to be at variance with a ruling idea in art that has however since dissolved. Today we are no longer left with the urge and with the possibility of breaking the mirror we call art history, as we no longer are in a position to replace this mirror easily.

Innovation, nevertheless, remains an ideal that however is too hastily pursued by merely escaping into other media. A video installation, to give just one example, may even quote painting without being accused of imitation. Today, the new already seems to happen by changing the medium instead of choosing innovation in substance. Video artists, to give again an example, may address topical issues of their society, which would be inaccessible for gallery art of the traditional kind.

But there is still another side to this. Art in posthistory often seems to happen by turning technology into art, in which case art allows for an imagination that one could call meta-technological. It does not seem that a post-technological age is in reach, even if technology looks meanwhile back to a history of its own which makes possible a kind of archeology. When Nam June Paik started to use TV items for his earliest installations, he already worked with still earlier TV sets that had gone out of use, thus turning around the claim of technology to look intentionally new and to invite for immediate usage. Instead he shifted the attention to a kind of history in technology where the latter had become available for memory. It may be that even technological tools allow the artist to apply personal expression much as he had done with paintbrush and palette. At least, it may be hoped that technology does not remain the last word in posthistory.

19 "Prospero's Books"

Technology and art in the meanwhile interact in new ways, in which tradition, as subject or topic, and mediality differ from each other and are played out against each other. For this symbiosis, a film from the early nineties may serve as an example. When Peter Greenaway choose Shakespeare's *The Tempest*, a venerable masterpiece of classical literature, as his subject, he nevertheless did not hesitate to introduce recent electronic technology and even to digitalize the film in such a way that it accepted a new appearance. This is the film he called *Prospero's Books*. In the accompanying publication he describes the "graphic paint box" as follows: "This machine combines the vocabulary of electronic image control with the art of pen-and-ink, paintbrush, and palette, so that it allows as personal a signature as they do." He added that the new procedure resembles and yet goes beyond the technique of collage.

Greenaway used the same technology to produce independent images that are taken from the film but transform the film's motifs and thus do not resemble film stills properly speaking. One such case is the "electronic collage" of a mythical being with a double body that Greenaway called Janus, the double-headed god who was able to look back into the past and forward into the future (fig. 46). In Greenaway's application, the figure resembles and, in a way, doubles the court dwarf of the Medici in the Boboli Gardens in Florence who, in the same collage, appears as emblem in its original appearance and not yet altered as a standing double figure, which Greenaway constructed with the help of the new technology. In the upper part, Shakespeare's air sprite Ariel looks out of a window in the Vittoriano at Rome as if he wanted to sneak through the title vignette into a book from Shakespeare's age. A Latin text running across the two bodies completes the hybrid of book and image.

It is significant that this Janus does not form a part of the film at all but belongs to the TV production called *A Walk trough Prospero's Library*, in which Greenaway reprocessed his own earlier film. The intention now was to introduce the mythological and historical characters of the "magic books" in Prospero's possession. Greenaway thus invented a new type of commentary. The artist commented on his own film in an

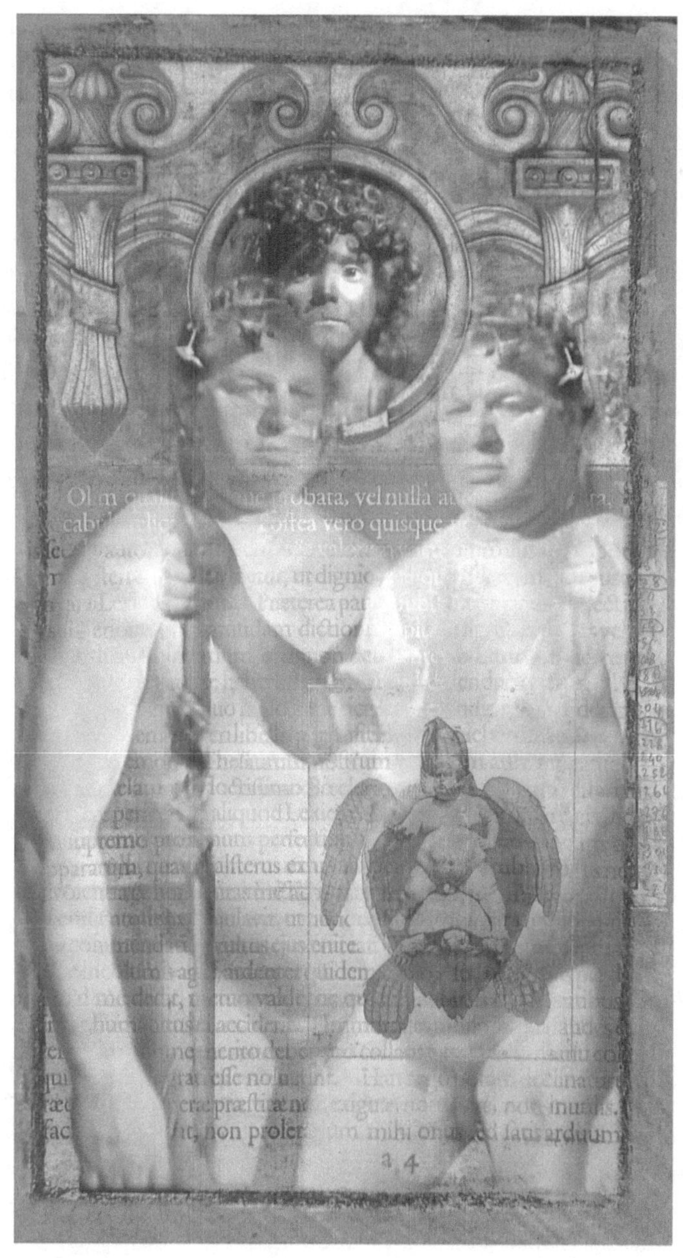

46. Peter Greenaway, *Janus*, 1992. High-Definition-Electronic Paintbox in Japan. Motius from the Boboli Gardens Fatman Turtle-Taxi.

accompanying book as well as in a supplementary video, probably preoccupied by the problem that he might have overtaxed the public's familiarity with a historical issue. Culture no longer seems to be able to mediate itself but demands commentaries to make up for the difficult access to its heritage.

But the video epilogue is not merely a commentary but also a continuation of the film with other artistic means and in other genres. Greenaway had still not reached the end of his metamorphic procedure when he was asked to device a new type of exhibition for the Biennial at Venice in 1993 (chapter 11). Here, the same video surprisingly appeared in the center of an installation which simultaneously turned into an exhibition. On this occasion, the so-called "original books" from the main film were displayed like props from a living theatre stage and thus offered a most confusing "memory" of the film as if the latter was of a quite different genre. The whole took place in the gothic palace from whose dark walls were flashing "television windows," as Greenaway called these hybrids of window and painting. One of them was "Janus," who in a large ektachrome as if behind an electronic window offered the distant view of an amalgam of many-layered cultural memories.

In his film *Prospero's Books* , Greenaway wanted to test the "visual literacies" which live in electronic technology, much as Shakespeare, so he wrote, developed a new language for the stage. The literacy in this case remains strictly linked to the text that Greenaway transforms into narrative and visuality, just as Prospero, the aged magician in island exile, animated the characters by the spoken word. Technology serves as a magic tool that brings the text to a new and unexpected life: but it is still the text, not the digital magic, that makes the play. Also Shakespeare makes us think of the books that Prospero was allowed to take along when going into exile. We thus are referred to another medium but Shakespeare does not reveal which kind of books Prospero owned. He only speaks of "volumes that I prize above my [lost] dukedom." This is the point where Greenaway begins to speculate. He invents twenty-four books, Prospero's Books, that represent a past culture, a baroque culture obsessed with books.

Art history is absent among these books, as is to be expected of literature from the seventeenth century, but ruins are the subject of the twentieth volume and thus refer us to past cultures. The whole film draws on the "essential and inevitable encyclopedia" characteristic of culture, as Greenaway maintains: on an encyclopedia of painters and architects who quoted and commented on each other. But Prospero, as Greenaway explains in the book, was a hidden self-portrait of Shakespeare, who in his late drama created a world of illusions, with other words, art. The inspiration for the film came from the aged Shakespearean actor John Gielgud, who performs not only the main character but also speaks other texts as well. We see Prospero in a setting (fig. 47) which shows him in his studio, where he looks up from the book of traveler's tales and animates the creatures of his imagination, that we see in a mirror, thus calling them into the life of art. There are many "cross-identifications" between Shakespeare and Prospero that now extend to Greenaway.

The homesick Prospero, as Greenaway tells us in his commentary, tends to interpret the island exile in the light of images of memory which bring back the culture of distant Italy. This may be called a metaphor of the "English Renaissance," which however accepts quite a new and contemporary meaning. In the original drama, the actor also played the director, who, by his mise-en-scène, even invented the plot. In the film, the hero also is the narrator who creates a world of illusion while speaking the script of the play. This superimposition of text and plot may remind us that there is no story that requires more than a single narrator, as we read in Jorge Louis Borges's short novel *Averrhoes's Search.* But it needs a narrative in order to interpret the world which would be meaningless without the help of a text.

The world as described in Prospero's encyclopedic books in a way resembles the computerized world, which today forms our "Ersatzwelt." The books did not only have a text but also contained illustrations and diagrams, which Greenaway revives in his film, though never abandoning the relation to a text that thus also serves as a hypertext. The words Prospero writes down generate all their inherent images which turn up in the film. The old illustrations of fauna and flora in the film turn into living examples, which however, while we see them in the film, fall back into cinematic images. The surface of a book page, which is repeatedly blended into the film scene, reminds us that even the film is but a new kind of illustration.

The filmic frame and the book page refer to each other whenever the films actors as living bodies build up a frame, much as the title pages of the old books were organized with a frame of figuration and ornament. The cinematic ornament emerges out of the symmetrical dance of their bodies. Immediately after, they move in the film between book and stage, since the page is backed by a stable stage that also serves as a library. The camera moves back and forth between a view of a book and a view of a stage. The film not only imitates text and theater but also develops a mise-en-scène with new filmic and digital means. No matter how much

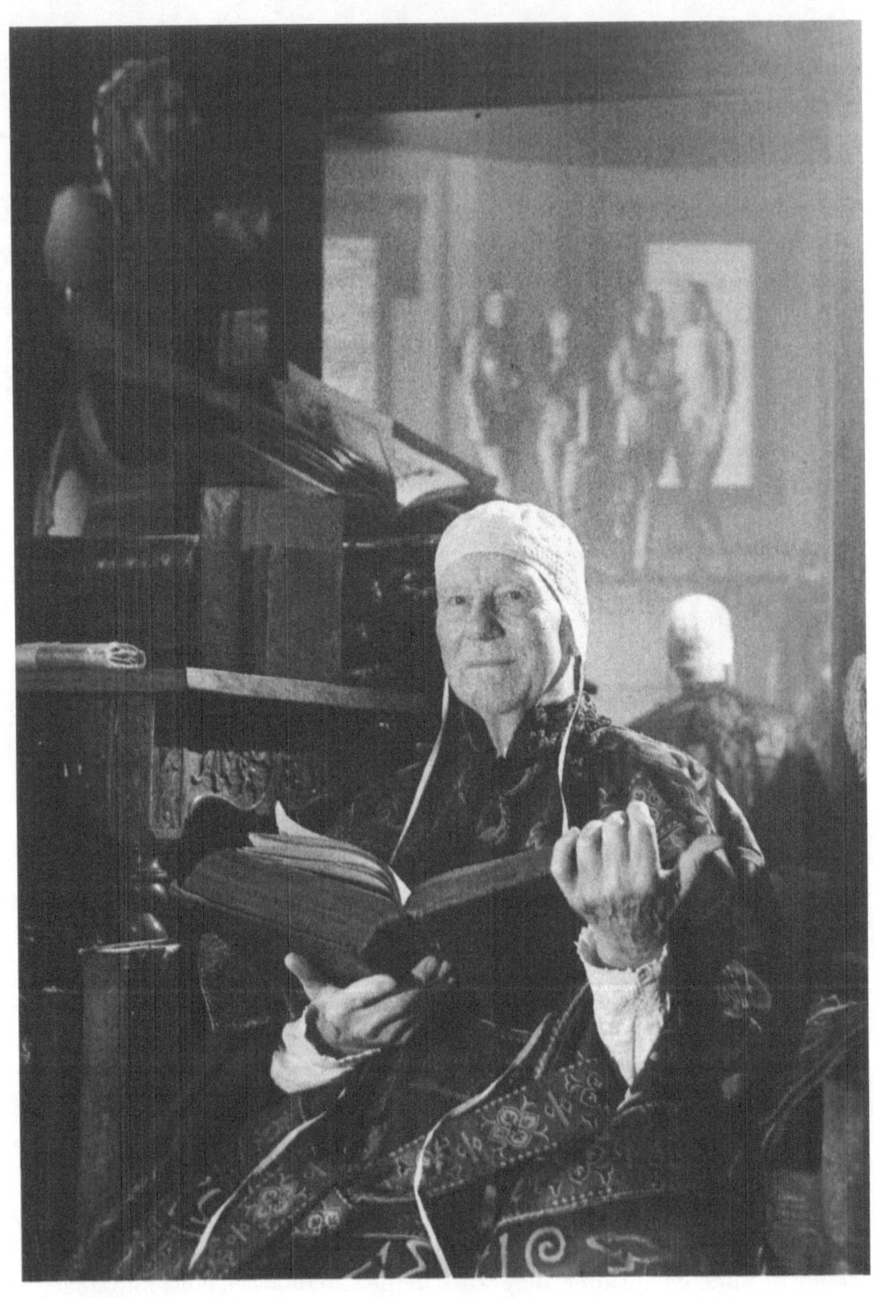

47. John Gielgud, movie still from Peter Greenaway, *Prospero's Books: A Film of Shakespeare's* The Tempest (London, 1991), 119.

reality the film captures, it remains a new type of play that lives from a new type of fiction. While other films are based on a screenplay that they make us forget, Greenaway's film performs and represents a text that also may be understood as a visible screenplay. At the end, when the reconciliation begins, the books have served their purpose, and the characters begin to speak. At this point of the story, the used-up books are being burned or drowned, until Prospero appears in close-up in front of the curtain and speaks Shakespeare's famous epilogue.

In his commentary, Greenaway repeatedly, and with a certain obsession, speaks of the problem of the frame. He would like to dispense with it and liberate us from the frame, which not only closes up its images but also restricts our vision. In his outdoor exhibitions, in which he wants us to step out of the cinema, he however needs to introduce a certain kind of frame once again. In my own essay, the narrative called art history forms a historical frame in which everything has assumed a "framed" and thus limited meaning. As we know, frame and image entertain ever new relations. Images need a frame in order to become images, just as a frame needs images to serve as a frame. But Greenaway describes Prospero's island as a world "full of retreating mirrors and mirror images. All the images that rise from the text, become as dizzyingly real as objects, facts, and events" when they seek their frame. We cannot help noticing that "everything consists of illusion, and is so continually fitted into a rectangle, a picture frame, a film image."

In the Venice exhibition *Watching Water* in which Janus was staged by an electronic window, Greenaway offered an imaginary dialogue not with Shakespeare, but with the Spanish artist Mario Fortuny (1871–1949), the sometime owner of the palazzo and the collector of that chaotic ensemble of costumes, pictures, and props of all kind that Greenaway brilliantly restaged with filmic means, that is, with film lighting. Fortuny was a man of the theater, creating costumes and lighting and, like Greenaway, had been a painter and a mind obsessed with culture. This constellation favored a secret conspiracy between the one and the other that inspired the unusual act of a filmic mise en-scène in the center of a collection, while the audience felt that they participated in a nonexistent film. In a small booklet that Greenaway wrote as introduction of this exhibition, he suggested that it would have appealed to Fortuny to move "in and out of history," as was the case with the strange collage of exhibition and nonfilm. Fortuny "took the historical quote so serious, as it must be taken in any cultural context."

20 Marco Polo and Other Cultures

This final chapter was originally written for another occasion, but the implication of its topic for the theme of the book will become apparent at once. The coexistence of non-Western art in the contemporary art scene has reached great importance within the two last decades, as can be seen from the newly emerging Biennials around the world. Thus art history, in its most recent application, can no longer neglect this situation. On the other hand, more attention is not enough, as it needs an engaging discourse to deal with such phenomena. It goes without saying that a discourse that integrates the new topic is not at hand. It cannot be invented at will, since art history, which one may call a peculiar artifact of thinking, has developed over a long span of time and within traditions of its own. It may be sufficient to state this embarrassing constellation and thus to confront art history with the present tense, which means with a new situation in the world.

The relevance of this topic will be emphasized in the context of primitivism. It was 1984 that William Rubin in his famous exhibition *Primitivism and 20th Century Art* for the last time concentrated on the old issue of "influence" of the so-called primitive on early modernism. Five years later, Jean-Hubert Martin for the first time presented the new panorama of Western and non-Western contemporary art in his two Paris exhibitions of 1989. He called them *Magiciens de la Terre* and permitted for each artist only the name, subject, and the date of a work. "Magician" was a cover name for avoiding the label of "artist" for members of such cultures where artist could not be defined with any degree of certainty. The connection with the topic of art history is obvious, since the claim to be an artist traditionally depended on the possibility of finding a place or his/her place in any history of art deserving this name. Some may wish to substitute the master narrative of a unified Western art history with universal claims, but the matter is not exhausted with such easy escapes. My book can only offer its implications and thus remain in a very tentative position in the face of the impossibility to aim at final answers.

CENTER AND PERIPHERY

In Italo Calvino's novel *The Invisible Cities,* the Venetian traveler Marco Polo converses with the Mongol ruler in the Imperial Gardens of China, always circling the question how to describe the world, or more precisely, the cities of the vast Mongol empire through which Marco Polo had passed. Finally, "Kubla Khan noticed that Marco Polo's cities all resembled each other" and, in fact, were practically interchangeable. Only later did he realize the reason for that similarity. Marco Polo never named the city he always had in mind, but confessed it freely when asked. "Every time I describe a city to you, I am talking about Venice."

When the historical Marco Polo wrote his *Travels,* he wrote for Venice, not about it. He wanted to impress upon his readers that he was describing a world they neither knew or could conceive of. But the exoticism that was already popular in the Middle Ages was merely the other side of the same coin. The exotic, as the completely other, made it possible that, seen from Venice, everything looked different. The relation between center and periphery, so much discussed today, has hardly changed since then despite all our experience of colonialism and postcolonialism. Today we can travel the world at lightning speed and summon distant lands into our homes at the push of a button. But does that mean that we understand the world any better? Or is the "electronic superhighway," of which the modern Marco Polo, Nam June Paik, speaks with such enthusiasm, merely another road paved with old prejudices, prejudices we can no more shake off than we can shed our selves?

The dialogue between cultures has become an occasion for surpassing one another in understanding the "other," whom one thus excludes from one's own world. The very harmony in this behavior however is a matter of fiction. The holy spirit, as in the Biblical Pentecost, would occur only if the modern apostles would speak in different tongues, instead of using only the single tongue of the world-dominating media, which, outside the West, can only be foreign language. But such a metaphor is deficient, as it is not the point to preach a single faith to the world—in our case, a faith in a global modernism in the name of Western art considered as a universal art. Socialism's attempt at another kind of globalism already failed, as long as it strove for power (if only the power of its ideology). Today we are trained in a remorseful idealism that willingly seems to submit to other cultures in the name of a polycentrism of cultures that is to compensate for the equality that was betrayed and lost.

The "rhetoric of universalism," as Hans Magnus Enzensberger calls it, is defective, since in Western use it would be only a liberal variant of the old hegemony. There is no universal way of thinking to accommodate the multiplicity of cultures, because every thinking is culturally coded, particularly in the West, where we still believe that the only justification to guide the other cultures is to have invented the idea of humanity. But the old division of the world was an act dear to both sides, since it allowed each to measure its own reality against an imaginary counterpart, thus permitting each the experience of itself. In his book on symbolic exchange, Jean Baudrillard makes the illuminating point that "the peoples of the Third World form the imaginary side of Western culture," and vice versa. The cultural prison in which the West took refuge is also revealed by Western practices of exhibition: their type of presenting other cultures subordinates them to a Western concept of art. We applaud when the result is satisfactory and forgive when it is not. But we consider "art" a transcultural matter against which all cultures can be measured under the same heading. Though we meanwhile are used to a climate of self-critical discussion or self-pity in which the catchphrases are right at hand, this long-trained practice sometimes pretends to know less than we meanwhile do. We cannot free ourselves from it, if only for the reason that with it we perform the idiosyncrasies of our own culture.

Sometimes we hope to find a way out of the dilemma by giving contemporary artists from other cultures credit for their different position in history. But here, too, the initiative is ours, and it is our view that is pseudo-benevolent. Whether we practice universalism or ghettoization, we cannot avoid taking a Western point of view also where non-Western art is exhibited in the West. Precisely for this reason, we must ask ourselves whether the art of other cultures (whether welcomed as exotic strangers or as members of the contemporary art scene) can be meaningfully represented in our institutions, which means translating them into our own culture. The problem does not disappear when one attempts to escape the art market. We prefer artists from other cultures when they already live in the West and have become successful in the Western art scene.

THE ART SCENE AS A PRODUCT OF SECULARIZATION

What about the much-discussed topic of "decontextualization"? Does it mean that we deprive non-Western artists of their own context when we exhibit them in our context? We cannot suggest that they arrive with their own context and exhibit their works in an improvised

Western enclave. We do not even know whether they still possess their own context at home. It is far more likely that they are already working for an art market that reproduces that of the West, whereby they have lost much and gained little. They incidentally are competing for an art market that we have long doubted to be still as vital, crisis-free, and unequivocally legitimate as foreign cultures may hope.

We could go one step further and concede that other cultures are now where we arrived more than two hundred years ago. At that time, the newly created art scene was a refuge for any art that had just lost its former context. It offered a substitute for the old context, in which art still had retained a living function. Churches and castles were turned into museums. A modicum of historical awareness thus rapidly relativizes the topical antithesis dividing the West from the rest of the world. Today's art scene was at that time nothing other than the product of a secularization that now has reached many other cultures. Items that find their way into the museums are already alienated from their original context, just as, conversely, a defunct culture can be recollected only in a museum of objects or in a descriptive literature—unless it is perpetuated in a (compensatory) ritual of so-called artistic recreation, which always embodies a kind of epilogue in a culture. This characterizes our own modern age, which embarked as much upon the memory of its past as it tended to liberate itself from such concerns and thus developed a view of distance: the distance from its own culture, its religion, and its myths.

But in the West we are dealing with a process that took centuries to run its course. This means that Western modernity, spread throughout the world by colonialism, can hardly provide a readymade solution for other cultures. If we take this idea at all seriously, we are compelled to draw the utopian conclusion that other cultures should produce their own modernity and bring forth a cultural alternative compatible with secularization, but not its Western simile. Only then could they create a new context for their own traditions and travel their own road to modernity. But for this, they lack the economic and social structures (and sometimes their own cultural heritage long ago annexed by the West, to the degree that it is material). The shadow of the West, inescapable for the time being, lies over them. Since no ready solution serving this part of the world is forthcoming, the West is left with a paradoxical responsibility for events that we should not and cannot control. In the same way, modernization, however gratefully the "others" may welcome it as an aid for their development, has so far amounted to colonialism in the guise of culture.

MODERNISM AND PRIMITIVISM

Modernism and primitivism, however intrinsically opposed they might be, nonetheless remain an inseparable pair of concepts. That is why we are so easily confused by art from other cultures that is obviously modern but equally obviously does not belong to our own history of art. If, rather than remaining authentic and archaic, such a society emulates modernism as if "illegitimately" (for only a society whose development is very advanced appears modern), we categorize it as hybrid. Even our concept of "art" is the product of secularization and reflexivity that has learned to play with its own fictions. In retrospect, we have declared even our own premodern images to be art; but we find it easier to identify with an art that reflects the skepticism of the modern mind. Up to now many artistic media have kept ties to this premodern tradition and thus also retained the physicality of painting or sculpture. But we are dissolving this presence in the virtual world of the electronic media. Western technology is, by the way, equally accessible to other cultures. Wherever the economic power constellation permits, former cultural frontiers become permeable.

Primitivism once arose as a label for a loss, for which compensation was sought in other cultures. Far from being a term of abuse, it is clogged with nostalgia. The Enlightenment age created the myth of the "noble savage," whom one welcomed in an idealized humanity. There was still no wish that he should be capable of producing art. Art was regarded as a Western priority for which only the West owned a proper ideal. Not even premodern Western art would satisfy this ideal. That is why initially the term "primitive" was applied even to old Western art that nourished the nostalgia for a lost naiveté of painted religion. The more the concept of art expanded (thus also including pre-Renaissance Italian painters), the more one looked for " primitive artists" in other cultures, who succeeded each other in relation to the broadening panorama of world travel.

This paved the way for the dialectics that have determined the course of modern art ever since. Art created under the banner of the avant-garde was equally the symbol of progress and the source for a utopian return to the roots. Thus, the young Picasso and his friends wanted to reinvent modern art precisely by introducing masks from tribal art. And it was artists who, in defiance of the ethnologists, declared these artifacts to be the only "true" art. Today we have long accepted such early attempts of integrating the pictorial production of primitive cultures into the "vocabulary" of modern art.

Because it fell in love with its own nostalgia, Western modernism appropriated what it did not own. It had to choose between two irreconcilable views, either classifying non-Western art as ethnic material or, conversely, aestheticizing it so as to insert it seamlessly into a Western concept of art. Either art was identical with Western art or it served as the welcome evidence of creative humanity, in the sense that André Malraux dreamed of a world art purged of all content and thus permitting every comparison. The connection between the two alternatives is self-explanatory. The respective concept of art is one invented by modernism, just like the ethnological concept we distinguish from that of art. Equally modern is the doubt whether we have invented a new and better culture or if we have lost all culture: in our case, whether we have freed art to be itself or if art can from now on be found only elsewhere, in the paradise of an unspoiled culture. The concepts of modern and primitive art thus are closely related because of their very antithesis.

NEW BOUNDARIES

But this description no longer corresponds with the present. We live in a postcolonial age in which the questions change but we still lack answers. Until now, we insisted on the privileged position of studying the others. After they are now producing modern art of their own, they return our glance at their free will. They thereby seize on a privilege that casts doubt on the accustomed division of the world. Sometimes we react defensively, for example, when we refer to a postcolonial decadence in former colonies that we secretly measure against a precolonial innocence. We look at every derivative of the West with suspicion, not least because we feel guilty of having driven other cultures out of a golden age in which everything looked naïve, authentic, and archaic. This involves our fear of losing not only "the others" but also ourselves after having so convincingly defined ourselves in the light of their otherness.

But who exactly are these others, culturally speaking? We can no longer discover them in the colonies, so we speak of the "third world" or, more delicately, of "the South." But such definitions, however cruelly they may be confirmed by economic reality, contain a misconception when we apply them to the discourse on cultures. The respective distinctions usually define a deficit inherent in a non-Western development, a retarded modernization, which, however, cannot be reconciled with the nostalgia of "genuine cultures." Such discussions also tend to neglect the fundamental distinctions between ancient high cultures and mere tribal cultures. Such collective concepts confidently ignore the great variety of still-existing live cultures. We can also conceive of a situation in which a technologically and scientifically advanced country, such as South Korea, becomes culturally alienated from itself and thus neither Western nor "other." Culture is not a mere phantom, even if the West no longer respects it as much as we used to respect the nation, which we cherished as our own invention.

Having come this far, we must ask ourselves what sort of modernism it is we are talking of. The West has long since fled into a so-called "postmodernism" and questioned not only its own belief in progress but also its concept of art, thus permitting a self-criticism, which however is denied as critique by the "others." Modernism with its self-confidence is over. The continuing crisis of art in a broader sense also is a crisis of representation, meaning the representation of our own values and creeds. Polemically speaking only the institutions are still functioning with any confidence. So-called "mass-culture" long ago effaced the carefully guarded boundary between high culture and consumption; thus even art succumbs to a populist temptation to abolish all the privileges previously adorning the face of culture. This weakens the West's claim to be distinct from the "others" who were estimated to produce only folk culture.

The crisis of modernism has also become the crisis of a discourse in art history that celebrated evolution, tradition, and innovation within the autonomous and linear course of art. Thus, art's universal truth as embodied in its form has lost much of its credibility. While the global expansion of technology feeds on the belief in information and its economic use, things are different in art. In its own time, the Enlightenment age congratulated itself with a universally valid aesthetic whose language was understood all over the world. After the setbacks inflicted by national cultures, modernism returned to this early ideal as its prevailing claim. Today, even in the West, the universalism propagated in this ideal of art has revealed its lack of substance. Art is still a practice of personal autonomy to the degree that it can hold up against the constraints of the art market. But this practice no longer possesses any formal models from which we could read the autonomy of the artistic creation. Pluralism is the source of a new freedom that also expresses itself in resistance to standards of art that conform with the market. Since art, in the best sense, still allows self-expression for its participants, it is also subject to cultural limits, while the technical media spread anonymously and globally. The old universalism that fed the Western belief in art disappears in the new globalism of cultural difference. The doubt in a still-valid universal ideal of art also threatens the bastion from whose heights we looked down on other cultures that presented themselves in a mythic state of prehistorical delay. The historical model we possessed could not be transferred to distant, allegedly ahistorical societies. This is why artists who nostalgically continue cultivating local tradition seem just as suspect as those who assimilate unconditionally to the West, thus occupying modern positions. We do not seriously credit local genealogies of image production ("art") as compatible with art history of the Western type, though, to give an example, China and Japan possess older tradition of art literature and art collection than the West. Are these genealogies still viable or will they be annihilated by a misunderstood modernism? Perhaps they will survive in a transformation that we, with the compass of our practiced clichés, will not even recognize.

TWO SCENARIOS

Our speculations about art in other parts of the world are guided by experiences limited to the Western art scene. After all, "others" are other because they think differently about the same, in our case, about art. The Western art scene is like a scenario dominated by the art market. The scenario is quite different in countries such as Morocco or Syria, where art neither owns institutions of sufficient standing nor can rely on an audience that responds to a sufficient degree. New Biennials claim to professionalize and institutionalize local art, but they are still going a long way from creating a global art scene, which, when successful, would transform the Western scenario as well.

On the one hand, there is the Western art market, powerful but susceptible to crisis, on which established names rise and fall like stock prices. Here the "historical and art historical position" of a work often matters more than the uncertain issue of quality. Such a position is an effect of what we call art history. Content is usually less relevant, unless it adds aura to the professional profile of a given work. Leaving aesthetic considerations in a general sense aside, the mere professionalism is decided by an international art scene ruled by the hierarchy of names and prices. Here, any bonus given to non-Western art is suspect because it endangers the prevailing currency of art. Pluralism calls for an amount of good will or credits some art with the charm of naiveté, a quality prized mostly by small investors. Although we may celebrate universalism, we secretly prefer to keep such universalism under control, that is, under our own control.

And there is the other scenario that only allows for preliminary speculations. Art is still a new experience in other cultures and must still prove its proper claims. It is being exposed to questions of and answers on private and public issues which are relevant in a particular place. In underdeveloped countries, art will stir interest primarily when admitting confessions, taboo-breaking, or else renewing memories or forgotten traditions, the more political and economic agents manipulate and control the local media. Art thus may reclaim a free space that is not yet controlled by other interests, but it can do so only to the degree that such local art is not yet neutralized as a professional area of its own. In contrast to the global media network, individual art may recover a political role whose value cannot be assessed in terms of market prices.

Bibliography

1. EPILOGUES FOR ART OR FOR ART HISTORY?

Epilogues appear when we speak of the "end," as in the "end of art" or the "end of the avant-garde" or in constructions beginning with the prefix "post-"; but they also play a role in book titles such as *On the Museum's Ruins*, as formulated by Douglas Crimp (1993); see chapter 11. On the "end of the avant-garde," see chapter 13; on the "end of history," chapter 18. Heinrich Klotz and Charles Jencks publicized the concept of postmodernism in the architecture debate of the 1970s. In the context of art, the concept of the postphotographic era already appears as the subtitle of W. J. T. Mitchell's study of the electronic media, *The Reconfigured Eye* (Cambridge, Mass., 1992). The term "posthuman" seemed an evil omen in the catch phrase of a new art movement exhibited in 1993 by J. Deitsch in the Deichtorhallen in Hamburg. Walter Benjamin's essay "Das Kunstwerk im Zeitalter seiner technischen Reproduzierbarkeit" (The Work of Art in the Age of Mechanical Reproduction), first and third versions, in Walter Benjamin, *Gesammelte Schriften* (Frankfurt am Main, 1991), 12: 413ff.; Hans Sedlmayr, *Verlust der Mitte: Die bildende Kunst des 19. und 20. Jahrhunderts als Symbol der Zeit* (Salzburg, 1948). On Gary Hill's body symbolism, see the installation *Inasmuch As It Is Always Already Taking Place* (1990); chapter 10. On Peter Greenaway's exhibitions, see chapter 11.

2. THE MEANING OF ART HISTORY IN TODAY'S CULTURE

On the history of art history, see, among others, Michael Podro, *The Critical Historians of Art* (New Haven and London, 1982); Mark W. Roskill, *What is Art History?* 2d ed. (Amherst, 1989); Vernon H. Minor, *Art History's History* (New York, 1994); Udo Kultermann, *Geschichte der Kunstgeschichte: Der Weg einer Wissenschaft*, 2d ed. (Munich, 1990); Heinrich Dilly, *Kunstgeschichte als Institution* (Frankfurt am Main, 1979); Germain Bazin, *Histoire de l'histoire de l'art de Vasari à nos jours*, 2d ed. (Paris, 1986). On the contemporary museum, see chapter 11; on the exhibition *High and Low*, chapter 9. The *Dictionary of Art* was announced by Macmillan Publishers Ltd. in March 1994.

On the situation of art theory, see Arthur C. Danto, *The Philosophical Disenfranchisement of Art* (New York, 1986); Charles Harrison and Paul Wood, eds., *Art in Theory* (Oxford, 1992); Dieter Henrich and Wolfgang Iser, eds., *Theorien der Kunst* (Frankfurt am Main, 1982).

Danto's essay ("Narratives of the End of Art") is reprinted in Arthur C. Danto, *Encounters and Reflections: Art in the Historical Present* (New York, 1990), 331ff.; cf. Danto, *The Transfiguration of the Common Place: A Philosophy of Art* (Cambridge, Mass., 1981). The interview with Peter Greenaway, entitled "New Media and Old Masters," was conducted by Sabine Daneck and Torsten Beyer in *Sight and Sound* 4, no. 7 (July 1994): 18–19. On the subject of *posthistoire*, see chapter 18. Cf. Donald Preziosi, *Rethinking Art History: Meditations on a Coy Sci-*

ence (New Haven and London, 1989), 156ff.; Alan Potts, *Flesh and the Ideal: Winckelmann and the Origins of Art History* (New Haven and London, 1994).

3. ART CRITICISM VERSUS ART HISTORY

For a description of ekphrasis, see Philostratus's unsurpassed text, *Imagines* (Eikones), in the Loeb Classical Library, edited with an English translation by A. Fairbanks (London and Cambridge, Mass., 1931); and on the Renaissance usage, Michaela J. Marek, *Ekphrasis und Herrscherallegorie: Antike Bildbeschreibungen im Werk Tizians und Leonardos* (Worms, 1985).

On the history of art criticism, Albert Dresdner's *Die Entstehung der Kunstkritik in Zusammenhang der Geschichte des europäischen Kunstlebens* (1915; Munich, 1968) is still a standard work, as is Lionello Venturi, *Storia della critica d'arte*, 2d rev. ed. (Turin, 1948). On Marinetti, Breton, and Duchamp, see Fillipo T. Marinetti, *Opera*, 4 vols., ed. Luciano de Maria (Milan, 1968); André Breton, *Le Surréalisme et la peinture* (Paris, 1928); Marcel Duchamp, *Die Schriften*, ed. Serge Stauffer (Zurich, 1981); and *Salt Seller: The Writings of Marcel Duchamp*, ed. Michel Sanouillet and Elmer Peterson (New York, 1973). See also Serge Stauffer, *Marcel Duchamp: Interviews und Statements* (Stuttgart, 1991); and Dieter Daniels, *Duchamp und die anderen* (Cologne, 1992).

Also on Duchamp, see my own study, "Das Kleid der Braut: Marcel Duchamps 'Großes Glas' als Travestie des Meisterwerks," in Hans M. Bachmayer, Dietmar Kamper, and Florian Rötzer, eds., *Nach der Destruktion des ästhetischen Scheins: Van Gogh, Malewitsch, Duchamp* (Munich, 1992), 70–90.

On concept art and Kosuth, cf. Joseph Kosuth, *Art after Philosophy and After: Collected Writings, 1966–1990*, ed. Gabriele Guercio (Cambridge, Mass., 1991), and idem, "Art after Philosophy," in *Studio International* 1969 (cf. Gerd de Vries [comp.], *Über Kunst: Künstlertexte zum veränderten Kunstverständnis nach 1965* [Cologne 1974], 90ff.) For texts on the subject of "art and language" by T. Atkinson, D. Bainbridge, and M. Baldwin, among others, see *Art and Language*, eds. Paul Maenz and Gerd de Vries (Cologne, 1972); and Vries, *Über Kunst.*

On the photographic reproduction of Kosuth's work, see Robert Atkins, *Art Speak: A Guide to Contemporary Ideas, Movements and Buzzwords* (New York, 1990), 64. Germano Celant, ed., *Art Povera: Conceptual, Actual or Impossible Art?* (London, 1969), 5. Achille Bonito Oliva, *Il sogno dell'arte: Tra avanguardia e transavanguardia* (Milan, 1981), showing a reproduction of Sandro Chia's painting *Ritratto di A. B. O.* (1980).

4. THE UNWELCOME HERITAGE OF MODERNISM: STYLE AND HISTORY

Alois Riegl, *Stilfragen: Grundlegungen zu einer Geschichte der Ornamentik* (Berlin, 1893), reissued as *Problems of Style: Foundations for a History of Ornament*, ed. David Castriota (Princeton, 1992). Heinrich Wölfflin, *Kunstgeschichtliche Grundbegriffe: Das Problem der Stilentwicklung in der neueren Kunst* (Munich, 1915), translated as *Principles of Art History: The Problem of the Development of Style in Later Art* (New York, 1932). On late antiquity, cf. studies by Franz Wickhoff and Alois Riegl.

On Max Raphael, see Klaus Binder's edition of Max Raphael's *Wie will ein Kunstwerk gesehen sein?* (Frankfurt am Main, 1984); also Max Raphael, "Aufbruch in die Gegenwart" and his "Marx, Picasso," both in the Suhrkamp *Werkausgabe* [Collected Works], ed. H. J. Heinrichs (Frankfurt am Main, 1989).

Julius Meier-Graefe, *Entwicklungsgeschichte der modernen Kunst* (1904, 1914–24) in a new edition by Hans Belting (Munich, 1987), with an epilogue in volume 2 (727–257); Werner Weisbach, *Impressionismus: Ein Problem der Malerei in der Antike und Neuzeit* (Berlin, 1910–11). My own contribution to the debate on representation is "Bilderstreit: Ein Streit um die Moderne," in *Bilderstreit: Widerspruch, Einheit und Fragment in der Kunst seit 1960*, exhibition catalog, eds. Siegfried Gohr and Johannes Gachnang (Cologne, 1989), 15–28.

The futurist manifestos of 1909 and 1911 were most recently printed in Harrison and Wood, *Art in Theory* (see under chapter 2), 145ff., 149ff.; also in this book are texts by Malevich and a whole collection of documents on the "Idea of the Modern World."

Julius Meier-Graefe, *Wohin treiben wir?* (Berlin, 1913). On Meier-Graefe, see Kenworth Moffett's biography, *Meier-Graefe as Art Critic* (Munich, 1973). The text of Thomas Mann's essay "On Myself" is found in Thomas Mann, *On Myself* (Frankfurt am Main, 1983), 75ff.

On modernist utopias, see Hubertus Gassner, ed., *Die Konstruktion der Utopie: Ästhetische Avantgarde und politische Utopie in den 20er Jahren* (Marburg, 1992). On Raoul Hausmann's work *The Spirit of our Age*, see *Raoul Hausmann*, exhibition catalog (Hanover, 1981); and Hanne Bergius, *Das Lachen Dadas: Die Berliner Dadaisten und ihre Aktionen* (Giessen, 1989); also the essay "Der Geist unserer Zeit" (1919) in *Dada in Europa*, exhibition catalog (Frankfurt am Main, 1978), 3.50.

On De Stijl, see Carten-Peter Warncke, *Das Ideal als Kunst: De Stijl, 1917–1931* (Cologne, 1990); Joost Baljeu, *Theo van Doesburg* (London and New York, 1974); the various manifestos of De Stijl in the periodical *De Stijl*, 1917–21; finally, the exhibition catalog *Theo van Doesburg* (Nuremberg, 1969), 155ff. On the history of Malevich's long-unpublished writings and of the Bauhaus book of 1927, see Hans von Riesen and Werner Haftmann, *Suprematismus—Die gegenstandslose Welt* (Cologne, 1962).

Myths in the modern age are discussed by Beat Wyss, *Mythologie der Aufklärung: Geheimlehren der Moderne* (Munich, 1993), but he restricts himself to Gnostic fantasies, poetic visions, and the theories found in Hans Arp's "Klassisches Lesebuch der Moderne"; this is printed in Carola Giedion-Welcker, ed., *Anthologie der Abseitigen* (Zurich, 1944).

On the development of iconology, see chapter 14.

On the failure of the avant-garde in the Soviet Union, see Boris Grois, *Gesamtkunstwerk Stalin* (Munich, 1988); on the same under National Socialism, see Hans Belting, "Die Krise des Sinns: Stand oder Widerstand der Kunst?" in *Widerstand: Denkbilder für die Zukunft*, exhibition catalog (Munich, 1993); idem, *Die Deutschen und ihre Kunst: Ein schwieriges Erbe* (Munich, 1992); Paul O. Rave, *Kunstdiktatur im Dritten Reich* (Hamburg, 1949); cf. also Peter-Klaus Schuster, ed., *Nationalsozialismus und "Entartete Kunst": Die "Kunststadt" München 1937*, exhibition catalog (Munich, 1987); Bazon Brock and Achim Preiß, eds., *Kunst auf Befehl? Dreiunddreißig bis Fünfundvierzig* (Munich, 1990); and Otto Thomae, *Die Propaganda-Maschinerie: Bildende Kunst und Öffentlichkeitsarbeit im Dritten Reich* (Berlin, 1978), with further bibliographies.

Theoretical reflections on Zeitgeist in the context of scientific development are found in Thomas Kuhn, *Die Entstehung des Neuen* (Frankfurt am Main, 1963); and, in particular, in Robert Merton, *Entwicklung und Wandel von Forschungsinteressen* (Frankfurt am Main, 1985).

5. THE LATE CULT OF MODERNISM: DOCUMENTA AND WESTERN ART

Stephanie Barron, *Entartete Kunst. Das Schicksal der Avantgarde im Nazi-Deutschland*, exhitibition catalog (Munich, 1991). Henrike Junge-Gent, ed., *Avantgarde und Publikum: Zur Rezeption avantgardistischer Kunst in Deutschland, 1905–1933* (Cologne, 1992).

Hugo Borger, Ekkehard Mai, and Stephan Waetzold, eds., *'45 und die Folgen: Kunstgeschichte eines Wiederbeginns* (Cologne, 1991). Jean Améry provides an important discussion of the intellectual situation at the middle of the century in *Geburt der Gegenwart: Gestalten und Gestaltungen der westlichen Zivilisation seit Kriegsende* (Olten, 1961).

Werner Haftmann and Arnold Bode, eds., *documenta: Kunst des 20. Jahrhunderts* (Munich, 1955); Bernd Klüser and Katharina Hegewisch, eds., *Die Kunst der Ausstellung: Eine Dokumentation dreissig exemplarischer Kunstausstellungen dieses Jahrhunderts* (Frankfurt am Main, 1991), see especially 116ff., W. Grasskamp on *Documenta 1.* V. Rattenmeyer, ed., *Documenta* (Kassel, 1984); Arnold Bode, *documenta Kassel* (Kassel, 1987); also Manfred Schneckenburgér, ed., *Documenta: Idee und Institution* (Munich, 1983). On Sedlmayr, see chapter 1. On José Ortega y Gasset, see his book *La deshumanisacion del arte: Ideas sobre la novela* (Madrid, 1925). Werner Haftmann's "Über das moderne Bild" was published in the *Frankfurter Allgemeine Zeitung*, 30 July 1955.

On the loss of modernism, see Jürgen Habermas, *Die neue Unübersichtlichkeit: Kleine politische Schriften V* (Frankfurt am Main, 1985).

On the early modernist exhibitions, see Eberhard Roters, *Stationen der Moderne: Die bedeutendsten Kunstausstellungen des 20. Jahrhunderts in Deutschland* (Berlin, n.d.).

See chapter 9 for a discussion of Jean Dubuffet and of the exhibition *This Is Tomorrow in London.*

The Cologne exhibition is *Westkunst: Zeitgenössische Kunst seit 1939* (1981), with an exhibition catalog edited by Lazlo Glozer.

Barnett Newman, "The Sublime Is Now," in John P. O'Neill, ed., *Barnett Newman: Selected Writings and Interviews* (New York, 1990), 170ff.

6. WESTERN ART: THE INTERVENTION OF THE UNITED STATES IN POSTWAR MODERNISM

On the general topic, see Siegfried Gohr, ed., *Europa-Amerika: Die Geschichte einer künstlerischen Faszination seit 1940*, exhibition catalog (Cologne, 1986). The photo of Adolph Gottlieb is by Aaron Siskind: cf. the Brooklyn Museum exhibition *Image and Reflection: Adolph Gottlieb's Pictographs and African Sculpture* (1989), with booklet guide.

The exhibition *The Ideographic Picture*, shown in the Betty Parsons Gallery in 1947, was preceded in 1946 by the exhibition *Northwest Coast Indian Paint-*

ing; cf. Barnett Newman, *Selected Writings and Interviews,* ed. J. P. O'Neill (New York, 1990), 107 ff., 170 ff.

On Jackson Pollock and also on the American Foundation of Modern Painters and Sculptors, see Steven Naifeh and Gregory White Smith, *Jackson Pollock: An American Saga* (London, 1990).

George Segal's work is discussed by Jean Lipman and Richard Marshall in *Art about Art* (New York, 1978), 111 (with illustration).

On the legacy of Clement Greenberg and abstract expressionism, see the so-called Critical Debate, edited and reissued in 1985 by Francis Frascina as *Pollock and After: The Critical Debate* (London, 1985). On Clement Greenberg, see his *Art and Culture: Critical Essays* (Boston, 1961), and *Perception and Judgments, 1939–1944,* vol. 1 of *The Collected Essays and Criticism,* ed. John O'Brian (Chicago, 1986). Criticism and countercriticism of American art can be found in Harold Rosenberg, *The Tradition of the New* (London, 1962), also idem, *The De-Definition of Art* (New York, 1972); Tom Wolfe, *The Painted Word* (New York, 1975); Calvin Tomkins, *Off the Wall: Robert Rauschenberg and the Art World of Our Times* (New York, 1981), idem, *The Scene: Reports on Postmodern Art* (New York, 1976); Suzi Gablik, *Has Modernism Failed?* (New York, 1984); James H. Beck, *The Tyranny of the Detail: Contemporary Art in an Urban Setting* (New York, 1992); cf. also Karl Gunnar Pontus Hultén, ed., *Paris-New York,* exhibition catalog (Paris, 1977).

On the Zero Group, cf. Anette Kuhn, *Zero: Eine Avantgarde der sechziger Jahre* (Frankfurt am Main, 1991); and Heiner Stachelhaus, *Zero: Heinz Mack, Otto Piene, Günther Uecker* (Düsseldorf, 1993). On Yves Klein, see Catherine Krahmer, *Der Fall Yves Klein: Zur Krise der Kunst* (Munich, 1974); cf. also the retrospective exhibition in the Center Pompidou, Paris, 1983.

On events around 1960 in Paris, see Jean-Paul Ameline, *Les Nouveaux Realistes,* exhibition catalog (Paris, 1992). The 1960 catalog *Les Nouveaux Realistes* was reprinted in Paris in 1986. For further reading on pop art (incl. Christopher Finch, *Pop Art* [London, 1968]), see Marco Livingstone, ed., *Pop Art* (Munich, 1992). The text of Meyer Schapiro's "Recent Abstract Painting" is found in his *Modern Art: 19th and 20th Century,* parts 1–2 (1956–57; New York, 1978), 213 ff.

Christos M. Joachimides and Norman Rosenthal, *Zeitgeist* (Berlin, 1982, previously published as *A New Spirit in Painting,* exhibition catalog (London, 1981); cf. Peter Fuller, *Images of God: The Consolations of Lost Illusions* (London, 1985). The exhibition *Binationale: Amerikanische Kunst der späten 80er Jahre* was shown in Dusseldorf and Cologne in 1988.

On Mapplethorpe, cf. *Mapplethorpe,* with an essay by Arthur C. Danto (New York, 1992); and Robert Hughes, *The Culture of Complaint: The Fraying of America* (New York and Oxford, 1993), which contains documentary contributions to the general debate. See also Richard Bolton, ed., *Culture Wars: Documents from the Recent Controversies in the Arts* (New York, 1992); also, Steven C. Dubin, *Arresting Images: Impolitic Art and Uncivil Actions* (New York, 1992). On U.S. society, see Gert Raeithel, *Geschichte der nordamerikanischen Kultur* (Weinheim, 1989). For obvious reasons, I will refrain from listing here any literature on Joseph Beuys and Andy Warhol.

7. EUROPE: EAST AND WEST AT THE WATERSHED OF ART HISTORY

On art of the former GDR (East Germany), see Hans Belting, *Die Deutschen und ihre Kunst* (Munich, 1992), with bibliography; idem, "Die Krise des Sinns: Stand oder Widerstand der Kunst?" in *Widerstand: Denkbilder für die Zukunft*, exhibition catalog (Munich, 1993), 23ff.; cf. also Améry in chapter 5 on the subject of Europe.

On the theme of "Eastern art," see Thomas Strauss, ed., *Westkunst-Ostkunst: Absonderung oder Integration?* (Munich, 1991), idem, "Ostkunst," *Idea* 7 (1989): 212ff.; *Europa, Europa: Das Jahrhundert der Avantgarde in Mittel- und Osteuropa*, exhibition catalog, 4 vols. (Bonn, 1994).

On the example of Hungary, see L. Beke, "The Hidden Dimensions of the Hungarian Art of the 1960s," in Ildikó Nagy, ed., *Harvanas évek: Új törekvések a magyar képzomuvészetben*, exhibition catalog (Budapest, 1991); Péter György and Gábor Pataki, *Az Európai Iskola és az elvont muvészek csoportja* [The European School] (Budapest, 1991); Péter György and Hedvig Turai, eds., *Staatskunstwerk: Kultur im Stalinismus* (Budapest, 1992).

On Russia, see Boris Grois in conversation with Il'ia Kabakov, "Rußland auf dem Buckel," in *Parkett* 34 (1992): 30ff.; Il'ia Kabakov and Boris Grois, *Die Kunst des Fliehens: Dialoge über Angst, das heilige Weiss und den sowjetischen Müll* (Munich and Vienna, 1991). On the Russians in New York, see, for example, *Alexander Kosolapov*, exhibition catalog (New York, 1990). On V. Komar and A. Melamid, see, for example, *Europa, Europa*, 1: 270ff. and 4: 67, with biographies and literature. For a long time, the Costakis Collection was the only source of information about the Russian avant-garde in the West; see *Russische Avantgarde aus der Sammlung Costakis*, exhibition catalog (Munich, 1984). On the Russian avant-garde in 1920s Berlin, see Fritz Mierau, *Russen in Berlin, 1918–1933: Eine kulturelle Begegnung* (Weinheim and Berlin, 1988).

W. A. L. Beeren, *Wanderlieder*, exhibition catalog (Amsterdam, 1991), contains Heiner Müller's "Stirb schneller, Europa," 80ff.; cf. also F. A. Hetting, "Wanderlieder," in *Kunstforum* (1992), with a photograph of the mural by Jon Grigorescu entitled *Recommandation pour Golonia*.

8. GLOBAL ART AND MINORITIES: A NEW GEOGRAPHY OF ART HISTORY

On "political correctness" and the role of minorities, see chapter 6. On Alfred H. Barr's catalogs in the Museum of Modern Art, see *Cubism and Abstract Art* (1936; New York, 1966); also *Fantastic Art, Dada, Surrealism* (New York,1936). On the influence of these European movements on North America, see William S. Rubin's exhibition catalog, *Dada, Surrealism and Their Heritage* (New York, 1968).

On feminist art history, see H. Spickernagel, "Gegenstandsdeutung," part 3 of *Kunstgeschichte: Eine Einführung*, ed. Wolfgang Kemp and Hans Belting (Berlin, 1985), 332ff. Cf. also Craig Owens, "The Discourse of Others: Feminists and Postmodernism," in Hal Foster, ed., *Postmodern Culture* (London, 1985), 57ff.

On regional art in the U.S.A., see the exhibition catalogs *Art in New Mexico, 1900–1945: Paths to Taos and Santa Fe* (Washington, D.C., 1986); and Luis R.

Cancel, ed., *The Latin American Spirit: Art and Artists in the United States, 1920–1970* (New York, 1988); cf. the highly controversial exhibition *The West as America: Reinterpreting Images of the Frontier* at the National Museum of American Art, Washington, D.C., 1991; the accompanying exhibition catalog was edited by William H. Truettner. Exhibitions on the Northwest have been staged repeatedly in Seattle in recent years.

Attempts to represent contemporary art in the third world should be distinguished from the project of a "global art history"; cf. the catalog *Il sud del mondo: L'altra arte contemporanea* (Milan, 1991), of an exhibition sponsored by UNESCO; also Marc Scheps, *Lateinamerikanische Kunst im 20. Jahrhundert* (Munich, 1993); and Susan M. Vogel, *Africa Explores: Twentieth Century African Art* (Munich, 1991); Jan Vansina, *Art History in Africa: An Introduction to Method* (London, 1984); the anthology *ART/artifact: African Art in Anthropology Collections,* with an introduction by Arthur C. Danto (New York, 1988); the exhibition catalog *Paris in Japan: The Paris Encounter with European Painting* (Tokyo and St. Louis, 1987).

On the "cultural archive," cf. Boris Grois, *Über das Neue: Versuch einer Kulturökonomie* (Munich, 1992). On the critique of "universalism," see Hans Magnus Enzensberger, *Aussichten auf den Bürgerkrieg* (Frankfurt am Main, 1993). On the problem of global culture, see Constantin von Barloewen, *Kulturgeschichte und Modernität Lateinamerikas: Technologie und Kultur im andinischen Raum* (Munich, 1992). On Malraux's "imaginary museum," see chapter 15. On the exhibition *"Primitivism" in Twentieth Century Art: Affinity of the Tribal and the Modern* in the Museum of Modern Art, see the introduction by William S. Rubin, "Modernist Primitivism," to the exhibition catalog of the same title (New York, 1984). Cf. also Karla Bilang, *Das Gegenbild: Die Begegnung der Avantgarde mit dem Ursprünglichen* (Leipzig, 1989). On "art planetaire," cf. Yves Michaud, *L'artiste et les commissaires: Quatre essais non pas sur l'art contemporain mais sur ceux qui s'en occupent* (Nîmes, 1989), 69ff.

On ethnic issues, see Clifford Geertz, *Die künstlichen Wilden: Der Anthropologe als Schriftsteller* (Frankfurt am Main, 1993). Sometimes ethnology is equated with the old theme of "exoticism"; see Götz Pochat, *Der Exotismus während des Mittelalters und der Renaissance* (Stockholm, 1970); and Fritz Kramer, *Verkehrte Welten: Zur imaginären Ethnologie des 19. Jahrhunderts* (Frankfurt am Main, 1981).

On primeval painting, see Denis Vialou, *Frühzeit des Menschen* (Munich, 1992); Venceslas Kruta, *Die Anfänge Europas* (Munich, 1992); plus a bold comparison with contemporary art in the exhibition *First Europeans: Frühe Kulturen—moderne Visionen* (Berlin, 1993). Theodor W. Adorno, "Theorien über den Ursprung der Kunst," in his *Ästhetische Theorie* (Frankfurt am Main, 1970), 480ff.

The exhibition *Magiciens de la Terre,* in Paris 1989, was accompanied by a detailed catalog. The illustration I have reproduced here was published in *Art in America* (July 1989): 90. See also the essay by E. Heartney, printed in the same issue.

On the "electronic super-highway" (*From Venice to Ulan Bator*), Venice, see the exhibition catalog by Klaus Bußmann and Florian Matzner, *Nam June Paik: Eine Data base,* exhibition catalog (Stuttgart, 1993). On the exhibition in Tokyo with the installation *The Eurasian Way* in the Watari-Um Gallery, see the review in *B. T.* [*Bijutsu Techo*] 45, no. 680 (1993): 105ff. The term "Eurasia" is, of course, inspired in part by Joseph Beuys's happenings of the 1960s; see Uwe M. Schneede, *Joseph Beuys: Die Aktionen. Kommentiertes Werkverzeichnis mit fotografischen Dokumentationen* (Stuttgart, 1994).

On diaspora art, see Ronald B. Kitaj, *First Diaspora Manifesto* (London, 1989).

9. THE MIRROR OF MASS CULTURE: ART'S REVOLT AGAINST ART HISTORY

The key texts on the various theories of modernism are collected in a convenient anthology edited by Harrison and Wood, *Art in Theory* (see under chapter 2). On Jean Dubuffet, see Jean Dubuffet, "Malerei in der Falle: Antikulturelle Positionen," in *Schriften*, ed. A. Franke (Bern, 1991), 1: 82ff, 95ff. The Chicago facsimile can be seen in Richard L. Feigen, ed., *Dubuffet and the Anticulture*, exhibition catalog (New York, 1969).

On art and mass culture in general, see Arthur C. Danto, *The Transfiguration of the Common Place* (Cambridge, Mass., 1981). On Eduardo Paolozzi, see W. Konnertz, *Eduardo Paolozzi* (Cologne, 1984), 33ff., 39 (on his stay in Paris), with an illustration of the collage I discuss; 69ff. (on the "Independence Group" and the beginnings of English pop art), with a discussion of the exhibition *This Is Tomorrow* (74ff.). On the exhibition of 1956, cf. S. Schmidt-Wulffen, in Klüser and Hegewisch, *Die Kunst der Ausstellung*, 126ff. Cf. also Christopher H. Finch, *Pop Art: Object and Image* (London, 1968); the exhibition catalog *Richard Hamilton: Studies-Studien, 1937–1977* (Bielefeld, 1978); Richard Hamilton, *Collected Works* (New York, 1983); Lawrence Alloway, in *Architecture Design* 28, no. 2 (1958), reprinted in Livingstone, *Pop Art*, (see under chapter 6), 160ff. The frequently reproduced collage by Richard Hamilton (cf. chapter 6) also appeared in the exhibition catalog *High and Low* (see below), plate 143, with commentary.

On art and advertising, see Uwe Geese and Harald Kimpel, *Kunst im Rahmen der Werbung* (Frankfurt am Main, 1982); Oskar Cöster, *Ad' Age, der Himmel auf Erden: Eine Theodizee der Werbung* (Hamburg, 1990); Holger Bonus and Dieter Ronte, *Die Wa(h)re Kunst: Markt, Kultur und Illusion* (Erlangen, 1991). On L. Boucher, "La publicité moderne," see *High and Low* (discussed below), plate 230 (photomontage in "L'art vivante," Jan. 1927, p. 193).

On the subject of design, I mention here only the literature on the Bauhaus and on the influence of the Bauhaus on the Hochschule für Gestaltung in Ulm during the 1950s. The exhibition by Kirk Varnedoe and Adam Gopnik, *High and Low—Popular Culture and Modern Art*, at the Museum of Modern Art in New York in 1991 contained the genres of graffiti, caricature, comics, and advertising. On this exhibition, see Arthur C. Danto, *High Art, Low Art and the Spirit of History* (see chapter 11). On the "Petit journal pour rire," see *Nadar*, exhibition catalog (Paris, 1994). On the history of the comic strip, see the bibliography of 102 titles in *High and Low*, 434ff.

On Clement Greenberg's essay on "Avantgarde und Kitsch," see the literature cited for chapter 6. Extensive literature is available on Robert Rauschenberg's silkscreens (see also the comment in chapter 12): cf. Roni Feinstein, *Robert Rauschen-*

berg: The Silkscreen Paintings, 1962–64, exhibition catalog (New York, 1990), with a list of further reading; on the poster for the Metropolitan Museum, see also Douglas Crimp, "On the Museum's Ruins," in the eponymous volume (cf. chapter 11), 44 ff. Texts by Rauschenberg in this context are found in Barbara Rose, *An Interview with Robert Rauschenberg* (New York, 1987).

10. THE TEMPORALITY OF VIDEO ART

In the jungle of literature that has already grown up on this topic, it is difficult to select introductory titles that stand out; in this area, too, the dominant ethos is one of fast production using a large team of authors. I mention, for instance, John Hanhardt, ed., *Video Culture: A Critical Investigation* (Rochester, N.Y., 1986); Sally Jo Fifer and Doug Hall, *Illuminating Video: An Essential Guide to Video Art* (Metuchen, N.J., 1990); Florian Rötzer, ed., *Digitaler Schein: Ästhetik der elektronischen Medien* (Frankfurt am Main, 1991); Gerda Lampalzer, *Videokunst: Historischer Überblick und theoretische Zugänge* (Vienna, 1992); Lori Zippay, *Artist's Video: An International Guide* (New York, 1991); *Video Denk-Raum Architiktur* (Zurich, 1994); and the ironically critical *Medien-Archiv* (Bensheim, 1993) by Agentur Bilwet and edited by D. Diederichsen; finally, the anthology by R. Bellour, et al., *Passages de l'image* (Paris, 1990). Ira Schneider and Beryl Korot, *Video Art: An Anthology* (New York and London, 1976), includes Nam June Paik's text (98) and an essay by D. Antin, "Video: The Distinctive Features of the Medium" (174–183). R. Krauss's "Video: The Aesthetics of Narcissism" is reprinted in Handardt (see above), 179 ff. On Fluxus, see, for example, H. Sohm, ed., *Happening und Fluxus* (Cologne, 1970); and E. Milman, ed., "Fluxus: A Conceptual Country," in *Visible Language* 26 (1992).

On Nam June Paik's videos *A Tribute to John Cage* (1973), *Merce by Merce by Paik* (1977), and *Merce and Merce* (1978), see, for example, Klaus Bußmann and Florian Matzner, *Nam June Paik, eine DATA base* (Stuttgart, 1993), 238 ff. For literature on Paik, see, for example, Wulf Herzogenrath, *Nam June Paik: Fluxus-Video* (Munich, 1983); Jean Paul Fargier, *Nam June Paik* (Paris, 1989); Paik's writings in Paik, *Niederschriften eines Kulturnomaden: Aphorismen, Briefe, Texte*, ed. Edith Decker (Cologne, 1992). On his conception of time, see Paik, *Time Collage* (Tokyo, 1984). There are countless publications on the TV-Buddha; on the Hydra-Buddha, see the questionable interpretation by M. Baudson, "Die Zeit—ein Spiegel," in Hannelore Paflik, ed., *Das Phänomen Zeit in Kunst und Wissenschaft* (Weinheim, 1987), 125 ff.

On Gary Hill's quotation, see the catalog *Gary Hill*, eds. Dorine Mignot, Eleonor Louis, and Toni Stoos (Amsterdam and Vienna, 1993), 13 ff, 37 ff (from which I have taken the other quotations); in the same catalog, 80 ff., L. Cooke on the installation *Inasmuch . . .* (1990). Cf. also the catalog of the Hirshhorn Museum in Washington (1994) and that of the Watari-Um Gallery in Tokyo, *I Believe It Is an Image* (Tokyo, 1992).

On Bill Viola's installations, see the catalog edited by Marie Luise Syring, *Bill Viola: Unseen Images* (Dusseldorf, 1993), and *Bill Viola*, the catalog of an exhibition held at the Salzburger Kunstverein (1994), edited by Alexander Pühringer with an essay by C. Montolio, "The Unspoken Language of the Body." The installation *Heaven and Earth* (D. Young Gallery, Seattle) exists in two editions: Y. Hendeles Art Foundation, Toronto; and Museum of Contemporary Art, San Diego; the same applies to *Slowly Turning Narrative* (Institute of Contemporary Art, Philadelphia, and Museo Nacional Reina Sofia, Madrid).

II. THE NARRATIVE OF ART IN THE NEW MUSEUM: THE SEARCH FOR A PROFILE

Claes Oldenburg, "The Store," in idem, *Store Days: Documents from The Store, 1961, and Ray Gun Theater, 1962* (New York, 1967). Ad Reinhardt, *Schriften und Gespräche*, ed. Thomas Kellein (Munich, 1984).

On the Museum of Modern Art, cf. the discourse by Arthur C. Danto, "High Art, Low Art and the Spirit of History," in idem, *Beyond the Brillo-Box: The Visual Arts in Posthistorical Perspective* (New York, 1992), 147ff.; plus the text "The Museum of Museums," 199ff.

On the contemporary museum and the museum crisis, see A. Preiß, K. Stamm, and F. G. Zehnder, *Das Museum: Die Entwicklung in den 80er Jahren* (Munich, 1990), in particular, the essay by Siegfried Gohr, "Das Kunstmuseum zwischen Avantgarde und Salon," 229ff.; H. Auer, ed., *Das Museum im technischen und sozialen Wandel unserer Zeit* (Munich, 1975); R. Mißelbeck, *Das Museum als Traditionsproduzent* (Bonn, 1980); Walter Grasskamp, *Museumsgründer und Museumsstürmer: Zur Sozialgeschichte des Kunstmuseums* (Munich, 1981); Helmut Börsch-Supan, *Kunstmuseen in der Krise: Chancen, Gefährdungen, Aufgaben in mageren Jahren* (Munich, 1993); S. E. Weil, *Rethinking the Museum and Other Meditations* (Washington, 1990); from another view, see Yves Michaud, *L'artiste et les commissaires: Quatre essais non pas sur l'art contemporain mais sur ceux qui s'en occupent* (Paris, 1989), 179ff. ("Après le musée, avant Disneyland").

On the earlier museum debate, cf. Gerhard Bott, ed., *Das Museum der Zukunft* (Cologne, 1970), containing W. Haftmann, "Das Museum der Gegenwart"; Ellen Spickernagel and Brigitte Walbe, eds., *Das Museum—Lernort contra Musentempel* (Gießen, 1970). For the Marxist viewpoint in the U.S.A., see the title essay by Douglas Crimp, "On the Museum's Ruins" (Cambridge, Mass., 1993), first published in *October* 13 (1990).

On museum architecture, see Heinrich Klotz, ed., *Neue Museumsbauten in der Bundesrepublik* (Stuttgart, 1985); J. M. Montana and J. Olivares, *Die Museumsbauten der neuen Generation* (Stuttgart, 1987).

There is extensive literature on market activities, for instance, Bonus and Ronte (see chapter 9); Jürgen Weber, *Entmündigung der Künstler: Geschichte und Funktionsweise der bürgerlichen Kunsteinrichtungen* (Munich, 1981); W. Pommerehne and B. S. Frey, *Musen und Märkte—Ansätze einer Ökonomik der Kunst* (Munich, 1993); cf. the famous court case to decide the legacy of Marc Rothko, in N. Seldes, *The Legacy of Marc Rothko* (New York, 1974).

On R. Wilson's museum dramatization, see his *Portrait, Still Life, Landscape*, exhibition catalog (Rotterdam, 1993), showing a photograph of room 3. On the exhibition *Peter Greenaway: Watching Water in the Palazzo Fortuny, Venice;* see the booklet of the same title and also the larger publication, with a preface by Luca M. Barbero (Milan, 1993); the latter shows the exhibition photograph reprinted here (23) and the *Janus* (81). The exhibition catalog *100 Objekte zeigen die Welt* was published in Stuttgart in 1992, and that of *The Stairs: The Location, Genf* appeared in London, 1994. On Greenaway's interview in the *Film Bulletin*, see chapter 2.

On the curiosity cabinet from today's perspective, see Horst Bredekamp, *Antikensehnsucht und Maschinenglauben: Die Geschichte der Kunstkammer und die Zukunft der Kunstgeschichte* (Berlin, 1993); and Victor I. Stoichita, *L'Instauration du tableau: Métapeinture à l'aube des temps modernes* (Paris, 1993), 90ff.

The exhibition of works by Gary Hill was shown in the Stedelijk Museum, Amsterdam, and in the Kunsthalle, Vienna, 1993–94 (with catalog). The exhibition in the Nationalgalerie, Berlin, summer 1994, was the subject of hot debate in *Die Zeit* and the *Frankfurter Allgemeine Zeitung.* Cf. descriptions of earlier controversies in the Nationalgalerie at the turn of the twentieth century on the topic of German art: among others, my book essay *Die Deutschen und ihre Kunst* (Munich, 1993). On the history of the Nationalgalerie, see Paul O. Rave, *Die Geschichte der Nationalgalerie Berlin* (Berlin, n.d.).

The controversy surrounding the icons in Moscow and the debate about the installation of new open-air museums for outmoded memorial statues in the former Communist states received only press coverage, as far as I am aware, and received no attention in academic literature.

On the exhibition *Europa-Europa,* cf. the references in chapter 7. On the controversy about the Museum of Modern Art's exhibition policy, see Crimp, "On the Museum's Ruins," 200ff. ("This is not a museum of art"); and Danto, op. cit.

The dubious new "museum art" challenges the contemporary museum to enter either into conflict or collusion with the original concept of the museum. Cf. Umberto Eco and Jean Baudrillard in *Museo dei Musei,* exhibition catalog (Florence, 1988)," an exhibition that consisted entirely of copies.

12. ART AND THE CRISIS OF MODERNISM

A. Danto, *After the End of Art: Contemporary Art and the Pale of History* (Princeton, 1997), pp. 14ff; cf. *The Transfiguration of the Commonplace* (Harvard, 1981), pp. 6f and *Beyond the Porillo-Box* (New York, 1992), pp. 5ff.

Hervé Fischer, *L'histoire de l'art est terminée* (Paris, 1978). On Guttoso's work, cf. *Guttoso: Das Gastmahl,* exhibition catalog (Frankfurt am Main, 1974), plate 3 (*Conversation with the Painters,* 1973). On Guttoso, see *Guttoso, Opere dal 1931 al 1981,* exhibition catalog (Venice, 1982).

On Richard Hamilton's drawing, *Picasso's Meniñas, Study III* (1973; 56 × 76 cm, in the collection of R. Donagh, Northend), cf. the catalog to the exhibition *Nachbilder* by G. Ahrens and K. Sello (Hanover, 1979), illustration on p. 205;, and *Richard Hamilton: A Complete Catalogue of Graphic Works, 1939–83* (Stuttgart and London, 1984), put out by Waddington Graphics and E. H. J. Mayer. André Malraux's *Das Haupt aus Obsidian* (Frankfurt am Main, 1975). The series *Meniñas* is found in the exhibition catalog *Picasso: Les Ménines, 1957* (Paris, 1959), published by the Galerie Louise Leiris; Jaime Sabartés, *Picasso: Las Meniñas y la vida* (Barcelona, 1982); and Josep Palaui i Fabre, *El Secreto de Las Meniñas de Picasso* (Barcelona, 1982). On Rauschenberg, cf. also chapter 9. His work *Persimmon,* in the exhibition catalog by Roni Feinstein, *Robert Rauschenberg: The Silkscreen Paintings, 1962–64* (New York, 1990), no. 56 and plate 29. The interview appeared in Barbara Rose, *An Interview with Robert Rauschenberg* (New York, 1987). The poster for the Metropolitan Museum can also be seen in Douglas Crimp, *On the Museum's Ruins* (Cambridge, Mass., 1993), 60f. and in *Art about Art,* see chapter 5. On Cindy Sherman's *History Portraits,* see Rosalind

Krauss and Norman Bryson, *Cindy Sherman, 1975–1993* (Munich, 1993), 173 ff.; Arthur C. Danto, *Cindy Sherman: History Portraits. Alte Meister und Postmoderne* (Munich, 1991); Christa Döttinger, "Cindy Sherman: History Portraits," M.A. thesis, Munich, 1993; and Hans Belting, *Thomas Struth. Museum Photographs* (Munich, 1993), 15.

13. ART HISTORIOGRAPHY AS TRADITION

Le vite de' più eccellenti pittori, scultori ed architettori, ed. Gaetano Milanesi (1568; Florence, 1906). On Vasari, see T. S. R. Boase, *Giorgio Vasari: The Man and the Book* (Princeton, 1971); and Hans Belting, "Vasari und die Folgen," in idem, *Das Ende der Kunstgeschichte?* (Munich, 1983), part 2.

Johann Joachim Winckelmann, *Geschichte der Kunst des Altertums* (1764; Darmstadt, 1972). On Winckelmann, see the biography by Wolfgang Leppmann, *Winckelmann* (New York, 1970); and the recent book by Potts (see above under chapter 2).

On the early history of the discipline, see Heinrich Dilly, *Kunstgeschichte als Institution: Studien zur Geschichte einer Disziplin* (Frankfurt am Main, 1979). On the Viennese School, see W. Hofmann, "Was bleibt von der 'Wiener Schule'?" in *Jahrbuch des Zentralinstitutes für Kunstgeschichte* (1986): 2: 273 ff. Cf. Wolfgang Kemp on Alois Riegl and E. Lachnit on J. von Schlosser in Heinrich Dilly, ed., *Altmeister moderner Kunstgeschichte* (Berlin, 1990); also, on J. Schlosser, *Kritische Berichte* IV (1988) passim; and *International Congress for Art History* (Vienna, 1983).

The connections between art history and exhibitions in the early years of the Louvre are discussed in Hans Belting, "L'Adieu d'Apollon," in *L'histoire de l'histoire de l'art*, ed. E. Pommier (Paris, 1994). Cf. also Paul Wescher, *Kunstraub unter Napoleon* (Berlin, 1978), and Pierre Lelièvre, *Vivant Denon* (Paris, 1993), with bibliography. On the Louvre catalogs, cf. Joseph Lavallée, ed., *Galerie du Musée Napoléon*, 10 vols. (Paris, 1804–1814), and Robillard-Péronville and Pierre Laurent, eds., *Le Musée Français*, 4 vols. (1803–1809): on this subject, see the M.A. thesis by C. Weissert (under my supervision), 1993. Luigi Lanzi's *Storia della pittura italiana* was translated into several other languages soon after its publication. Johann David Passavant's art history appeared in 1820 in Heidelberg and Speyer; on this, see Hans Belting, "Vasari und die Folgen," in idem, *Das Ende der Kunstgeschichte?*.

J. Schlobach, "Die klassisch-humanistische Zyklentheorie und ihre Anfechtung durch das Fortschrittsbewußtsein der französischen Frühaufklärung," in *Theorie der Geschichte 2: Historische Prozesse* (Munich, 1978), 127 ff.; on Winckelmann, see chapter 12.

Hans Robert Jauss, *Literaturgeschichte als Provokation* (Frankfurt am Main, 1970), 153 f. G. W. F. Hegel, *Vorlesungen über die Ästhetik*, ed. Heinrich G. Hotho (1836; Berlin, 1953), especially, 1: 32, 2, 231 ff., 244 f.; see also the study edition by Eva Moldenhauer and Karl M. Michel, eds., *Werke* (Frankfurt am Main, 1969). Cf. inter alia Werner Koepsel, *Die Rezeption der Hegelschen Ästhetik im 20. Jahrhundert* (Bonn, 1975); J. Simmen, *Kunst—Ideal oder Augenschein: Systematik, Sprache, Malerei. Ein Versuch zu Hegels Ästhetik* (Berlin, 1980); and Beat Wyss, *Hegel's Art History and the Critique of Modernism* (Cambridge, Mass.,

1999). Cf. also Wolf Lepenies, *Aufstieg und Fall der Intellektuellen in Europa* (Frankfurt am Main, 1992), 73ff.

On the contradiction between the development of truth and the practice of copying an ancient artistic canon, see Adorno, *Ästhetische Theorie*, 309f. On early criticism of Hegel, cf. the idealistic viewpoint of Benedetto Croce, *Lebendiges und Totes in Hegels Philosophie* (Heidelberg, 1909), 106. Cf. also G. Vanni, *Das Ende der Moderne* (Stuttgart, 1990), 57f.

Quatremère's text was reissued by Jean-Louis Déotte, *Considérations morales sur la destination desouvrages de l'art ; suivi de, Lettres sur l'enlèvement des ouvrages de l'art antique à Athènes et à Rome* (Paris, 1989). On Quatremère, see E. Pommier, *Lettres à Miranda* (Paris, 1989), and idem, *L'art de la liberté* (Paris, 1991).

On the history of the avant-garde, see D. D. Egbert, "The Idea of 'Avantgarde' in Art and Politics" in *American Historical Review* 73 (1967): 339ff.; Hans Egon Holthusen's anthology *Avant-garde: Geschichte und Krise einer Idee* (Munich, 1966); and Thomas B. Hess and John Ashbery, *Avant-Garde Art* (London, 1967). On the criticism of and the crisis within the movement, see Harold Rosenberg, *The Anxious Object: Art Today and Its Audience* (New York, 1964), 25ff. ("Past and Possibility"); idem, *The De-definition of Art: Action Art to Pop to Earthworks* (New York, 1972), 212ff. ("D. M. Z. Vanguardism"); Christopher Finch, "On the Absence of an Avant-Garde," in *Art Studies for an Editor: Twenty-five Essays in Memory of M. S. Fox* (New York, 1975), 168ff.; Eduard Beaucamp, *Das Dilemma der Avantgarde: Aufsätze zur bildenden Kunst* (Frankfurt am Main, 1976); T. W. Gaethgens, "Wo ist die Avantgarde?" *Kunstchronik* 30 (1977): 472ff.; S. N. Hadjinicolaou, "L'ideologie de l'Avantgardisme," *Histoire et Critique des Arts* (July 1978); see also the special issue "Fine delle Avanguardie?" of the periodical *Ulisse* 32, no. 4 (1978); K. Honneg, "Abschied von der Avantgarde," *Kunstforum* 40 (1980), 86ff.; finally, Achille Bonito Oliva, *Tra Avanguardia e Transavanguardia* (Milan, 1981). Subsequent publications include Jean Clair, *Considérations sur l'état des Beaux-Arts: Critique de la modernité* (Paris, 1983); Suzi Gablik, *Has Modernism Failed?* (London, 1984); Diana Crane, *The Transformation of the Avant-Garde: The New York Art World, 1940–1945* (Chicago, 1987); Andrew Benjamin, *Art, Mimesis and the Avant-Garde: Aspects of a Philosophy of Difference* (London, 1991).

The turning point in the discussion is marked by Soby and Rosenberg: James T. Soby, *Modern Art and the New Past* (Norman, Okla., 1957), describes the meaning of tradition for modernism, while Harold Rosenberg, *The Tradition of the New* (London, 1962), attacks acquiescence in the notion of modernism as a new tradition.

On the discussion of style in art criticism, see Werner Hager and Norbert Knopp, eds., *Beiträge zum Problem des Stilpluralismus* (Munich, 1977). On fascination with style in the early modern age, cf. the success of W. Worringer's doctoral dissertation, "Abstraktion und Einfühlung: Ein Beitrag zur Stilpsychologie" (Ph.D. diss., 1908). Cf. also M. Schapiro, "Style," in H. Kroeber, ed., *Anthropology Today: An Encyclopedic Inventory* (Chicago 1953), 287ff.; Jan Bialostocki, *Stil und Ikonographie: Studien zur Kunstwissenschaft* (Dresden, 1978); J. Adolf Schmoll gen. Eisenwerth, *Epochengrenzen und Kontinuität: Studien zur Kunstgeschichte* (Munich, 1985); Friedrich Möbius and Helga Sciurie, eds., *Stil und Epoche: Periodisierungsfragen* (Dresden, 1989).

14. METHODS AND GAMES OF AN ACADEMIC DISCIPLINE

On Wölfflin, see Meinhold Lurz, *Heinrich Wölfflin, Biographie einer Kunsttheorie* (Worms, 1981); and several essays by Martin Warnke, for example, "On Heinrich Wölfflin," *Representation* 27 (1989): 172ff.

Adorno's remark is found in *Ästhetische Theorie,* 336. On Alois Riegl (*Spätrömische Kunstindustrie* [Vienna, 1901], and *Gesammelte Aufsätze,* ed. Karl M. Swoboda [Vienna, 1929]), see W. Sauerländer, "Alois Riegl und die Entstehung der autonomen Kunstgeschichte," in *Fin de siècle: Zu Literatur und Kunst der Jahrhundertwende,* ed. Roger Bauer (Frankfurt am Main, 1977), 125ff.; also Margaret R. Olin, "Alois Riegl and the Crisis of Representation in Art Theory, 1880–1905" (Ph.D. dissertation, University of Chicago, 1982).

Henri Focillon, *La vie des formes* (Paris, 1939); George Kubler, *The Shape of Time: Remarks on the History of Things* (New Haven, 1962). Siegfried Kracauer, *Geschichte— vor den letzten Dingen* (Frankfurt am Main, 1971), 162ff., and Adorno, *Ästhetische Theorie,* 310ff. On Berenson, see David A. Brown, *Berenson and the Connoisseurship of Italian Painting* (Washington, D.C., 1979); *Bernhard Berenson: Entwurf zu einem Selbstbildnis* (Frankfurt am Main, 1953); Meryle Secrest, *Being Bernhard Berenson: A Biography* (London, 1979).

On iconology, see Erwin Panofsky, "Iconography and Iconology," reprinted in idem, *The History of Art as a Humanist Discipline* (New York, 1957); Ekkehard Kaemmerling, ed., *Bildende Kunst als Zeichensystem,* vol. 1, *Ikonographie und Ikonologie: Theorien, Entwicklung, Probleme* (Cologne, 1979); J. K. Eberlein, "Ikonologie," in Hans. Belting, et al., *Kunstgeschichte: Eine Einführung* (Berlin, 1986), 164ff.; Andreas Beyer, ed., *Die Lesbarkeit der Kunst: Zur Geistes-Gegenwart der Ikonologie* (Berlin, 1992).

On Neo-Platonism, see the controversy outlined in Horst Bredekamp's writings on this theme. On the subject of "art history as a humanist discipline," see Max Dvorák, *Kunstgeschichte als Geistesgeschichte: Kunstgeschichte als Geistesgeschichte* (Munich, 1924).

On philosophical hermeneutics, see Hans Georg Gadamer, *Wahrheit und Methode* (Tübingen, 1960), and idem, "Hermeneutik," in *Historisches Wörterbuch der Philosophie,* ed. Joachim Ritter, vol. 3 (1973), col. 106ff. On the hermeneutic tradition, see Wilhelm Dilthey, *Die Einbildungskraft des Dichters* (1887), in *Gesammelte Schriften,* 6th ed. (1964), 6: 105; also idem, *Die Entstehung der Hermeneutik,* ibid., 1.5: 7ff.; cf. also Joachim Wach, *Das Verstehen: Grundzüge einer Geschichte der hermeneutischen Theorien des 19. Jahrhunderts* (Tübingen, 1926), and Paul Ricoeur, *Hermeneutik und Strukturalismus,* vols. 1–2 (Munich, 1973–74). On the application of hermeneutics to art history, see Hans Sedlmayr, *Zu einer strengen Kunstwissenschaft* (1931), reprinted in idem, *Kunst und Wahrheit,* 2d ed. (Mittenwald, 1978), 107. The subject has since been treated comprehensively by Oskar Bätschmann, *Einführung in die kunstgeschichtliche Hermeneutik,* 3d ed. (1984; Darmstadt, 1988).

Art psychology began optimistically with Ernst Kris's *Psychoanalytic Explorations in Art* (New York, 1952); and Rudolf Arnheim, *Kunst und Sehen* (Berlin, 1965). A contemporary study is found in Rosalind E. Krauss, *The Optical Unconscious* (Cambridge, Mass., 1993), with theses on modern art. Among Ernst H. Gombrich's works, see especially *Art and Illusion: A Study of Pictorial Representation* (Princeton, 1960); his other writings do not relate directly to this theme.

The visual arts' relation to reality is not to be equated with the customary realism. For a social-historical definition of reality, see Peter L. Berger and Thomas Luckmann, *The Social Construction of Reality: Treatise in the Sociology of Knowledge* (New York, 1967). The debate on realism is found in Reinhold Grimm and Jost Hermand, eds., *Realismustheorie in Literatur, Malerei, Musik und Politik* (Stuttgart, 1975). For approaches to a sociology of modern art, see Arnold Gehlen, *Zeitbilder*, 3d ed. (Frankfurt am Main, 1960); and Peter Gay, *Art and Act: On Causes in History—Manet, Gropius, Mondrian* (New York, 1976). The nineteenth-century situation is seen from an entirely different perspective by Barbara Novak, *Nature and Culture: American Landscape and Painting, 1825–1875* (London, 1980); T. Clark, *The Painting of Modern Life: Paris in the Art of Manet and His Followers* (Princeton, 1984); Michael Fried, *Courbet's Realism* (Chicago, 1990).

Arnold Hauser, *The Social History of Art and Literature, Vol. 1: Prehistoric Times, Ancient-Oriental Urban Cultures, Greece and Rome, the Middle Ages* (New York, 1951); cf. also Frederick Antal, *Florentine Painting and Its Social Background* (London, 1947); Francis Haskell, *Patrons and Painters: A Study in the Relations between Italian Art and Society in the Age of the Baroque* (Oxford, 1963); E. Castelnuovo, *Arte, industria, rivoluzioni: Temi di storia sociale dell'arte* (Turin, 1985); Jutta Held and Norbert Schneider, *Sozialgeschichte der Malerei vom Spätmittelalter bis ins 20. Jahrhundert* (Cologne, 1993). On reception history, see Wolfgang Kemp, *Der Anteil des Betrachters* (Munich, 1983), and idem, ed., *Der Betrachter ist im Bild* (Cologne, 1985). The topic became popular in German literary studies with Hans R. Jauss's *Literaturgeschichte als Provokation* (Frankfurt am Main, 1970).

On Susan Sontag, see idem, *On Photography* (New York, 1973), 144; cf. ibid., 153 ff., on the "image world" in the media. On the theory of photography, cf. studies by W. Kemp, R. Barthes, and V. Flusser. On Norman Bryson, cf. his studies *Word and Image: French Painting of the Ancien Régime* (Cambridge, Mass., 1981), and *Vision and Painting: The Logic of the Gaze* (New Haven, 1983). On Louis Marin, see his *Détruire la peinture* (Paris, 1977), and *L'opacité de la peinture* (Paris, 1990). On Minor's book, see chapter 2.

15. WORK OF ART OR HISTORY OF ART?

On ekphrasis, see chapter 3. On Duchamp, also chapter 3; cf. Jean François Lyotard, *Die TRANSformatoren Duchamp* (Stuttgart, 1987), and Yves Arman, *Marcel Duchamp Plays and Wins = Joue et gagne* (Paris, 1984), with a "ready-made" casting a shadow on the cover image.

On Fernand Léger, see Christopher Green, *Léger and the Avant-Garde* (New Haven and London, 1976), and the "Hommage à Fernand Léger," special issue of *XXe Siècle* [Paris] (1971). The photo reproduced here in the appendix to the first *Documenta* catalog, 1955. The writings of Léger are found in *Fonctions de la peinture* (Paris, 1965), in an English translation with an introduction by Edward F. Fry, *Functions of Painting* (New York, 1973), with index. On Poussin's self-portrait, see Stoichita, *L'instauration du tableau*, 228 ff., and the essays by W. Kemp, V. I. Stoichita, and M. Winner in Matthias Winner, ed., *Der Künstler über sich in seinem Werk* (Weinheim, 1992), passim.

On Wölfflin, see chapter 13; on his concept of style, see the literature mentioned for chapter 4 above.

André Malraux, *Le Musée imaginaire de la sculpture mondiale* (written during the Second World War), 3 vols. (Paris, 1947); first part of the trilogy, *Les Voix du silence.* Georges Duthuit, *Le Musée inimaginable,* 3 vols. (Paris, 1956).

The seminal writings of Charles de Tolnay still have not found wide recognition and have therefore not yet appeared in a collected edition; cf., for example, "Remarques sur la Joconde," *Revue des Arts* 2 (1952): 18ff., or "Le Jugement dernier de Michel Ange," *Art Quarterly* (1940): 125ff. Michel Foucault, *Les mots et les choses* (Paris, 1966), chapter 1, "Les suivantes," 19ff. Unfortunately, Foucault's linguistic style is practically untranslatable, which has resulted in misunderstanding and mistaken criticism of the work he has done in art scholarship.

Peter Weiss, *Die Ästhetik des Widerstands: Roman,* vol. 1 (Frankfurt am Main, 1975), 3 vols. in 1 (Frankfurt am Main, 1988), 332ff. On Weiss, see Gunilla Palmstierna-Weiss and Jürgen Schutte, *Peter Weiss, Leben und Werk* (Frankfurt am Main, 1991). Julian Barnes, *A History of the World in 10½ Chapters* (New York and London, 1989), passim.

On Jean Luc Godard's film *Passion* (1982), see his writings in *J. L. Godard par J. L. G.,* ed. A. Bergala, in *Cahiers du Cinéma* (1985), 484ff.; Jean Louis Leutrat, *Des traces qui nous ressemblent* (Paris, 1990); Joachin Paech, *Passion, oder, Die Einbildung des Jean-Luc Godard,* Cinematograph, vol. 6 (Frankfurt am Main, 1989).

Jean Rivette's film *La Belle Noiseuse* (1991) is based on Honoré de Balzac's 1831 novella *Le Chef-d'oeuvre inconnu.* On Yves Klein, see Krahmer (chapter 6) and also the catalog to the 1983 retrospective exhibition in the Center Pompidou, with texts on 189ff., and "Quelques extraits de mon journal en 1957," in the catalog *Art et Création* [Paris] no. 1 (1968).

16. ART HISTORY VERSUS MEDIA STUDIES

For literature on the social history of art and references to Jauss, also for references to Susan Sontag, see chapter 13.

On the discussion of images, there is a wealth of recent titles from various disciplines, which cannot be gathered under a common denominator here. The following may be helpful to begin with: the anthology *The Language of Images,* ed. W. J. T. Mitchell (Chicago, 1974); Nelson Goodman, *Languages of Art: An Approach to a Theory of Symbols* (Indianapolis, 1968); various publications by V. Flusser on technological images; and Claude Lévi-Strauss, *Regarder—écouter— lire* (Paris 1993).

It is difficult to give references that can already be representative on the subject of media theory and media history. Cf. in particular the anthology *Aisthesis: Wahrnehmung heute oder Perspektiven einer anderen Ästhetik,* ed. Karlheinz Barck et al. (Leipzig, 1991), and Norbert W. Bolz, *Theorie der neuen Medien* (Munich, 1990).

The history of the image is still in its early stages; cf. also Hans Belting and Christiane Kruse, *Die Erfindung des Gemäldes: Das erste Jahrhundert niederländischer Malerei* (Munich, 1994); Werner Busch, ed., *Funkkolleg Kunst: Eine Geschichte der Kunst im Wandel ihrer Funktionen,* vols. 1–2, with a supplement dealing with the history of artistic function (Munich, 1987), and idem, *Das sentimentalische Bild: Die Krise der Kunst im 18. Jahrhundert und die Geburt der*

Moderne (Munich, 1993): or Joseph Leo Koerner, *The Moment of Self-Portraiture in German Renaissance Art* (Chicago, 1993). For a French perspective, cf. the interdisciplinary anthology *Destins de l'image*, in the series Nouvelle Revue de Psychoanalyse, no. 44 (n.p., 1991). On D. Teniers's "Theatrum Pictoricum" (Antwerp, 1660), see Stoichita (as in chapter 13), chapter 6. On the curiosity cabinet, cf. also Bredekamp, *Antikensehnsucht und Maschinenglauben* (chapter 11).

17. THE MYTH OF MODERNISM IN THE MIRROR OF ART HISTORY

On early histories of modern art, including H. Thode and Julius Meier-Graefe, see my introduction to Meier-Graefe's *Entwicklungsgeschichte* (as in chapter 4); on Sedlmayr, see chapter 1. Gottfried Boehm, "Die Krise der Repräsentation," in Lorenz Dittmann, ed., *Kategorien und Methoden der deutschen Kunstgeschichte, 1900–1930* (Wiesbaden, 1985), 113ff. Finally, see the essays in Monika Wagner, ed., *Moderne Kunst: Das Funkkolleg zum Verständnis der Gegenwartskunst*, 2 vols. (Reinbek, 1992).

The partisans of modernism were, above all, Wilhelm Hausenstein (*Die bildende Kunst der Gegenwart. Malerei, Plastik, Zeichnung* [Stuttgart, 1914]); C. Einstein (for example, *Die bildende Kunst des 20. Jahrhunderts* [Berlin, 1927]); and Herbert E. Read (*The Anatomy of Art. An Introduction to the Problems of Art and Aesthetics* [London, 1932], *Art and Society*, 3d. ed. [London, 1956], *The Philosophy of Modern Art* [London, 1964], *Icon and Idea* [London, 1955]). After the Second World War, the principal theorists are Werner Haftmann (*Skizzenbuch: Zur Kultur der Gegenwart* [Munich, 1960], *Malerei im 20. Jahrhundert* [Munich, 1954]), followed by Giulio C. Argan (*L'arte moderna, 1770–1970* [Florence, 1970]), and Werner Hofmann (*Zeichen und Gestalt: Die Malerei des 20. Jahrhunderts* [Vienna, 1956], *Die Grundlagen der modernen Kunst* [Stuttgart, 1966], and *Von der Nachahmung zur Erfindung der Wirklichkeit* [Hamburg, 1970]).

On the art history of the avant-garde, see chapter 13; on Harold Rosenberg, chapter 6. On the realism debate during the 1930s, see *Paris-Paris*, exhibition catalog (Paris, 1981). On Fernand Léger, see chapter 13. On the "farewell to the painting," see Nikolai M. Tarabukin, *Ot Mol'berta do mashine* (From the Easel to the Machine) (Moscow, 1923); cf. also Hofmann, *Von der Nachahmung zur Erfindung der Wirklichkeit;* M. Pleynet, "Disparation du tableau," in *Art International* (1968); Wolfgang Drechsler and Peter Weibel, eds., *Bildlicht: Malerei zwischen Material und Immaterialität*, exhibition catalog (Vienna, 1991).

18. POSTMODERNISM OR POSTHISTORY

On the modernism debate, see, for example, Michael Fried, "Art and Objecthood," in *Artforum* (1967), and V. Burgin, in *Studio International* (October 1969); here the issue was the definitions of the work of art and of attitudes to art as a whole. What D. Judd called the "disinterest in doing it again" was associated with the concept of the end of art history: D. Judd, "Specific Objects," in *Arts Yearbook* 8 (1965). On performance art, see chapter 10.

For a comment on "art and life," see Allan Kaprow, *Assemblage, Environment and Happening* (New York, 1965); Wolf Vostell, *Happening und Leben* (Cologne, 1970); and Jürgen Schilling, *Aktionskunst. Identität von Kunst und Leben? Eine Dokumentation* (Lucerne, 1978). Rosenberg, *The Anxious Object.* On Jean

Tinguely, see also B. Klüver, "The Garden Party," in Karl Gunnar Pontus Hultén, *A Magic Stronger than Death* (Milan, 1987), 74ff., with numerous illustrations.

On Achille Bonito Oliva and G. Celant, see chapter 3 Claude Lévi-Strauss, *Tristes tropiques* (Paris, 1955). Günter Metken, *Spurensicherung: Kunst als Anthropologie und Selbsterforschung* (Cologne, 1977).

On quotation and paraphrase, see the exhibition catalog *D'Après: Omaggi e dissacrazioni nell'arte contemporanea*, (Lugano, 1971); "E. Weiss, Kunst in Kunst —Das Zitat in der Pop Art," in *Aachener Kunstblätter* 40 (1971); the exhibitions *Kunst und Künstler als Thema der Kunst: Dialoge-Kopie* (Dresden, 1970); *Bilder nach Bildern: Druckgraphik und die Vermittlung von Kunst* (Münster, 1976); *Original und Fälschung* (Bonn, 1974); *Art about Art* (New York, 1978), with a catalog by Jean Lipman and Richard Marshall that includes an essay by Leo Steinberg); *Nachbilder—Vom Nutzen und Nachteil des Zitierens für die Kunst* (Kunstverein Hanover, 1979); and *Mona Lisa im 20. Jahrhundert* (Duisburg, 1978). See also Hans Belting, "Larry Rivers und die Historie in der modernen Kunst," in *Art International* 25 (1982), 72ff.; and Charles N. Mason's book *Themes and Variations* (1976). The painting by Gorella was published in *Nachbilder*, 192.

On "political correctness" and on the exhibitions *A New Spirit in Painting* and *Zeitgeist*, see chapter 6. The exhibition *Zeitlos* was shown in Berlin in 1989. On R. Atkins's *Art Speak* (p. 55 on "Body Art"), see chapter 3. On the exhibition *Widerstand* (Resistance) see chapter 7. Cf. Ziva Amishai-Maisels, *Depiction and Interpretation: The Influence of the Holocaust on the Visual Arts* (Oxford and New York, 1993), and the symposium "Kunst und Natur—Natur und Ökologie" in the Sprengel Museum, Hanover, 1993. On "mixed exhibitions," see J. Clair's projects in Paris (L'âme au corps, 1993) and at the Venice Biennale: on this topic, cf. chapter 11.

On postmodern architecture, see Heinrich Klotz: *Moderne und Postmoderne: Architektur der Gegenwart, 1960–1980* (Frankfurt am Main, 1984). On *posthistoire*, cf. Gehlen, *Zeitbilder*, 1986, idem, "Ende der Geschichte?" in idem, *Einblicke* (Frankfurt am Main, 1975), 115ff.; Wolf Lepenies, *Melancholie und Gesellschaft* (Frankfurt am Main, 1969); H. Lefèvre, *La fin de l'histoire Epilogomènes* (Paris, 1970); Lutz Niethammer, *Posthistoire: Ist die Geschichte zu Ende?* (Reinbek, 1989); Wolf Lepenies, *Aufstieg und Fall der Intellektuellen in Europa* (Frankfurt am Main, 1992), 73ff. One should also remember the viewpoints of artists such as D. Judd (see above) and H. Fischer (see chapter 12).

19. "PROSPERO'S BOOKS"

Peter Greenaway's catalogs and exhibition guidebooks are described in chapter 11. The screenplay *Prospero's Books: A Film of Shakespeare's* The Tempest (London, 1991), includes an introduction (9ff.), a commentary on paintbox software (28ff.), and the illustration replicated in this book. On the image and the frame, similar problems of staging a work of art are described in the valuable anthology by Catherine Lawless et al., *L'oeuvre et son accrochage*, in the series Cahiers du Musée nationale d'art moderne, nos. 17–18 (Paris, 1983). On Shakespeare's *The Tempest*, cf. *The Oxford Shakespeare* (Oxford, 1987), with textual commentary.

20. MARCO POLO AND OTHER CULTURES

Chapter 20 is translated from my essay, "Eine globale Kunslrgene? Marco Polo ued die endven Kultüren," in *Neue bildende Kemst* 4/5, 1995, p. 13ff. Cf. also W. Rubin, *"Primitivism" in 20th Century Art* (Museum of Modern Art, N. York, 1984); J. H. Martin, *Magiciens de la Terre* (Centre Pompidou, Paris 1989); H. Belting, *Die Ausstelluug von Kultüren*, in *Jahrbuch Wissenscheftskolleg* (Berlin, 1995), pp. 214 ff. and H. Belting, "Hybride Kunst? Ein Block hiutes die globale Fassade," in M. Scheps, ed., *Global Art-Rheinland 2000* (Cologne, 1999), pp. 324 ff.; S. Errington, *The Death of Authentic Primitive Art and Other Tales of Progress* (Univ. of Calif., 1998).

Index

Page references to figures are indicated by f.

www.ingramcontent.com/pod-product-compliance
Lightning Source LLC
LaVergne TN
LVHW091131080826
845145LV00008B/2118

* 9 7 8 0 2 2 6 0 4 1 8 5 8 *